CULINARY
NEW MEXICO

Fulcrum Publishing
Golden, Colorado

D0190183

To
Theresa L. Wilson,
The Wilson School

Jean Sudrann,
Mount Holyoke College

and Great Teachers Everywhere

Text and images copyright © 2004 Sally Moore

The information in *Culinary New Mexico* is accurate as of April 2005. Prices, hours of operation, addresses, phone numbers, Web sites, and other items change rapidly. If something in the book is incorrect, please write to the author in care of Fulcrum Publishing, 16100 Table Mountain Parkway, Suite 300, Golden, Colorado, 80403 or contact her at smcuisine@earthlink.net.

Library of Congress Cataloging-in-Publication Data

Moore, Sally, 1936-
  Culinary New Mexico : the ultimate food lover's guide / Sally Moore.
    p. cm.
  ISBN 1-55591-491-8
  1. Restaurants—New Mexico—Guidebooks. 2. Cookery, American—Southwestern style. 3. Cookery—New Mexico. I. Title.
  TX907.3.N6M66 2005
  647.95789—dc22

                                    2004024227

Printed in the United States of America
0 9 8 7 6 5 4 3 2 1

Editorial: Faith Marcovecchio, Katie Raymond
Design: Ann W. Douden, Jack Lenzo
Cover image: Sally Moore

Fulcrum Publishing
16100 Table Mountain Parkway, Suite 300
Golden, Colorado 80403
(800) 992-2908 • (303) 277-1623
www.fulcrum-books.com

TABLE OF CONTENTS

ACKNOWLEDGMENTS

I'd like to thank all the chefs and restaurant owners who took time from their busy schedules to share their thoughts with me. Some came up from the ranks and others from great culinary institutes, but all had that passion that defines a professional in the culinary arts.

Representatives of the New Mexico travel industry helped immensely by providing itinerary guidance and moral support. So thanks to Patty Romero, New Mexico Department of Tourism; Tania Armenta, the Albuquerque Convention and Visitors Bureau; Steve Lewis, Impressions Advertising for the Santa Fe Convention and Visitors Bureau; Steve Fuhlendorf, the Taos County Chamber of Commerce; Debbie Dusenbery, Farmington Convention and Visitors Bureau; Susan Russell, City of Roswell Tourism; Chris Faivre, Las Cruces Convention and Visitors Bureau; Cissy McAndrew, Silver City Chamber of Commerce; and Antionette Gallegos, Las Vegas/San Miguel Chamber of Commerce.

For acting as the family executive chef and always supporting me as I completed this work, undying gratitude to my husband.

This book stems from a late-in-life love affair with New Mexico: its people, its mountains and deserts, and especially its cuisine. Everything from its endless vistas to its bold, assertive flavors told me I'd found my own version of Utopia. New Mexico, that most exotic of states, was an education not easily learned for a born and bred easterner whose roots go back to 17th century New England. Before moving West I didn't know posole from potholes.

Traveling the state and learning from home cooks and world-famous chefs, I compiled notes, recipes, and experience. Gradually, the boisterous savors of the Southwest became as much a part of me as brown eyes and freckles. *Culinary New Mexico* is my remembrance of past gustatory pleasures and my gift to you, the reader.

Knowing something of the land and its history is imperative to understanding its cuisine. New Mexico is not all desert, or mountains, or forests. It is all of the above. With 122,666 square miles, it is the fifth largest state. It has a diverse landscape which includes sections of the Rocky Mountains, the Great Plains, the Colorado Plateau, and six of the seven climatic life zones, from the lower Sonoran (2,876 to 5,000 feet) to the arctic/alpine (higher than 12,000 feet). Each zone has its own cast of plants and animals, and as you might imagine, farms in each zone have their own set of rules for plant selection and growth.

The Rio Grande, which runs from its headwaters in southern Colorado to Brownsville, Texas, on the Gulf of Mexico, cleaves the state in two from east to west. In its more northern reaches, or *rio arriba*, it can be a raging torrent, but once it reaches the plains, or *rio abajo*, it slows to a broad, silty stream. The lifeblood of many civilizations from Archaic to modern times, the river has been indispensable to the state's growth.

The history of man in New Mexico begins around 12,000 B.C. or earlier. Crude tools and animal bones of prehistoric big-game hunters were found at Sandia Cave, near Albuquerque, and finely chipped projectile points were discovered at the Folsom Site in the northeast and the Clovis Site near Anderson Basin.

Toward the latter part of the Archaic period, the concept of agriculture filtered up from Mexico, and dependence on game lessened. Groups became more sedentary and built semi-permanent dwellings such as pit houses. Over time these evolved into the cliff dwellings and freestanding apartment complexes of the Ancestral Puebloan people.

By A.D. 1500, rumors of great Indian civilizations and gold brought the Spanish to New Mexico. Their first encounter with Native Americans occurred in 1539, when a Franciscan friar, Marcos de Niza, led a party from northern Mexico into today's Arizona and New Mexico. At Hàwikuh, near Zuni, his party was repulsed and the good friar fled back to Mexico.

In response to the priest's exaggerated tales of riches, in 1540 Francisco Vàsques de Coronado, governor of Nueva Galicia, Mexico, led 300 soldiers and 800 Indians from Compostela to Hàwikuh. He found no cities of gold, only the pueblos whose straw-enriched adobe glistened in the sun.

Following the *entrada* (Spanish entry), Don Juan de Oñate marched north accompanied by troops, priests, colonists, and cattle to secure New Mexico by the cross and the sword, and in 1609 Don Pedro de Peralta established Santa Fe as the capital of the region.

The Spanish maintained dominance until 1680, when under the leadership of Popé, a San Juan Indian living at Taos, the pueblos revolted, expelled their oppressors, and killed many of the priests. The Spanish reestablished control in 1692, when Captain General Diego de Vargas Zapata Lujan Ponce de León y Contreras led a small army from El Paso, subdued the pueblos along the way, and easily wrested control of Santa Fe from the Indians.

With the signing of the Treaty of Córdova on August 12, 1821, Mexico received its independence from Spain, and New Mexico became a part of the new nation. The Mexican regime lasted until 1846, when U.S. Army Brig. Gen. Stephen Kearny led the Army of the West down the Santa Fe Trail and declared New Mexico a U.S. territory. The Treaty of Guadalupe Hidalgo ratified this at the end of the Mexican War.

During the long territorial period, the people of New Mexico tried many times to gain admittance to the Union, but it wasn't until January 7, 1912, that President William Howard Taft signed the bill admitting New Mexico as the 47th state.

With its history, it is easy to see why New Mexico is so culturally diverse, its Hispanic, Anglo, and Indian population supplemented by a 21st century infusion of African Americans, Middle Easterners, and Asians. This rich cultural tapestry is intrinsically woven into its cuisine.

State symbols range from daisies to dinosaurs, but only one in 50 has an official state question. New Mexicans ask, "red or green?" Do you want your chile served red-ripened in the sun or harvested green and sassy? And it is our dedication to that glorious capsicum that most differentiates our cuisine from the general catchall often labeled as southwestern food.

What makes New Mexico dishes different from, say, Tex-Mex, Arizona Mex, or Old Mexican? The signature component is chile, especially green chile, which is eaten as a food rather than as a spice. Chili (spelled with an *i*) bears little resemblance to chile. A stew most favored in cookoffs and barbecues in such diverse locales as Dallas and Cincinnati, it's traditionally flavored with chili powder, a mixture of ground chiles, cumin, garlic, and oregano. Ingredients may include beans, tomatoes, meat, and even spaghetti or macaroni.

Contrary to accepted opinion, chiles are fruits, not vegetables. Roasted, peeled, and served as a condiment or as the main ingredient in sauces or green-chile stew, they are everywhere. Red chiles are simply ripened green chiles. They are usually dried and packaged or roped into *ristras*. The usual method of preparation is hydrating the pods in hot water, pureeing the mixture in a food processor or blender, and cooking down the puree with oil or lard. The results are a basic sauce served over dishes such as enchiladas and huevos rancheros.

Worldwide there are more than 200 varieties of chile. Individual tolerance to peppers' pungency varies, and many believe it increases with consumption. The heat is concentrated in the seeds and veins and is measured in Scoville Units. A bell pepper comes in at zero and some varieties of habañeros come in at a blistering 577,000 units. The jalapeño, which most New Mexicans consider relatively mild, registers 25,000 units. The most common chiles found in our markets are New Mexico Big Jims and Sandias (also called Anaheims), poblanos (when dried called anchos), serranos, and jalapeños (dubbed chipotle when dried and smoked). More exotic varieties such as *piquin, cascabel,* and *de arbol* are also available.

Pepper is the common vernacular for both chiles and the black pepper. How did this confusing state of affairs develop? Chile and sweet peppers are members of the genus *Capsicum.* The black pepper that graces every American tabletop is *Piper nigrum,* a totally different genus.

Black pepper was once so valuable that it was measured against gold. When Columbus sailed west, one of his goals was to find a route to the Far East where *Piper nigrum* grew. The native population called the plant he found in the New World *aji,* and Columbus took it back to the Iberian Peninsula mistaking it for black pepper. However wrongful his discovery, the chile soon became popular and its use soon spread around the world.

A debate rages as to how chiles found their way into what is now the United States. It is widely believed that the Spanish brought the peppers to Mexico and the early explorers carried them north. This ties in with the story that Capitán General Don Juan de Oñate, who founded Santa Fe in 1598, was responsible for transporting the chiles up from Old Mexico.

Another theory is that Aztec long-distance traders, or *pochteca*, brought them north as goods for barter. Native Americans have an oral tradition of chile use dating back many hundreds of years.

The chiltepin, a wild chile pepper, traditionally has been found in Sonora and southern Arizona. However, chiltepin cultivation depends on so many rigorous factors of soil, climate, and location that no historical record exists of them north of their native territory. No matter their origin, chiles have a firm base in both Native American and southwestern cuisine.

New Mexican food is one of the earliest examples of "fusion" cuisine, combining the foods of Native Americans, the Spanish, and Mexicans. When the Spanish moved north from Mexico City, they found Native Americans existing on game, plants harvested in the wild, and on cultivated plants such as piñon nuts, corn, beans, and squash. The Europeans introduced many new foodstuffs including cattle, pigs, chickens, wheat, grapes, and apples. Today's New Mexican cuisine is a blend of all these elements with a few Asian, French, Italian, Caribbean, Creole, Cajun, and Far Eastern influences thrown in for good measure.

Although our regional cuisine is world famous, it is not the whole story. In *Culinary New Mexico* you will find a celebration of our remarkable variety. In our restaurants, you'll discover something for every taste and pocketbook from an elegant Santa Fe bistro to a modest mom-and-pop *taquería*.

North, south, east, and west, we've scouted out stores specializing in cookware and utensils and visited food and wine festivals in your behalf. We've tracked down the best retail butchers, bakers, and candlestick makers; taken classes at cooking schools; and haunted farmers' markets. We've done the legwork, leaving you free to enjoy the inimitable experience that is New Mexico cuisine.

What you will find in this book

Bakeries, *Panaderías*, and *Tortillerías*

Thanks to the widespread popularity of southwestern cuisine, tortillas are not difficult to find. As their popularity spreads, they are appearing on grocery shelves from New Jersey to California. According to the Tortilla Industry Association, tortillas currently outsell bagels, pita bread, and English muffins. In the land of the tortilla, finding a place to purchase a fresh, homemade product was our goal. We want you to be able to taste the real thing, not a preservative-filled cardboard disk that has been sitting on the shelf for more than a week.

Unearthing a first-rate classic bakery is more difficult than finding a good tortilla. In Mexico, bread, or *pan*, was often the province of the elite because wheat was so much harder and more expensive to grow. The general populace ate corn tortillas, and this influence carried over into New Mexico for many years. Fortunately for bread lovers everywhere, bakers educated in the European tradition have come to New Mexico lured by our stellar climate and relaxed lifestyle. They have established islands of excellence in the more populated areas of Albuquerque, Santa Fe, and Taos.

New Mexico retailers can be divided into several classes: tortilla makers, or *tortillerías*; general bakeries; bread bakeries; sweet shops; and *panaderías*, the Hispanic bakeries specializing in traditional Mexican breads and *pan dulces*.

Tortilla makers produce yellow, blue, and white corn tortillas and flour tortillas in a range of sizes, some plain and others flavored with ingredients varying from strawberry to piñon.

General bakeries offer cakes, pies, bread, cookies, and pastries. Some bakeries concentrate on special occasion cakes.

Bread specialists range from small artisanal operations to large companies baking in quantities sufficient to supply discerning restaurants. You'll find their loaves range from farmhouse rye, French baguettes, and challah to the more unusual, such as green-chile sourdough.

Panaderías will have specialties such as *bizcochitos*, the anise-flavored New Mexico state cookie. Mexican sweet bread (*pan dulce*) appears as *conchas* (shells), *llaves* (keys), *besos* (kisses), *orejas* (ears), or *pan de muerto* for Day of the Dead celebrations. There are numerous *galletas* such as *tres leches*, a very sweet cake made from condensed, evaporated, and fresh milk.

And we can't forget those numerous operations that combine a bakery with a café or coffee bar, where you can relax with a good cup of joe and a scone or bear claw.

Breweries and Brewpubs

New Mexico's 17 breweries and brewpubs are scattered statewide from Socorro to Taos. Most serve beer and food, although some are microbreweries and may or may not have food, tasting rooms, or beer to go.

Carnicerías

Today much of our meat comes from the supermarket, precut and protected by plastic wrap. Here in New Mexico we're fortunate to have both independent ranchers raising organic beef, chicken, and lamb and Hispanic *carnicerías*. In our friendly neighborhood *carnicerías* you'll find common Mexican cuts such as *chuleta del siete* (a seven-bone cut), *paleta* (shoulder steak), *arrachera* (flank steak for fajitas), chorizo (spicy pork sausage), and more esoteric items such as tripe for menudo as well as ox and pig hocks. In addition, the *carnicerías* often stock a complement of herbs and spices, dried chiles, salsas, candy, soft drinks, and Mexican-style cheeses such as *cotija*, *asadero*, Oaxaca, *fresco*, *panela*, and my favorite, *menonita*.

Cooking Classes

Taking a cooking class is both fun and rewarding. You learn new recipes and get an insight into techniques that might have eluded you in the past. Every year our most famous kitchen doyennes, Susan Curtis of Santa Fe and Jane Butel of Albuquerque, turn out hundreds of cooks experienced in the art and science of New Mexican cooking.

You can learn about chiles and how to make a variety of dishes from posole to chile rellenos. Other chefs in other locales tackle classes ranging from sushi making to creating bistro soups and breads. Some classes are participatory, others demonstration.

Cookware Stores

Where do you go when the recipe calls for a paella pan and nothing else will do? The cookware store, of course. For a state with a population of only 1.6 million, *mas o menos*, we are fortunate to have a selection of well-stocked vendors of china, glass, pots and pans, cookbooks, linens, and kitchen accessories.

Albuquerque, Santa Fe, and Taos have the greatest number of stores, carrying everything from upscale Le Creuset pots to simple spatulas. In addition to their kitchenware, most conduct cooking classes on a full- or part-time basis.

Dining

Were I to detail every good restaurant in the state, this guide would grow to encyclopedic proportions. I must admit to subjective selection. What I've tried to accomplish is a representation of those restaurants that I believe give good value, whether it be white tablecloth service in Santa Fe or enchiladas at a small family-owned café in the hinterlands. Of course, I'll give special representation to those restaurants serving New Mexican cuisine, but you will also find listings for all forms of international cuisine.

Restaurants are notoriously fickle, changing hours, menus, and owners with frequency. Please bear this in mind and call to confirm details. Nothing spoils plans worse than finding a dining place completely booked or closed when you wish to visit. If you find closures, relocations, or just plain bad food or service in our listings, please let us know at smcuisine@earthlink.net.

Wineries

New Mexico is one of the oldest wine-producing regions in the country. Fray Gracia de Zuniga, a Franciscan, and Antonio de Arteaga, a Capuchin monk, planted the first grapevines in 1629. This was 140 years before historians date the first California vines.

By the middle of the 19th century, New Mexico was producing more wine than California, but vineyard flooding and the resulting alkaline deposits and root rot tolled a decades-long death knell on the state industry. It wasn't until 1978 that New Mexico had a rebirth of its wine production, and now there are 19 wineries producing almost 350,000 gallons of wine per year.

New Mexico Wine Growers Association sponsors wine festivals throughout the state as well as providing information on tasting and tours.

Events

You're seldom at a loss for some food-related event to attend in New Mexico. From the Whole Enchilada Fiesta in Las Cruces to the Chile Festival in Hatch, there's usually something cooking at plaza or fairground.

Recipes

Culinary New Mexico is not a cookbook, but it was too hard to resist including a few select recipes. Some are foundations of New Mexican cooking while others are gleaned with permission from chefs and restaurateurs. All should be within the capabilities of the home cook.

Appendices

Indian Feast Days

New Mexico's Pueblo Indians live in 19 villages, most located in the northern part of the state bordering the Rio Grande. They speak five distinct languages: Zuni (Zuni), Towa (Jemez), Tewa (Nambe, Pojoaque, San Ildefonso, San Juan, Santa Clara, and Tesuque), Tiwa (Isleta, Picuris, Sandia, and Taos), and Keresan (Acoma, Cochiti, Laguna, San Felipe, Santa Ana, Santo Domingo, and Zia).

They are a deeply religious and private people, always gracious, but preferring to keep their beliefs secret. On certain days of the year, they celebrate the feast day of their patron saint with dances and special foods. During these days the public is welcome into the pueblo, and if you are invited into a home for a meal, you should accept, eat, thank the hosts, and depart quickly. If you wish to be a welcome guest on feast days or at any time throughout the year, keep the following cautions in mind:

- Native American territory is part of a sovereign nation. Observe all posted requests or regulations, especially speed limits and prohibitions against photography, sketching, or recording. Photography is an especially sensitive issue. If permitted, images are only for private use, not to be reproduced or sold without written permission from the tribe, a difficult and time-consuming process.
- Many pueblos charge an admission fee for regular visitations. This may or may not be waived on feast days. Some charge a photo fee, while others allow no photography, sketching, or recording at all.
- Try to check in at the tribal office or call the pueblo governor's office or the tourist center prior to visiting. Some pueblos welcome visitors, others do not except on feast days.
- Certain areas of the pueblo may be off limits, and these restrictions may or may not be posted. Generally, restricted areas include cemeteries, kivas, and private homes.
- Tribes hold traditions, customs, and religion in high regard. Some actions and/or questions may be offensive. Dances are religious ceremonies, not performances. When attending, remain silent and do not applaud. And do not walk across the dance area, look into kivas (ceremonial chambers), or talk to the dancers or onlookers during the ceremonies. Photography of the dances is generally not allowed due to their religious nature.
- The best time to visit a pueblo is on feast days, which are held annually, regardless of the day of the week.
- Do not bring alcohol, pets, or drugs onto the pueblo.
- Finally, these communities are not theme parks. They are people's homes and should be treated with respect.

Albuquerque's International Balloon Fiesta

**Jane Butel Southwestern
Cooking School**

Vineyards
Ponderosa

Satellite Coffee
Albuquerque

ALBUQUERQUE:
THE DUKE CITY

With a population of nearly 500,000, Albuquerque is New Mexico's largest city. Named in 1706 for the Duke of Alburquerque, viceroy to the king of Spain, it is beautifully situated between the Sandia Mountains to the east and a volcanic escarpment etched with ancient petroglyphs to the west. On either side of the Rio Grande, the cottonwood bosque, a green ribbon of life, provides cooling shade and an oasis in the midst of the city. Albuquerque's setting and quality of life are superb, but its image problem has traditionally suffered in comparison to its nearby neighbor Santa Fe.

Perhaps the best way to illustrate the difference between the cities is to draw an analogy between two women "of a certain age." Both wear their years well, but that's where the similarity ends. Santa Fe is the wealthy dowager, a classic beauty who retains her peerless presence with elegant attire and immaculate grooming. Albuquerque is your best friend's mama, straightforward, gracious, and unpretentious. She may have a few wrinkles and a no-longer-shapely figure, but she will always greet you with a warm *abrazo*.

Albuquerque is a town of neighborhoods. Old Town with its shaded plaza, bandstand, and shops celebrates where the city began. Downtown is the heart of the business district. South Valley is a blend of small industry and agricultural enterprise. North Valley encompasses some of the areas priciest real estate. The North Valley's Los Ranchos is a city within the city, a rural enclave of estates and horse farms. West Mesa, which includes Taylor Ranch, is the area boomtown, filled with shops, restaurants, and the largest mall in New Mexico.

Likewise, Albuquerque's culinary reputation has suffered in comparison to Santa Fe, and until recently there was some truth to that notion. However, in the past decade more chefs have discovered the boost to their business that Albuquerque's steady, year-round, loyal local

CULINARY NEW MEXICO

clientele provides. Access to locally grown fresh produce is about even for both cities, but since Albuquerque has the state's only major airport, the city has a transport edge on produce, fish, and meat from other areas.

Bakeries, *Panaderías*, and *Tortillerías*

Bakeries

French Riviera Bakery, Inc.

Daniel Reymonenq is a second-generation baker who learned his skills from his father in Toulon, France. He came to the States in 1971 and was drafted into the Marine Corps, where he worked in many of the world's trouble spots. After discharge, he settled in Taos where he was employed at the Austing Haus and the Saint Bernard restaurants. He moved to Albuquerque and opened his French Riviera Bakery on 4th Street in 1992. Currently, he bakes around 500 loaves a day that he retails from his shop and sells to local restaurants. His selection of Old World breads includes many types and configurations: alpine, *alpinette*, baguette, boule, *couronne*, *épices*, *fougasse*, Parisian, peasant loaf, rye, and six grain.

You'll find pastry shelves containing croissants, brioche, *pain de campagne*, napoleons, linzertorte, strudel, éclairs, profiteroles, Danish pastry, and tarts. For the holidays he'll do a *bûche de Noël* and for weddings, a *croquembouche*. All baked goods are preservative free, made from scratch using only pure butter as shortening.

French Riviera Bakery, Inc., 4208 4th Street NW, Albuquerque, 87107; (505) 343-0112.

Le Paris French Bakery & Deli

Parisians Philippe and Aude Laau arrived fresh from Europe in 1999 and opened their bake shop, first on San Pedro and finally on Eubank, where they have a larger floor plan. A combination of café and bakery, the store is a little bit of France in Albuquerque. It's a welcoming atmosphere with its cream colored walls, a wheat sheaf wall frieze, French and U.S. flags, and a collection of miniature Eiffel towers. A case filled with bread, cookies, pastries, and cakes lines one wall, and the dining area extends into another room with its bistro tables and white-and-blue color scheme.

They bake Parisian, Parmesan, *alpinette, miche,* herb and garlic, and baguette loaves. On weekends, they will add epis, sun bread, and *marguerites* (flower-shaped loaves). Pastries include palmiers, scones, turnovers, croissants, brioche, *sacristans,* strudel, profiteroles, *chou a la crème,* tarts, cheesecake, cookies, and meringues. No preservatives are used.

The café serves a bistro menu with quiche, salads, soups, and nine varieties of sandwiches. Try their Asiago Bisque paired with the Royal Sandwich of turkey, ham, and cheese, or the Rustic with house-made pâté and tomato. All sandwiches are served with the tiny pickles called cornichons, which you don't find in many U.S. delis. In addition, they serve breakfast, which features omelets, crêpes, and egg dishes. Closed Sunday.

Le Paris French Bakery & Deli, 1439 Eubank Boulevard NE, Albuquerque, 87112; (505) 299-4141.

Swiss Alps Bakery

The dream of owning his own bakery stayed with Raimond Pepe from his boyhood in a small village near Zurich, Switzerland, through his baking apprenticeship. His working experience ranged from Swiss high-tech operations to places without electricity in Thailand. For 16 years, he traveled and gained experience, always searching for a place he could call his own. One day he saw an advertisement for a bakery for sale in Albuquerque, and in April 1999 he made the decision to move his family west and set up shop.

The Swiss Alps Bakery is the fruit of his labors, and a better Old World bakery couldn't be found anywhere. Raimond specializes in dark breads such as rye, pumpernickel, and farmer's loaves. (Author's favorite: his *ciabatoni.*) In addition, he bakes traditional Italian and French breads; sourdough; and specialty breads such as sunflower, walnut, Calabrese, and challah. His pastries make you drool just looking at them. He does napoleons, rum balls, éclairs, beehives, tíramisu, fruit tarts, profiteroles, brownies, strudel—the list is almost endless. His Danish pastries are diet breakers, especially the Swiss nut rolls, almond horns, and Swiss delights. Of course, he does cakes—Black Forest, hazelnut, mocha, and chocolate.

In addition to staffing his shop, you'll also find him or his wife, Soraida, summer Saturday mornings at the Los Rancho de Albuquerque farmers' market.

Swiss Alps Bakery, 6607 Menaul Boulevard NE, Albuquerque, 87110; (505) 881-3063.

Panaderías

Golden Crown Panadería

Tucked away in a neighborhood of modest homes in the old Sawmill District, the Golden Crown Panadería is housed in an aged adobe flamboyantly decorated with a riot of Mexican vines and flowers. Owner Pratt Morales is the one-man dynamo in charge. A former Air Force accountant, Morales knew counting numbers wasn't in his future. He says, "The accounting profession didn't allow for creativity. I wasn't in love with it."

Baking fascinated him, and wherever he was stationed, he visited bake and bread shops for whatever knowledge he could garner. When a bakery in Albuquerque went out of business after a half a century, Morales bought the operation and jumped in cold, learning as he went. He has been at his current location on Mountain Road for the past 12 years, and he is living his dream, baking bread that is "nutritious, delicious, and beautiful."

His breads fill all those requirements. Using a recipe for hard-crust Italian loaves, he makes baguettes, epis, rustic shapes, and *bolillos*, the Mexican roll that he does in both large and small dinner-roll sizes. He loves to "give life to his bread" by creating bread sculptures for special events. He has crafted Thanksgiving roasted turkeys, castles for visiting dignitaries, and once a whole state fair booth made entirely of bread.

His *pièce de résistance* is his green-chile bread, which is decorated with a coyote howling at the moon. "I wanted to create a bread that captured the aroma of green chiles roasting," he explains. "I use fresh tomatoes, onions, cilantro, green chile, Parmesan cheese, and spices. The secret is my method of incorporating these ingredients without making the dough soggy."

In addition to bread, Morales bakes Hispanic specialties such as crisp flautas stuffed with fruits and Bavarian cream; tasty empanadas in assorted flavors; powder sugar–coated Mexican wedding cookies; *bizcochitos* in anise, chocolate, and cappuccino; and other delights. His *bizcochitos* are famous for their elimination of what most consider a key ingredient: lard. Wanting a healthier alternative, he experimented with many possibilities before settling on a soy replacement. "Most customers swear they can't tell the difference," he says. Open only Tuesday through Saturday.

Golden Crown Panadería, 1103 Mountain Road NW, Albuquerque, 87102; (505) 243-2424; www.goldencrown.biz.

Pastelandia

If you are searching for a *panadería* like you found in Mexico, Pastelandia is the place to go. Remember how in Mexico City, Oaxaca, or Guadalajara you'd search out a bakery by the yeasty smells emanating from the ovens? You'd wander in and there would be rack after rack of sweet rolls in all configurations with myriad decorations from icing to colored sugars. The person behind the counter did not wait on you but pointed to a stack of small trays and tongs used to make the selections, which you took to the cashier. Pastelandia is just like those Mexican shops.

Little English is spoken, but the drill is obvious. The bakery is immaculately clean and the help accommodating even if you can't speak Spanish. By exact count one day, we numbered 30 different types of sweet rolls, or *pan dulce*, plus several trays of *bizcochitos*.

Pastelandia, 139 Coors Boulevard SW, Albuquerque, 87121; (505) 836-3933.

Tortillerías

Tortillas are now almost mainstream, and you no longer have to search high and low for this basic product of the Hispanic kitchen. Years ago in the East I had to use regular cornmeal, a rolling pin, and a fry pan to make tortillas for enchiladas. They were really quite terrible.

Although considerably more available now, the grocery store variety cannot hold a candle to the freshly made product. Albuquerque has a number of *tortillerías*, large and small, from the Albuquerque Tortilla Company, which makes nearly 1.5 million corn and flour tortillas a day, to the little neighborhood store handing them right off the *comal*. To sift the wheat from the chaff, we visited them and did a taste test on both the corn and flour varieties.

Dos Hermanos

Dos Hermanos's platter-sized flour tortillas are close on the heels of the Frontier's. With four locations throughout the metro area, you don't have far to drive for your tortilla fix. More expensive than most (but larger than most), Dos Hermanos's tortillas are hand-rolled and made from a special family recipe.

The restaurants themselves are basic, with take-out and ordering counters and no-frills seating. Owner Robert Martinez created Dos Hermanos in 1992, and many of his recipes come from his mother, Jessie, who has a restaurant in Española. Their most popular item is the burrito, using those delicious flour tortillas, and many Duke City residents favor their tamales, which sell out during the holiday season.

Dos Hermanos, 6211 4th NW, Albuquerque, 87107; (505) 345-4588; 7600 Jefferson NE, 87109; (505) 828-1166; 2435 Wyoming NE, 87112; (505) 294-8945; 5010 Cutler NE, 87110; (505) 881-2202; www.redorgreen.com.

The Frontier Restaurant

First place for flour tortillas goes to the Frontier Restaurant. Located on Central Avenue across the street from the University of New Mexico bookstore, the Frontier has been an Albuquerque tradition since 1971. It covers a city block and is open 24 hours a day. You'll find it packed with college students eating, chatting, and pouring over books. The unusual order counter features a series of stations with flashing green lights signaling the next available clerk. Lines wind out the door at busy times, but the action is swift.

Some of their specialties include fresh-squeezed orange juice, plate-sized sweet rolls swimming in butter, and belly-busting breakfast burritos filled with scrambled eggs, melted cheese, hash browns, and green chile. However, it's their wonderful, light flour tortillas that bring us back time after time. A semi-automatic tortilla machine runs constantly, shaping and baking the dough into light, fluffy rounds that sell by the dozen. Their flavor, freshness, and consistency cannot be beaten.

The Frontier Restaurant, 2400 Central SE, Albuquerque, 87106; (505) 266-0550; www.frontierrestaurant.com.

Tortillería Cuauhtemoc

Coming in a respectable third in the flour tortilla taste test but first in the corn tortilla test, tiny Tortillería Cuauhtemoc sells only tortillas. Located east of the river in the South Valley, it is housed in a simple storefront. No English is spoken. You walk in, and if you're fluent in Spanish, you order. If you're linguistically challenged, you pick out your order and watch the cash register for the total. Flour tortillas are sold by the dozen. Corn tortillas come only in packages of 36. Piping hot, fragrant, and wrapped in unglazed paper, they are the essence of corn.

Tortillería Cuauhtemoc, 844 Bridge Street SW, (near National Spanish Cultural Center), Albuquerque, 87105; (505) 254-9940.

Breweries and Brewpubs

Assets Grille and Brewing Company

Albuquerque and vicinity have a fine roster of breweries and brewpubs. Assets Grille and Brewing Company is one of the earliest leaders in bringing craft-brewed beer to the state in 1993. Brewmaster Daniel Jaramillo produces nine standard beers that rotate by season. A recent roster includes Albuquerque Pale Ale, Duke City Amber, Kaktus Kolsch, Pablos Porter, Rio Grand Copper Ale, Roadrunner Ale, and Sandia Stout. Do you want to take some home? They sell half- and full-gallon growlers, 5- and 15-gallon kegs for off-premises consumption.

The restaurant always features five or six of their own beers, a handsome copper and wood bar, and seating at a dozen or so tables and booths. An outdoor patio opens up in warm weather.

Assets Grille and Brewing Company, 6910 Montgomery Boulevard NE, Albuquerque, 87109; (505) 889-6400.

Chama River Brewing Co.

Chama River Brewing Co. has locations in Albuquerque and Santa Fe. Ted Rice handles the responsibilities of head brewer in the Duke City, while Cullen Dwyer fills that job in Santa Fe. They produce High Altitude Pale Ale, which they describe as "altitude with an attitude— aggressively brewed with Centennial hops for bold beer lovers and hopheads."

Their Honeymoon Wheat Ale is dry, crisp, and delicately spiced with coriander and orange peel. Plaza Porter has chocolate and smoke tones with a balance of hops and malt for a subtle aroma and quick finish. End of the Trail Brown Ale is a dark beer with a light taste, and their Atomic Blonde Ale is a medium-bodied barley beer infused with American hops for balanced bitterness. In the Albuquerque location, brewmaster Rice holds Friday night brew tours.

Lunch specials meld southwestern enchiladas, tacos, carne adovada, and huevos rancheros with all-American entrées such as fish-and-chips and home-style meatloaf. The dinner menu expands the Southwest selections and adds specials including cedar plank salmon, T-bone and strip steaks, and a ribs and chicken basket.

Chama River Brewing Co., 4939 Pan American, Albuquerque, 87109; (505) 342-1800; Café & Brewery, 4056 Cerrillos Road, Santa Fe, 87507; (505) 438-1800; Downtown Café, 133 Water Street, Santa Fe, 87501; (505) 984-1800; www.riochamabrewery.com.

Kelly's Brewery

The hangout in Nob Hill you see jumping with thirtysomethings is Kelly's Brew Pub. If the building resembles an old auto dealership, that's because it was. Constructed as a Ford automotive center on historic Route 66, Kelly's served the needs of another generation's motorists with its big bays and Texaco service. The great old building fulfilled many purposes until 1997 when Janice and Dennis Bonfantine took it over and transformed it into a brewery and restaurant. The original Texaco sign is still out front with "Kelly's" emblazoned in the star in place of the original "T."

As one of the largest breweries in the state, they have 20 styles of beer constantly available: Blonde Ale, Golden Ale, Red Ale, Apricot Ale, ESB (extra strong/special bitter), Hefeweizen, Dunkleweizen, Belgian Pale Ale, Belgian Dubbel, British Pale Ale, Indian Pale Ale, Amber Ale, Altbier, Scottish Ale, Brown Ale, Black Ale, Bitter, Robust Porter, Oatmeal Stout, and Imperial Stout. In addition, they do seasonal specials such as Oktoberfest. In 2002, they produced 1,010 barrels, or 2,020 kegs (a barrel equals 31 gallons). On a busy Friday night, they have been known to finish off 25 kegs.

Another Kelly's special feature is their Brew Your Own Beer facility, the only one in the state. Customers may choose a beer recipe and, using the in-house ingredients, brew their own beer. The first operation takes about two hours, and the product is allowed to ferment for two weeks. The customer returns and performs the bottling operation, which results in a full keg of beer.

The restaurant's menu specializes in pub fare: appetizers such as jalapeño poppers and chicken wings, soups and salads, and sandwiches ranging from Kelly's Club to an ostrich burger. Dinners run from steak to bratwurst with sauerkraut.

Kelly's Brewery, 3222 Central Avenue SE, Albuquerque, 87106; (505) 262-2739.

Milagro Brewery and Milagro Grill

Milagro Brewery and Milagro Grill are just north of Albuquerque in Bernalillo. The brewery is located below the restaurant, and seats in the lounge overlook the brew house and the huge copper vats. Brewmaster Robert Lee, who trained at the American Brewers' Guild in Woodland, California, makes 20 different styles of beer, three of which are always on tap: Milagro Gold, a pale ale; Milagro Silver, a Kolsch; and Milagro Bronze, a porter. Seasonal additions might include Hefeweizen, English Brown Ale, Milagro Copper (a bitter), Extra Stout, Weizenbock, 80 Schilling Scottish Ale, English Indian Pale Ale, MSB (Milagro special bitter), Fallfest, Sandia Blonde Ale, Platinum Blonde Ale, Diablo de Oro (Belgian strong), and Barleywine. All his malt is English floor-malted, which gives it a better taste and superior quality.

The Milagro Grill occupies the major portion of the upstairs building, with dining rooms and a patio that have a combined occupancy of 400. The dining rooms, lounge area, and patio all have a panoramic views of the Sandia Mountains. The lunch menu includes fish-and-chips, green-chile enchiladas, fish tacos, a variety of wraps, and bratwurst made with their own Milagro Bronze. For dinner entrées, you'd find Angus New York strip steak, Chicken Marsala, Roast Loin of Pork, and a daily fish special.

Milagro Brewery and Milagro Grill, 1016 Paseo del Rio West (U.S. 550), Bernalillo, 87004; (505) 867-7200; www.milagrobrewing.com.

CULINARY
NEW MEXICO

Il Vicino

Il Vicino is a restaurant group that includes two restaurant locations in Albuquerque and one each in Santa Fe, New Mexico; Clayton, Missouri; Wichita, Kansas; and Denver and Colorado Springs, Colorado. They brew their own specialty beers. The brewery for all New Mexico locations is on Vassar Street in Albuquerque, where a taproom is available for sampling and purchase of pints, half-gallon growlers, and kegs in 5- and 15 ¹/₂-gallon sizes.

Albuquerque brewmaster Brady McKeown makes a variety of styles, although in the taproom they feature six: the Wet Mountain India Pale Ale, Slow Down Brown Ale, Irish Red Ale, Pigtail Blonde Ale, and two special selections, usually a porter and a stout. The taproom is open noon to 7:00 P.M. Tuesday through Friday and 1:00 to 5:00 P.M. Saturday.

Il Vicino Restaurants, 3403 Central NE, Albuquerque, 87106; (505) 266-7855; 11225 Montgomery NE, Albuquerque, 87111; (505) 271-0882; Brewing Company Tap Room, 4000 Vassar Street NE, Albuquerque, 87107; (505) 830-4629; www.ilvicino.com.

Butcher Shops and Carnicerias

If you've never been inside one of Albuquerque's Mexican butcher shops, you will find the meat selections a mystery. First, there is bewildering number of cuts, most of which have unfamiliar Spanish names. Second, the cuts resembling steak or chuck are thinner and have bones in odd places. Third, you'll notice more "innards," such as tongue, tripe, and liver. However, if you are looking for authentic ingredients for a special Mexican or New Mexican meal, the *carnicería* is the place to go.

Carniceria Familia Mexicana

One of the best is Ron Baca's Carniceria Familia Mexicana at the SoLo Shopping Center on Bridge Street. Ron has been in business six years, and he typifies his customer base as 70 percent native Mexican, 20 percent Hispanic, and the remaining 10 percent Anglo. His 48-foot refrigerated meat case is immaculate and beautifully arranged in sections for beef, pork, sausage, chicken and poultry, fish and shrimp, and Mexican as well as Mennonite cheese. He sells 20,000 pounds of meat a week, so his offerings are always fresh. His best seller is *chuleta de siete*, an inexpensive cut used for carne adovada and carne asada.

The store isn't large, but it's packed with all varieties of Mexican-style canned goods, produce, tortillas, hot sauces, and chiles, some of which aren't easily available elsewhere. Special masa flour for tamales is in stock as well as the more common tortilla masa. They even stock Bimbo Bread, Mexico's answer to our Wonder Bread, as well as Mexican cookware including metates and *comals*. Huge, colorful piñatas hang from the ceiling. It helps if you speak Spanish, but Ron or one of his butchers usually can help in English. Open daily.

Carniceria Familia Mexicana, 1720 Bridge Boulevard SW, Albuquerque, 87105; (505) 244-3107.

El Mesquite Mercado Y Carniceria

Sergio Burmudez and his family emigrated from Sonora, Mexico, in 1999 and immediately stunned the community by opening four stores, one right after the other. Scattered through the city and in nearby Los Lunas, these Hispanic supermarkets are stocked with groceries and produce at the front and massive meat counters stretching the width of the back. Thankfully for gringos, the meat selections are bilingually labeled so even if the butcher does speak English you can tell the spareribs from the beef shanks. Their encyclopedic selection covers all things Latino, and they bake their own tortillas. There are snack bars serving all the usual noshes.

El Mesquite Mercado Y Carniceria, 3645 Isleta Boulevard SW, Albuquerque, 87105; (505) 877-0980; 201 San Pedro SE, Suite B-1, Albuquerque, 87108; (505) 255-1163; 4401 4th Street, Albuquerque, 87107; (505) 344-3235; 1910 Main Street "A", Los Lunas, 87031; (505) 565-0990.

Chocolatier

Theobroma Chocolatier

Theobroma Chocolatier in the Glenwood Village Shopping Center is a chocoholic's heaven. Charles and Heidi Weck's little store is packed floor to ceiling with gift baskets and bags, chocolate sculptures, molded items, and special seasonal fruit dipped in chocolate. Self-taught chocolatiers, the Wecks use only the best, Peters Ultra Swiss Chocolate, and all pieces are hand-dipped, not enrobed.

The exceptionally attractive packaging is done in house, and

Charles says "Our items are dual gifts. You enjoy the chocolate and use the containers after the fact. I believe chocolate is the highest impact gift you can give. Most people will not buy the luxury chocolate for themselves, so when it's received, it's so much more special."

The Wecks have more than 300 molds for various occasions and seasons. Of course, everyone knows the chocolate bunnies, but have you ever seen a chocolate "sweet tooth," a pair of cowboy boots, a guitar, a tennis racquet, or a "chocoholic diet pill"?

Charles reports that his all-time best seller is the Chocolat y Maiz, which, unbelievably, is dark or milk chocolate–coated cornflakes. Other favorites are the dark chocolate buttercream truffles dusted with French Brut Cocoa Powder and the Cortez Crunch, which has a layer of dark chocolate, a layer of chocolate caramel, and a layer of milk chocolate. It is topped with crushed chocolate cookie topping.

Additionally, they sell Taos Cow, a regional premium ice cream, in seven flavors, including their store special that mixes the Cow's regular dark chocolate with a bit of Amaretto. Closed Sunday.

Theobroma Chocolatier, 12611 Montgomery NE, Albuquerque, 87111; (505) 293-6545.

Cooking Schools

Le Café Miche

Tuesday evenings Chef Claus Hjortkjaer puts on his *toque blanche* and teaches a two-hour demonstration class at the Wine Bar of Le Café Miche. For a three-course dinner with wine pairing, he might tackle steamed mussels, lamb shanks, and a dessert of crème caramel. At class end, students enjoy the fruits of his labor.

Le Café Miche, 1431 Wyoming NE, Albuquerque, 87112; (505) 299-6088; www.lecafemiche.com.

Jane Butel Southwestern Cooking School

The Jane Butel Cooking School of Albuquerque specializes in weekend and weeklong hands-on instruction with Jane or her staff of internationally trained guest chefs and teachers. Housed in a spacious 2,000-square-foot facility in the historic La Posada de Albuquerque hotel downtown, the school has a mirrored demonstration area plus six complete workstations with sink, stove, and utensils. Classes are broken up into groups of three or four, with each group working at one of the stations under supervision of the teacher.

The traditional weekend class begins Friday with a welcome reception and a discussion of the history and traditions of the ingredients to be used. After Saturday or Sunday's continental breakfast with Jane and her staff, the rest of the morning is spent preparing selected popular dishes for your luncheon. An expanded weeklong version is available Sunday through Friday, and the school offers some evening programs on culinary techniques, barbecue, and southwestern smoking and grilling.

Jane Butel Southwestern Cooking School, 125 2nd Street NW, Albuquerque, 87102; (505) 243-2622 or (800) 472-8229; www.janebutel.com.

CULINARY
NEW MEXICO

Now We're Cooking

Now We're Cooking, a fab cookware store at the Northtown Mall, has two-hour demonstration classes most Thursday evenings. Programs feature guest chefs such as Claus Hjortkjaer of Le Café Miche and store staff. You'll find subjects ranging from "fearless baking" to light pasta sauces, rolling your own sushi, how to use Thanksgiving leftovers, and more.

Now We're Cooking, 5901 Wyoming Boulevard NE, Albuquerque, 87109; (505) 857-9625.

Soirée Personal Caterers

On Saturday mornings, Albuquerque's National Restaurant Supply Company opens its kitchens to Jennifer and Craig Sharp of Soirée Personal Caterers, who teach a two-hour hands-on class. Topics have included quick breads, heavenly potatoes (gnocchi and blinis), hors d'oeuvres, and sushi. They also run three-hour classes in a Monday series that addresses single subjects such as cheese and poultry preparation.

Soirée Personal Caterers, National Restaurant Supply Company, 2513 Comanche Road NE, Albuquerque, 87107; (505) 922-9367.

Vivace

Vivace, that bastion of regional Italian cooking, runs Sunday cooking schools with Chef Gordon Schutte of Vivace and experts in wine pairing, seafood selection, and more. You might learn about Italian grilling, how to do a fast Italian dinner in less than 30 minutes, or the best way to construct an Italian salad.

"We've really had a great time with the classes and wine tastings we have been doing," says Gordon, "and this is another way for our friends to come together and enjoy our cuisine while mastering some of the techniques for their own kitchens."

Vivace, 3118 Central Avenue SE, Albuquerque, 87106; (505) 268-5965.

Cookware

Now We're Cooking

Now We're Cooking is Albuquerque's premier cookware store. Yes, you'll find cooking basics at any one of the city's department stores, but if you're searching for a brioche mold or a shrimp deveiner, you won't go astray at Now We're Cooking.

Owner Nancy Herring opened the store in 1998, rationalizing that "it sounded like a fun thing to do." She takes pride in keeping her shelves brimming over with cookware, including Cuisinart, Chantal, and the Le Creuset you see so often on the Food Channel; cutlery including Henckels and Wusthof; electronics for food preparation and specialty use; kitchen tools; cookbooks; and more. The store carries an eye-boggling array of gadgets, and as mystifying as many appear, every employee knows their function and will be happy to demonstrate.

Now We're Cooking, 5901 Wyoming Boulevard NE, Albuquerque, 87109; (505) 857-9625.

Dining

New American and Contemporary Global

Ambrozia

Ambrozia is both the food of the gods and a fine little restaurant hugging the edges of Old Town. Opened on Christmas Eve by owner and chef Sam Etheridge, Ambrozia lives up to its name with imaginative creations and elegant presentation. Housed in an old adobe fronting Rio Grande Boulevard, the multiple rooms celebrate the building's historic character and present a cozy, romantic dining experience.

Chef Sam has an impeccable pedigree, graduating from the Fort Lauderdale School of Culinary Arts and working as assistant chef and manager in Johnny Vincence's Florida restaurant. After coming to New Mexico, he headed kitchens at Portabello, Bien Sur, and Kanome.

At Ambrozia he concentrates on wine-based food, matching ingredients to the body, acidity, and overtones of vintages. He changes his menu frequently, depending on what is fresh and in season. A unique lunch dish is his Burgers à Trois, three mini-burgers, one with green chile and cheddar; one with mushrooms and Swiss cheese; and one with vine-ripened tomatoes, proscuitto, and fresh mozzarella. The dish is accompanied by potatoes prepared three different ways. Another great lunch treat is the Cuban Sandwich with roasted pork loin, smoked ham, Swiss cheese, sweet and spicy pickles, and mustard sauce on crispy grilled bread.

Etheridge is tremendously creative, pairing unusual ingredients in a very iconoclastic manner. One example is his Lobster Corn Dog. He dips skewered lobster tails in a jalapeño corn batter, deep-fries them, and serves them with chipotle ketchup, mustard cream, and avocado remoulade. Another unusual appetizer is his Pancetta-Wrapped Jumbo Shrimp served over white cheddar grits with a molasses chile glaze.

Combining tastes of Italy and Asia, he features dinner entrées such as his Mushroom Taster: Portobello Mushrooms and smoked mozzarella lasagna with a drizzle of truffle oil, Edamame Dumplings in a shitake mushroom soy broth, and an Oyster Mushroom and Artichoke Tart with chile glaze. Echos of the Old West appear in his buffalo rib eye, seared in a cast-iron skillet and served with cowboy beans, red wine–braised collard greens, tempura mushroom sate, and a buffalo jerky sauce.

Desserts are no less extraordinary. "Coffee and Donuts" are beignets stuffed with chocolate ganache and served with *dulce de leche* custard, espresso whipped cream, and vanilla crème anglaise, and the Irish Chocolate Bomb features a flourless truffle cake with Bailey's Irish cream mousse, Guiness ice cream, and Irish whiskey gelée.

Etheridge's four-course weekend brunch is one of the most popular in Albuquerque. The first course is a selection of breads, croissants, pastries, and sweet rolls. The second course showcases French toast, Pig in a Pancake (sage sausage dipped in pancake batter and served with three kinds of syrup), Bagel and Lox Three Ways (citrus cured, smoked, and chile glazed), and Chicken-Fried Duck (buttermilk-soaked fried duck breast over potato hash with tomato-bacon vinaigrette). A third course tenders huevos rancheros, Ambrozia Benedict, steak and eggs, or biscuits and gravy. These are not your grandma's soakers. Etheridge crafts green-chile and cheddar biscuits, stuffs them with soft scrambled eggs, and tops them with foie gras country gravy. The fourth course, if you're still hungry, lists a fruit and cheese sampler, ice cream, a sweet crêpe, or (are you ready for this?) a batter-fried peanut butter and jelly sandwich.

Ambrozia schedules prix fixe dinners and special event celebrations. There's an extensive wine list ranging from a rare Bordeaux Saint Julien Chateau Ducru-Beaucaillon FR '96 to a more down-to-earth Dry Creek Merlot '99. In addition, you have a wide choice of more than 30 vintages available by the glass.

Ambrozia Café and Wine Bar, 108 Rio Grande Boulevard NW, Albuquerque, 87104; (505) 242-6560.

The Artichoke Café

The Artichoke Café is a little off the beaten path on Central in the historic Huning Highland District, between downtown and the University of New Mexico area. However, you will find, as have so many city professionals and businesspeople, that it's well worth the trip. Housed in an old adobe with a crisp blue awning, the Artichoke is a sophisticated place to eat and greet. The interior is expansive and is divided into several dining rooms, all clothed in the same pale green as its namesake vegetable. Accents of purple and beige follow the tonality of the artichoke's leaves. Rotating art graces the walls.

Owner Terry Keene and owner and chef Pat Keene purchased the building in 1989 from Addy Ames who ran a cookware store and small lunchtime café. Through the years, they have expanded the space so that they can now seat 120.

Terry and Pat entered the restaurant business the hard way. Terry started out as a waiter at the Montana Mining Company steakhouse chain and gradually advanced to manager of franchises in Albuquerque, El Paso, and Tulsa.

While running a restaurant in Hoboken, New Jersey, with Terry, Pat attended the New York Restaurant School to secure her chef's credentials, which served her well when they opened the Artichoke. Pat continued as executive chef until several years ago, when the growth of the business determined that another hand was needed, and Richard Winters was hired to head the kitchen. Pat still confers on menu planning, but Richard does the day-to-day food preparation.

Pat defines Artichoke cuisine as "New American," inspired by a variety of ethnicities. The emphasis is on fresh ingredients, carefully prepared. Starters might include Steamed Artichoke (of course) with three dipping sauces; French Onion Soup Gratinee with imported Gruyère; or the popular Roasted Garlic with Montrachet Goat Cheese, bruschette, and roasted red peppers with extra-virgin olive oil. Dinner entrées always include two fish dishes, one the chef's seafood special of the day and the other a variation on salmon.

House-made ravioli is another featured item, and it's delicious. Ours was stuffed with artichoke puree and ricotta, bathed in a sauce of garlic, tomato concasse, arugula, fresh marjoram, white wine, and butter, and finished with hazelnuts and shaved Parmigianno-Reggiano.

A lunch standby is their classic Salad Niçoise with tuna, new potatoes, tomatoes, Niçoise olives, capers, hard-boiled egg, artichoke hearts, haricot vert, and anchovies over mixed greens with Dijon vinaigrette. Sandwiches include Grilled Eggplant with fresh mozzarella, roasted red peppers, and garlic caper aioli on fresh rosemary focaccia. For the carnivore there's Smoked Pork Loin with grilled red onion, Fontina cheese, arugula, and coarse-grain mustard.

Lunch is Monday through Friday and dinner, Monday through Saturday. Closed Sunday.

The Artichoke Café, 424 Central Avenue SE, Albuquerque, 87102; (505) 243-0200; www.artichokecafe.com.

Café Bodega

When Matt and Barbara Besse-Brewer closed their popular Café de las Placitas on a hillside several miles north of Albuquerque, many devoted customers went into temporary mourning. They brightened up considerably when the talented duo moved to town and opened Café Bodega on Montgomery. Nothing was lost in the exchange. In fact, the food and service at the Café Bodega surpassed even their previous top-notch efforts. Matt, a native of Farmington, trained at the California Culinary Academy and worked at several restaurants in San Francisco before returning to New Mexico.

You would never guess that the café is situated in a former

International House of Pancakes. The transformation into a sophisticated, elegant space is complete with arches dividing waiting area, dining room, demo kitchen, and servers' station. The color scheme is smoky tones of green, beige, and mauve, and eye-catching art breaks up and brightens the walls. Opera music at a discreet volume plays in the background.

The food is faultless, sometimes combining elements of different cuisines on a single plate. Matt makes everything in house including the pillowy soft loaves of bread and fabulous desserts. His signature appetizer is the Hangtown Fry, a modern rendition of a classic. Matt serves plump, large fried oysters with thick-sliced bacon and a bit of greens to be rolled in crêpes, fajita style. His most popular entrée is the Duck Confit with Fontina and leek ravioli, served in a wild mushroom and sage broth with a dab of marinara. The duck is meltingly tender, the mushrooms plentiful, and the ravioli radiating cheesy goodness. This is sooo marvelous you'll find yourself sopping up every little bit of sauce.

The extensive wine list has selections from Spain, Italy, France, California, Oregon, and New Mexico, and the dessert menu features Matt's justly famous crème brûlée. Closed Sunday and Monday. Open for lunch Tuesday through Friday, dinner Tuesday through Saturday.

Café Bodega, Granada Square, 4243 Montgomery Boulevard NE, Albuquerque, 87109; (505) 872-1710.

The Flying Star Cafés

The Flying Star Cafés are scattered around Albuquerque like a come-to-earth meteor shower. Like meteors, they are brilliant—in both concept and execution. If you envisioned a great place to gather with your friends, enjoy a good meal for less than $10, or catch up on the latest papers and magazines, you'd design a café like the Flying Star and make it accessible.

Mark and Jean Bernstein have done just that. From humble beginnings as a Nob Hill ice cream parlor and bakery, Flying Star has grown to six restaurants and three Satellite Coffee locations. The combination of fun, funky, energetic design pairs 1950s retro essentials with elements from the West and space. The mood is bright and sophisticated. Jean says, "Our designers have compared the atmosphere to a train station. Come as you are and be what you want to be."

When queried how the expansion occurred, Jean says, "We just listened to our customers. They showed the way, and it was trial by fire. We aimed for great food, great value, and no pretense." Keeping quality up at so many cafés and coffee shops is a difficult matter simplified by centralizing the baking in one location and constructing a commissary in another.

Flying Star's baked goods are legend, and you must pass a fully loaded case of pastries, cookies, cakes, and pies before placing your order at a counter. Best sellers include the Chocolate Mousse Cake, the Key Lime Pie, and the giant éclairs, each weighing a pound and filled with creamy custard. Few can resist that temptation.

The menu changes with the seasons and availability of ingredients. Jean and Mark publish a newsletter listing daily and weekly specials as well as special events. What might you find? There are always a couple soups of the day and both regular and vegetarian entrées. "We bake our own bagels and make our breads fresh daily. Our smoked salmon is house cured. I call our food interpretive international," Jean states. "Our pastry chef is Dutch and our sous chef French-Chinese with Italian training."

This multinationalism results in dishes such as Rio Grande Tamale Pie one day and Pasta Mediterranean another. Eastern influence shows up in their Hidden Treasure Rice Bowl, based on a chef's dream. It combines peas, onions, red peppers, carrots, and roasted potatoes in a rich, red coconut curry sauce hiding under a mountain of Chinese rice and with a fresh chicken breast perched on top.

The Flying Star Cafés and Satellite Coffee shops produce the best java in town, roasting their own blend from Sumatra beans and producing more than 80,000 pounds per year. The flavor and aroma are truly exceptional. As one habitué exclaimed, "This is serious coffee!"

What's the difference between the cafés and coffee shops? Jean puts it succinctly: "We felt we were losing the coffee shop portion of our business to the likes of Starbucks. Some found the high energy of our Flying Stars too much and wanted a calmer, more relaxed atmosphere. They'll find this at the Satellites." Satellites serve all the usual tea and coffee beverages, pastries, daily meat and vegetarian soups, quiche specials, and stuffed croissants.

Flying Star Cafés, 3416 Central Avenue SE, Albuquerque, 87106; (505) 255-6633; 4501 Juan Tabo NE, Albuquerque, 87111; (505) 275-8311; 4026 Rio Grande NW, Albuquerque, 87107; (505) 344-6714; 8100 Menaul Boulevard NE, Albuquerque, 87110; (505) 293-6911; 723 Silver SW, Albuquerque, 87108; 2201 Louisiana NE, Albuquerque, 87110; Satellite Coffee, 3513 Central Avenue NE, Albuquerque, 87106; (505) 256-0345; 1628 Alameda Boulevard NW, Albuquerque, 87114; (505) 899-1001; 8405 Montgomery Boulevard NE, Albuquerque, 87111; (505) 296-7654; www.flyingstarcafe.com.

Graze by Jennifer James and Jennifer James Contemporary Cuisine

Jennifer James is a multitalented chef whose versatility is evident in her two restaurants, Graze and Jennifer James Contemporary Cuisine, dissimilar in appearance but similar in culinary style. Graze by Jennifer James at 3128 Central Avenue SE features "small plates," where meals or noshes may be made up of one or many dishes. Try the Pâté Grand-

Mère, a smooth blend of marinated French chicken livers and pork, served with fig walnut bread, cornichons, and coarse mustard.

If that doesn't satisfy your appetite, you could add an entrée by pairing the Deviled Eggs with Caviar Garnish with the Duck Confit—duck legs marinated three days in spices and herbs, covered with duck fat, cooked in a slow oven for three hours, and crisped before serving with the house chutney. Perhaps you're ready for an afternoon pick-me-up of the Crème Caramel with ginger ice cream and chocolate chip cookies warm from the oven. It's difficult to make selections with so many tempting choices.

Graze's décor is industrial with big windows and high ceilings softened by a grass-green and gold color scheme. Metal tables and chairs contribute to the casual atmosphere. Jennifer James Contemporary Cuisine has completely different ambiance. Located in an old adobe house, it has a cozy, warm feel with warm yellow walls and slate tile floor. The ambiance is more European than New Mexican, and the menu amplifies many of the small bites you'll find at Graze.

On the "big plates" you'll find dishes such as Pan-Seared Niman Ranch Pork with savory apple bread pudding and herbed Brussels sprouts; Orange Roasted Ruby Trout with a golden beet, fennel, and sunflower seed salad; or Braised Ancho Chile Rubbed Venison Osso Buco with buttery yams and pickled red onions and cranberries.

Chef James received her culinary training on the job, first at Gourmet To Go in Saint Louis and at Chef du Jour and Le Café Miche in Albuquerque. "Our food is prepared by professional culinarians using fresh produce delivered daily. It's simple and straight to the point," she says. "I want to bring good food and good wine to a greater range of people and take the pretentiousness out of fine dining."

Graze is open 11:00 A.M. until 11:00 P.M. Tuesday through Saturday.

Jennifer James Contemporary Cuisine is open for dinner Tuesday through Saturday at 5:00 P.M. Reservations recommended.

Graze by Jennifer James, 3128 Central Avenue SE, Albuquerque, 87106; (505) 268-4729. Jennifer James Contemporary Cuisine, 2813 San Mateo NE, Albuquerque, 87110; (505) 884-3665; www.grazejj.com.

Prairie Star

Prairie Star is an exquisite restaurant on Santa Ana Pueblo land. Here's a winning combination of a beautiful setting and New Mexican cuisine transformed by the hand of a master chef into southwestern-inspired New American cuisine.

The adobe house once was the property of Mrs. Eva Wade Duke, who built the original small adobe structure with her own hands. Eventually she sold the property, and it was purchased by Harold Brooks in 1947. Brooks, who owned a local photo lab, hired an architect, and with a labor force of Indians from Santa Ana, Sandia, and Zia Pueblos constructed the present two-story, 6,000-square-foot adobe. Indians from Jemez Pueblo cut the house's 156 vigas from San Juan Mesa on the east fork of the Jemez River. Time passed and more owners came and went until the property became part of the Santa Ana Golf Corporation.

Completely remodeled to accommodate its new use, Prairie Star retains those characteristics that make it an excellent example of New Mexican Mission architecture: exposed vigas, full *latilla* (small peeled poles used as lath) ceilings, and hand-carved fireplaces and *bancos*. At any time of day the view of the Sandias is breathtaking, and at night the twinkling lights of the distant city create a romantic atmosphere.

Executive Chef Heath Van Riper has created a menu to warm the heart of any gastronome. You might start with a Roasted Tomato Salad with Spanish goat cheese, living watercress, roasted garlic crackers, basil syrup, and truffle oil, or try their Smoked Sweet Potato Chowder with green chile, chives, smoked bacon, and Styrian pumpkin seed oil. Entrées provide something for everyone from the carnivore to the vegetarian. A house special is their New Zealand Lamb T-Bones served with baked sweet potato torte, seared snow pea shoots, mint and pomegranate essences, and tart, sun-dried tomato jam.

On a recent evening, a friend from Boulder and author of *Culinary Colorado* pronounced the Muscovy Duck Breast with French Amarena cherries and micromint salad the best duck she'd ever eaten. Another diner opted for the Oyster Mushroom Terrine with cilantro-scented grits, Spanish chèvre, seared baby spinach, and roasted red pepper coulis. A third person ordered the Pepper Dusted Veal Chops with honey crisp apples, caramelized fennel hash, long beans, lingonberries, and cinnamon beurre noisette. All were remarkable.

Chef Van Riper's early experiences were on a Wyoming ranch where he learned the value of freshness and the style of scratch cooking. He says, "I have found the pursuit of a great meal isn't magic or a great chef's secret. I believe it is determined by the amount of passion put into the food. I have held this philosophy true to me, and it is all my passion that I extend to our customers."

Sommelier Samuel McFall has developed one of the area's finest and most innovative wine programs, boasting Riedel stemware, nearly 30 wines by the glass, and more than 450 selections, which currently comprise 2,000 bottles. Chef Van Riper and the Prairie Star culinary team have joined Sommelier McFall to create specially scheduled prix fixe wine-pairing dinners. Contact the restaurant for dates and times.

Prairie Star, 288 Prairie Star Road, Santa Anna Pueblo, 87004 (a short drive north of Albuquerque); (505) 867-3327; www.santaanagolf.com.

CULINARY
NEW MEXICO

The Range Café

The Range has been a regional favorite since it opened its first location in 1992 in Bernalillo. With the motto "serving ordinary food done extraordinarily well," Tom Fenton, a former musician with the Last Mile Ramblers, and Matt DiGregory, an ex–film school graduate, have expanded their operation to include two Albuquerque eateries. Their story is an exercise in perseverance.

Bernalillo in 1992 was a sleepy Hispanic town whose greatest claim to fame was Rose's Pottery Shop and Silva's Saloon. Matt and Tom were brave pioneers when they rented an old adobe building on the town's main street and set up shop. The locals anxiously waited to see what the gringos had in mind. To everyone's surprise, the small café was a hit, and before long crowds lined the sidewalk, waiting for tables.

In 1995, the café underwent a much-needed face-lift with new tables and chairs and new hardwood floors. Then at 2:30 the morning of May 30, disaster struck. The building burned to the ground, new accoutrements and all. Help poured in from all sides. A benefit was organized by three local bed-and-breakfasts. There was an art auction, and hundreds of people showed up to raise more than $10,000.

Rebuilding at the former spot was not practical due to size restrictions, but Mary Ann Bessom, proprietor of the Old Convent Art Gallery, offered a space in the historic building. Two months after the fire, the Range was back in business.

Hampered by a cramped kitchen and the lack of a beer and wine license due to the proximity of a church, Matt and Tom once again looked for a permanent home. They found it in an old building owned by Rose and Antoinette Silva, which once housed a soda fountain, jewelry-manufacturing company, and the Lovato Drugstore. After renovation, the Range opened in December 1996, its third home in four years.

Thankfully, the remaining years have been smooth sailing with the opening of Albuquerque Range restaurants on 4200 Wyoming Boulevard NE in 2000 and on 2200 Menaul Boulevard NE in 2004.

The menu at all three locations is identical and might be characterized as the kind of food Mom would have produced had she been a talented and innovative chef. Open for breakfast, lunch, and dinner, the Range is especially popular for weekend brunch. After 11:00 A.M., you can order starters ranging from Green-Chile Chicken Stew to New Mexico Taco Salad. There are "north of the border" offerings including burritos, chimichangas, chile rellenos, enchiladas, and a combination plate. Sandwiches include the aptly named Rio Grande Gorge, a six-ounce grilled patty served open-faced on a flour tortilla with green chile, cheddar cheese, and grilled onions. A personal favorite is their Vegetarian Portobello Mushroom Burger, a grilled mushroom cap with red wine–sautéed red onions and poblano chile aioli, served on a bun.

Evening specials include dishes such as Range Scallops, sautéed scallops bathed in cilantro-lime cream sauce with grilled tomatoes and served over red-chile linguine with pine nuts and Parmesan. A perennial favorite, Tom's Meatloaf, is always on the menu, as are their Country Fried Steak, Pan-Seared Trout, and DiGregory's Gramma's Spaghetti and Meatballs.

For dessert, you may choose from their selection of fresh-baked pastries including a delicious French Apple Tarte Tatin; Life by Chocolate, three types of chocolate and raspberry mousse layered and glazed with a rich ganache; or Death by Lemon, a shortbread crust filled with a baked lemon custard and glazed with apricot preserves. In addition, they serve superpremium Taos Cow ice cream.

Whichever Range Café you choose, you can't help but be charmed by the funky décor and bustling atmosphere. If you're in a hurry, call ahead for takeout.

The Range Café, 925 Camino del Pueblo, Bernalillo, 87004; (505) 867-1700; 4200 Wyoming Boulevard NE, Albuquerque, 87111; (505) 293-2633; 2200 Menaul Boulevard NE, Albuquerque, 87107; (505) 888-1660; www.rangecafe.com.

Seasons Rotisserie and Grill

Seasons Rotisserie and Grill in San Felipe Plaza on the outskirts of Old Town is an elegant, sophisticated bistro providing great food in a relaxed environment. With its attractive main dining room decorated in soft earth tones and its popular warm-weather rooftop cantina bar, it draws a crowd of professionals and travelers to the Duke City.

Executive Chef Bob Petersen specializes in rotisserie food with a continental-American flare. You'll find items prepared by pan roasting, sautéing, and spit roasting over an oak wood fire. With a culinary style rooted in the American classics, the food at Seasons is more about taste and less about changing restaurant trends. Appetizers might include Minced Honey Duck Lettuce Wraps with an orange-chile dipping sauce or a Mushroom and Taleggio Napoleon of potato-chive pancakes anointed with truffle oil. One of their most popular entrées is the Blue Cheese–Crusted Beef Filet with fingerling potatoes, pan-roasted squash, and a roasted garlic port glaze. Other tempting dishes include the Double-Cut Pork Chop with rosemary roasted potatoes and cider-braised red cabbage or their Braised Colorado Lamb Shank with Parmesan polenta, herbed salad, and gremolata of lamb jus and lemon-mint. Vegetarian options are available such as the house-made Butternut Squash Ravioli with shitake mushrooms, Swiss chard, toasted hazelnuts, and aged Jack cheese.

As the weather warms, the rooftop cantina opens with a menu of starters, salads, sandwiches, and entrées such as Grilled Salmon Filet and Grilled Beef Flank Steak with horseradish mashed potatoes, portobello sauce, and fried onion strings. Their drink list features variations on classic cocktails including the martini, Manhattan, and daiquiri.

Seasons is owned by CEO Roger Roessler and partners Kevin Roessler and Luke Longley. The corporation operates a restaurant in Durango, Colorado, in addition to Zinc Wine Bar and Bistro on Albuquerque's Nob Hill. Amy Nordby, a former Geronimo chef, manages the Old Town business.

Seasons Rotisserie and Grill, 2031 Mountain Road NW, Albuquerque, 87104; (505) 766-5100; www.seasonsonthenet.com.

Barbecue

Quarters BBQ

Everyone has his own favorite barbecue emporium, but Albuquerque's Quarters ranks high on our list. Quarters began in 1970 when Connie Nellos opened his small restaurant in what had been Mrs. Zamora's Ice Cream Parlor on Yale Street. Business was good, and in 1980 Connie expanded by building a large eatery and liquor store on Wyoming Boulevard. A new West Side location opened in 2002, its distinctive modern design engineered by Connie's son Nicholas, whose young life was tragically ended that year in a random act of violence by two itinerant gang members.

Each restaurant boasts its own smoker, designed by Connie. The iron behemoths are fired with oak or fruitwood, and their special design allows different meats to be cooked at optimum temperatures. "We don't chintz on products," Connie says. "There's no way our customers can leave hungry or unhappy."

Portions are notoriously generous. You can choose from sandwiches, platters, and dinners, and selections include ribs, chicken, hot links, brisket, seafood, or any combination thereof. A side of coleslaw, baked beans, cottage cheese, potato salad, onion rings, or macaroni and cheese accompanies orders.

A personal favorite is the Quarters famous BBQ Spare Rib Sandwich with six succulent ribs bathed in Quarters's spicy sauce, resting on a slice of Texas toast. Specials include Monday and Tuesday's 16-ounce T-bone or 12-ounce prime rib and the Saturday lunch special of a burger and a beer.

Each restaurant has an attached liquor store, and Quarters is the largest independent dealer in spirits and wine in the state. Eating at Quarters provides an opportunity to choose a wine from their encyclopedic collection and enjoy it with your meal for a small corkage fee.

Each restaurant has its own ambiance, but all are casual, comfortable hangouts. The West Side location has a popular summertime patio overlooking the Sandia Mountains.

Quarters BBQ, 3700 Ellison Road NW (West Side), Albuquerque, 87114; (505) 897-3341; 4516 Wyoming Boulevard NE, Albuquerque, 87111; (505) 299-9864; and 801 Yale Boulevard SE, Albuquerque, 87106; (505) 843-7505.

Chinese

Chow's Chinese Bistro

You are treading in uncertain waters when you wander far from major cities where the Chinese settled and introduced a style of fine dining dating back thousands of years. Albuquerque, like many medium-sized cities without Chinatowns, has many Chinese restaurants catering to American tastes but few presenting the true scope and variety of China's regional cuisine.

Chow's Chinese Bistro is one establishment that has adjusted its menu to American tastes without losing its roots. Both Chow's, in Albuquerque and Santa Fe, are owned by Richard and Lucy Zeng. Richard emigrated from China 16 years ago, where he had studied language and literature at the university. He worked in San Francisco first as a reporter and later at the famous Peking Palace before settling in Albuquerque and opening his two restaurants. "One of my goals here is to teach more people about China, its splendid history and culture. I see them going through cuisine to culture."

Chow's specializes in "contemporary recipes" with healthy ingredients. It's fusion cooking incorporating elements of Japanese, Thai, Mexican, French, Italian, and American cuisine to create a completely new style.

On the menu you might find a traditional dish such as dumplings or pot stickers, but at Chow's they will be filled with ground turkey and carrots and tossed with a pesto spinach sauce. New Wave Scallops are wok-fried with steamed bok choy and red-chile rings in a coconut milk sauce. Mongolian Lamb combines tender stir-fried lamb slices, yellow onions, and scallions in a rich, savory sauce. Desserts mix Chinese delicacies such as green tea ice cream with all-American selections such as mud pie.

The décor is subdued. There are no fiery reds and paper lanterns. The ivory walls with framed scenes of waterfalls make a soothing ambiance, and a wall aquarium displays indolent fish swimming back and forth.

Chow's Chinese Bistro, 1950 Juan Tabo Boulevard NE, Albuquerque, 87117; (505) 298-3000; 720 Saint Michaels Drive, Ste. Q, Santa Fe, 87505; (505) 471-7120; www.mychows.com.

Ming Dynasty

Unlike Chow's, the Ming Dynasty is quintessential Chinese with an encyclopedic menu of more than 250 examples of Szechwan and Cantonese cuisine. Owned by Minh Tang, who was born in Vietnam to southern Chinese parents, the restaurant mirrors traditional décor with a moon gate entrance surmounted by a gold dragon and phoenix.

Although the regular offerings are quite good (we'll forgive them for catering to the uninitiated with chow mein and chop suey), the weekend dim sum brunch elevates this restaurant above similar establishments.

For the unversed, dim sum is the equivalent of Spanish tapas and consists of a variety of sweet and savory steamed, baked, and fried tidbits. Translated from the Cantonese, *dim sum* means "dot hearts," small treats that warm the heart. Ming Dynasty serves them in the traditional manner with servers bringing carts to your table. Diners point to the items they'd like to try and the dishes are set in the center of the table for all to enjoy. Lighter morsels are usually brought first. You might begin with *gyoza, siu mai*, and pot stickers—boiled, steamed, and pan-fried dumplings—and go on to *bao*, more substantial steamed buns containing meats, vegetables, and sweet bean paste or egg yolks. The very adventurous might even attempt stewed chicken feet, a delicacy. The traditional method of calculating your tab by counting dishes is not used at Ming Dynasty. Rather, the server makes notations on a pad as dishes are completed and cleared.

Hours are quirky. Call to confirm. Dim Sum served 11:00 A.M. to 3:00 P.M., Friday through Saturday. Closed Tuesday.

Ming Dynasty, 1551 Eubank Boulevard NE, Albuquerque, 87112; (505) 296-0298.

CULINARY NEW MEXICO

French

It's a fact that unless you're a native, you just can't eat chile every day, no matter how fine it is. That's when you start wondering what else is available. Of all cultures, perhaps the French have the reputation of being the best classic cooks. A French restaurant in the land of the enchilada? Suspend disbelief. Albuquerque is not without its *cuisine française.*

Le Café Miche

The Duke City's best-loved French restaurant is Le Café Miche, located, of all places, in a strip mall on Wyoming Boulevard. All vestiges of commercial development vanish once you set foot in the door. To the right of the host's stand, an elegant wine bar in forest green and maroon awaits. The several refined dining rooms carry the dark green theme in banquettes and accessories. Pure-white walls are pierced with large openings, giving the feeling of space, and live plants and fresh flower arrangements are everywhere. Glistening white napery covers the tables during both lunch and dinner. The whole effect is sophisticated and charming.

Owners Claus and Linda Hjortkjaer originally opened Le Café Miche in 1996. Chef Claus is a Dane who studied classic French cuisine in Denmark. When asked if he ever cooked his national dishes, he said, "I trained in the Escoffier school. I wouldn't know how to do Danish—all that fish, root vegetables, and pork." Prior to coming to Albuquerque, Claus worked in Taos at the old Casa Cordova (now Momentitos de la Vida) and the Thunderbird. In Santa Fe, he chefed at La Fonda Hotel and the Compound on Canyon Road. Café Miche initially had just eight tables, with Linda as server and Claus cooking. Today the restaurant employs 38, and the original small storefront now encompasses a greater part of the building.

The food is perfection, beautifully cooked and presented. The dinner appetizer menu includes such favorites as Frogs Legs Provençal, French Onion Soup, Gravlaks with mustard sauce, or Pan-Seared Foie Gras served over brioche, sautéed spinach, and garlic. The Rack of Lamb encrusted in Dijon mustard, breadcrumbs, and garlic and the Veal Scaloppini in Oscar, picatta, or Marsala styles are their best-selling entrées.

You'll also find French dishes not usually encountered in a city the size of Albuquerque. If you have a hankering for Veal Sweetbreads in Amontillado sherry-tomato démi-glace, they have it. Or if you'd prefer a Bouillabaisse of scallops, clams, mussels, shrimp, and fresh fish du jour in a saffron broth garnished with rouille crostini, they can provide. Their wine list is one of the most extensive in town.

The lunch menu starters list a soup du jour as well as the onion soup, and Escargot Poached in White Wine and served in a French crock with garlic Pernod butter sauce. There's a selection of crêpes including Grilled Salmon topped with fresh fruit relish and crème fraîche and Coq au Vin with free-range chicken braised in red wine with pearl onions, carrots, and bacon. Salads are not your usual greens and dressing. The Duck Confit Salad has a leg of duck over market greens tossed in white truffle oil and aged balsamic vinegar. The Crab Cake Salad is comprised of two sautéed patties served over greens with a curry aioli, fresh carrot salad, and Belgium endive. The Claus Salad has mozzarella and tomatoes dressed with balsamic vinaigrette on butter lettuce. A quiche du jour is presented daily.

Sandwiches run from regular deli style to the exotic, such as Chicken and Duck Liver Pâté on a sesame roll or Grilled Chicken Saltimbocca served warm with proscuitto ham, fresh mozzarella, and aioli sage. Some entrées repeat dinner selections, for example the Veal Picatta, Oscar, or Marsala, but there are always specials recited by your waitperson. An unusual and delectable entrée is the Braised Pork Shank served over garlic mashed potatoes. The rich sauce is a mirepoix of leeks, celery, carrots, and onions reduced with tomato and sun-dried prunes. If you love osso buco, you will go wild for this!

Le Café Miche has been rated the best French restaurant in the state for three years in a row by Zagat Survey and has been given the Award of Excellence by *Wine Spectator* magazine. Chef Claus publishes a monthly newsletter with all their many special events, the subjects of his Tuesday evening cooking classes, and monthly wine-pairing dinner. There's jazz every Thursday, Friday, and Saturday nights in the wine bar. Lunch is served Monday through Friday; dinner and wine bar, Tuesday through Sunday.

Le Café Miche, 1431 Wyoming Boulevard NE, Albuquerque, 87112; (505) 299-6088; www.lecafemiche.com.

Café Voila

Located in the Marketplace at Journal Center, Café Voila is tucked into a corner of the mini-mall that services the Albuquerque Publishing Company and the concentration of office buildings in the area. Owned by Debbie and Christian Tournier, Café Voila is a French restaurant that tailors its lunch offerings to the nature of its business clientele while serving a classic French menu at dinner.

Chef Christian received his training at a French hotel school near Dijon and came to the States in 1999 to open the French Corner Bakery in Albuquerque, which he later sold before purchasing La Cuisine Restaurant. That place was too small and had limited parking, so when Café Voila became available in 2003, he moved his operation there.

Lunch is their busiest time, and to aid in the process of snappy service, the café provides take-out sheets for their sandwiches, soups, crêpes, quiches, salads, and pastas. The spacious dining rooms have butter colored walls and accents in dark green and wine. An outdoor patio takes overflow and sun bunnies in moderate weather. There's an attractive wine bar with counter and banquette seating.

The midday menu lists two types of soup, French onion and the daily special. Quiches are served with house salad, and they run from leek and salmon to tomatoes, basil, and mozzarella. The hot crêpes include chicken and vegetables in a light cream sauce, vegetarian Crêpes Ratatouille, and Crêpes Salmon with leeks in a cream sauce. Salads range from Niçoise to Waldorf, and pastas run from Spaghetti Napolitania to Rainbow Lasagna with meat sauce. There are two grilled steaks, rib eye and T-bone, seared with your choice of red wine démi-glace, blue cheese, or green peppercorn sauce, and several fish dishes including Fish-and-Chips and Grilled or Poached Salmon with sorrel sauce.

The dinner menu has openers of Bisque of Lobster, homemade Duck Terrine, and Shallow Fried Frog Legs with butter garlic and parsley. Entrées include Mussels in Wine, Herbs, and Garlic, Dover Sole in

Lemon Butter, traditional French Pepper Steak with brandy and cream, Veal with Creamy Morel Mushroom Sauce, and Braised Rack of Lamb with a red wine démi-glace. You have a choice of cheese plate or dessert menu that lists Profiteroles with hot chocolate sauce and whipped cream, Crêpes Suzette, Crème Brûlée, Chocolate Mousse, or Fresh Fruit Tart. All dishes are made from scratch from soups to sauce. Closed Sunday and Monday dinner.

> Café Voila, 7600 Jefferson Street NE, Albuquerque, 87109; (505) 821-2666; http://site.voila.fr/cafe.voila.

Le Crêpe Michel

If you're touring Old Town and are looking for something special, saunter down San Felipe Street to La Crêpe Michel, hidden away in the back of San Felipe North Plaza. The tiny restaurant is owned by Chef Claudie Zamet, born in Roubaix, France, near the Belgian border and raised in the Near East, mainly Lebanon. She arrived in the States in 1974 to attend Purdue University, where she trained as a biochemist and physiologist.

Years passed, she traveled the world, married, and raised a family before landing in Albuquerque, where she discovered a small French restaurant for sale. In 1987 she purchased La Crêpe Michel and began her restaurant career using recipes passed down from the previous owner. Lack of professional culinary training has not hurt her at all. Her food is prepared using the freshest available ingredients and her own *bec fin* as criterion.

For a restaurant with "crêpe" in its name, you'd expect a wide selection of sweet and savory crêpes, and you wouldn't be disappointed. A favorite is Crêpe de Saumon Fumé aux Pommes, smoked salmon with grated apples, fresh cream, and capers. Vegetarians might prefer the Crêpe a la Ratatouille: zucchini, eggplant, onion, bell peppers, and tomatoes sautéed in pure olive oil and the spices of Provence. Sweet crêpes run from Crêpe au Chocolat with melted Ghiradelli chocolate and Chantilly cream to Crêpe Poire Belle-Helene with vanilla ice cream, a pear, melted chocolate, and Chantilly cream. Crêpes are available lunch and dinner.

Additionally, the lunch menu features salads such as Salade Mesclun, organic mixed greens with warm goat cheese on croutons, or Salade d'Endive au Roquefort et Noix, Belgian endives with Roquefort cheese and walnuts. French onion soup is always on the menu, and daily there's a quiche and soup du jour.

The dinner menu adds appetizers including a homemade pâté with marinated pork, veal, and chicken liver, baked with herbs and spices; Les Escargot, a half dozen snails in garlic butter sauce with mushrooms; or Rilette de Saumon, a homemade salmon pâté with smoked and poached fresh salmon in a dill-yogurt sauce. Entrées depend on what is seasonal and fresh. You might find Sardines au Persillade, Grilled Salmon, Mediterranean Mussels in garlic and white wine, or a tender Filet de Boeuf. Claudie cooks what she knows and likes. She's not a fan of pasta, and you'll never find it on her menu. Her best-selling desserts are her flavored crème brûlée and fruit charlottes.

The restaurant is located in one of Old Town's historic adobe homes. The front dining room has pink walls trimmed in white and decorated with Parisian prints. The back room or atrium was once a patio and still has a living tree growing from the brick floor. The atmosphere is reminiscent of a garden. Closed Monday and Sunday nights.

Le Crêpe Michel, 400 San Felipe Street NW, Albuquerque, 87104; (505) 242-1251.

Indian

Bombay Grill: Cuisine of India

Transforming a second-rate Chinese eatery into an elegant and sophisticated Indian restaurant on Albuquerque's west side took effort and planning, but owner Narendra Kloty has succeeded beautifully. The subdued lighting, dark wood accents, and the gentle splash of the charming fountain set the scene for gracious dining at lunch or dinner. Attentive but non-intrusive service completes the picture.

The menu follows traditional Indian offerings. Appetizers include vegetable Samosas, *papadums*, and Chicken Pakora. Entrées run from vegetarian dishes such as Saag Paneer to tandoori specialties, chicken, lamb, and seafood. There's a luncheon buffet with selections changing daily.

Bombay Grill: Cuisine of India, 3600 NM 528, Albuquerque, 87114; (505) 899-6900.

India Palace

If you're shy about venturing into the mysterious world of Indian spices and special cooking methods, you should try India Palace, an Albuquerque favorite. Owned for the past eight years by Baldev Singh, the unimposing restaurant on the edge of Montgomery Crossings Mall is always full of satisfied diners, whether for its lunch buffet or dinner service.

The building houses both a restaurant and a store selling hard-to-find Indian spices, ghee, beans, dal, and rice. The restaurant features Indian motifs with a rich wine color scheme. The waitstaff is exceptional. Dressed in conservative black pants and vests with white shirts and ties, they present a professional appearance, even at the lunch buffet, where you'll dine with white cloth service.

India Palace specializes in tandoori dishes. The tandoor is a tall cylindrical clay oven fired by charcoal, where the temperature at the bottom is maintained at 800° F. The process involves baking, roasting, and grilling simultaneously and requires a skilled cook.

Even if you're not fond of lunch buffets, you need not be concerned with encountering cold, stale, or depleted food at India Palace. The lunch crowd moves so quickly that you'll see previous selections constantly replaced and new dishes emerge from the kitchen. There's a good selection from which to choose. You will find condiments such as onion chutney, *raita* (a combination of house-made yogurt, carrot, tomato, onions, and cucumber), tamarind chutney, and mint chutney. Hot dishes might include Chana Masala (chickpeas in a blend of spices), Zucchini Masala, Saag Paneer (freshly chopped spinach with cubes of homemade cheese and fresh spice), Lamb Vindaloo roasted in spices with red chiles and tamarind paste, Butter Chicken (tandoori chicken cooked in a creamy tomato sauce and flavored with smoked fenugreek leaves), Basmati Rice and Peas, and for dessert, a creamy Mango Custard.

Although the menu warns of spicy dishes, we did not find the food excessively hot, but we're New Mexicans and adjusted to chiles. For cooked-to-order dishes, they will adjust the heat to taste. The menu is extensive, with a huge selection of vegetarian specialties. You'll find beef, lamb, chicken, and seafood specialties in addition to extraordinary combo dinners such as the Royal Banquet spread and the Punjabi Thali.

A second India Palace opened in 2004 to feed curry-addicted west-siders. Located in the Corrales Shopping Center on the corner of NM 528 and Coors Boulevard, the restaurant echoes the menu and fine service of its progenitor.

India Palace, 4410 Wyoming Boulevard NE, Albuquerque, 87111; (505) 271-5009; 10701 Coors Boulevard NW, Suite 23, Albuquerque, 87114; (505) 898-4188.

Italian

Vivace

When you're searching for Italian food in Albuquerque, you will have many choices, but if you're seeking well-prepared classic regional Italian food, there is only one place to go, Vivace, owned by Carol and Gordon Schutte. Vivace is located in Nob Hill's busy shopping area, and its atmosphere is casual, akin to a trattoria. Gordon describes his restaurant by saying, "Vivace is Mama's kitchen."

When you choose Vivace, you won't be disappointed with the results. Schutte is executive chef, and he prepares your meal to order—no soggy, warmed-over pasta or red sauce bubbling like lava on the back burner. Schutte considers Marcella Hazen, the doyenne of Italian cooking, his inspiration, and many of his recipes are adaptations of her classics. "She wrote the Bible," he says.

The menu follows the classic Italian form: *antipasti, insalate,* pasta, *il second,* or a *prezzo fisso delgiorno,* a special fixed price meal of *antipasto, primo piatto,* and *secondo.* Pastas may be ordered as first-course portions. You might start with Verdure Grigliata, herb marinated vegetables grilled with cracked anise seed and served with smoked provolone and Parmesan crackers, followed by Insalata di Spinaci, spinach salad with a dressing of warm honey, pancetta, caramelized red onions, and roasted shallots. Your pasta could be a simple Gnocchi alla Bettola, potato dumplings with a tomato and garlic cream sauce and a splash of vodka, and you could select as your main course Pollo Lemoncello, rosemary marinated chicken grilled and topped with a Lemoncello and Grand Marnier glaze.

Vivace is noted for its demonstration cooking classes and special events pairing authentic Italian foods with great wines. The group gathers at the restaurant to watch Chef Gordon cook and discuss the fine points of palate. "We have really had a great time with the classes and wine tastings we have been doing," says Schutte, "and this is another way for our friends to come together and enjoy our cuisine while mastering some of the techniques for their own kitchens. And it's just a lot of fun!"

Vivace, 3118 Central Avenue SE, Albuquerque, 87106; (505) 268-5965.

CULINARY
NEW MEXICO

Middle Eastern

Middle East Bakery

Judging by its name, you'd expect Middle East Bakery to be just that—a bakery specializing in the flatbreads of that region. You'd be partially correct. The grocery and restaurant does carry a wide selection of pitas and in-house baked desserts, such as baklava, but the reason for its mention in the dining listings is its small café serving longtime favorites such as hummus, tabbouleh, falafel, and gyros as well as chicken shawarma (gyros with chicken) and moussaka. The combination plates are very reasonable and run the gamut from spinach pie with tabbouleh and hummus to the Mujaddara Plate with rice and lentils. Their hummus is divine, creamy with just a hint of garlic, and the falafel moist and chewy.

Owner Mustafa Musleh is a former engineer with Intel in Rio Rancho. He has expanded the café from a few helter-skelter tables into a pleasant eating area, which can now seat as many as 20. The grocery section is expansive, carrying all those products necessary for mid-East cuisine.

Middle East Bakery, 5017 Menaul Boulevard NE, Albuquerque, 87110; (505) 883-4537.

New Mexican

Little Anita's New Mexican Foods

You will find Little Anita restaurants scattered throughout Albuquerque and Santa Fe. In their large manufacturing plant near the airport, they cook up the chile that defines their cuisine. The red is delicious: earth-red, finely textured, with hints of heat and smoke, and with that dusty graininess that says "handmade." The best foods at Little Anita's take advantage of chile heat. An example is the carne adovada enchiladas, filled with red-velvet chunks of pork, rich in adobo paste (ground chile, garlic, and a bit of vinegar), then grilled.

Other highlights include chile rellenos, stuffed with white New Mexican cheese and with a finely filigreed fried batter that resembles the Ethiopian bread *injera*; tamales, fat with beef; refried beans noted for their earthiness and deep flavor; and fresh salsa.

Larry and Jane Guitierrez culled the restaurant's name from a restaurant run by Larry's mother, Anita, who had eight New Mexican restaurants in northern Virginia. Their original restaurant started out as a pizza palace on the corner of Rio Bravo and Isleta. Realizing they couldn't compete with the chains, they looked at their demographics and switched to New Mexican food based on old family recipes. From such small beginnings came seven restaurants in Albuquerque, one in Santa Fe, and an outlier in Denver managed by Larry's son.

> **Little Anita's New Mexican Foods (dine in or take out), 3314 Isleta Boulevard SW, Albuquerque, 87105; (505) 877-1773; 2105 Mountain Road NW, Albuquerque, 87104; (505) 242-3102; 10200 Corrales Road NW, Albuquerque, 87114; (505) 899-2670; 2000 Menaul Boulevard NE, Albuquerque, 87107; (505) 837-9459; 1105 Juan Tabo Boulevard NE, Albuquerque, 87112; (505) 292-4111; 2811 Cerrillos Road, Santa Fe, 87507; (505) 473-4505. A Little Anita's offering takeout only is on 6131 4th Street NW, Albuquerque, 87107; (505) 345-4567.**

El Modelo

If we were to list all the good New Mexican restaurants in Albuquerque, we'd need a tome devoted to just that. No matter whom you query about a favorite, you'll almost always get a different answer. Although some will dispute the choices of establishments we've included, few will argue about El Modelo.

El Modelo is not strictly a restaurant. It has no tables and chairs, merely a take-out counter and a small warm-weather patio. But look beyond that counter to the huge industrial-size kitchen. This is where the magic occurs. A score of employees are chopping meat, stirring sauce, making tamales, and constructing enchiladas. Another three or four man the counter and take orders from the steady stream of customers who seem to show up at all hours.

El Modelo is an Albuquerque tradition started in 1929 by Carmen Garcia. The establishment has always been located south of downtown near the rail yards. It has been in its present location since 1947, and the construction of the National Hispanic Cultural Center nearby makes it a natural for hungry museum mavens.

The current owner, Virginia Chittim, is an Anglo, but she has hired Hispanic cooks who keep Carmen's recipes and techniques intact. You can stop for a morning nosh of huevos rancheros or a breakfast burrito, or you can fill your take-out container with orders of tostadas, enchiladas, stuffed sopapillas, or chile spareribs.

Their Burritos de Carne Desebrada (beef brisket cooked in green chile) are so good you'll be yelling for more, and El Modelo is one of the few places you can find an authentic *chicharron* burrito (made from pork skin twice deep-fried to make it crisp). Their tamales are legend: creamy masa with delicious pork and red-chile filling. They are huge, moist, and perfectly spiced. Tacos are another specialty, and they are unusual—made with a flat tostada shell and topped with a fresh green bean mixture, chili meat, and lettuce. In addition, their posole and menudo are superior. All items may be purchased singly, by the plate, or by the dozen. Sauces and *sopas* come in pint and quart sizes. For the home cook, they sell tortillas, their red and green-chile sauces, wonderful refried pinto beans, masa, cornhusks for tamales, chile pods, *mixtamle* (precooked white corn), and more.

Don't pass up this place. It may be slightly out of the way, but it produces the best New Mexican food in Albuquerque. Closed Sunday.

El Modelo, 1715 2nd Street SW, Albuquerque, 87102;
(505) 242-1843.

Monroe's New Mexican Food

What's a restaurant serving good New Mexican food doing with the name Monroe's? Certainly you'd expect something more ethnic, but when Miguel Diaz purchased the operation in 1979, it had been owned and operated by Monroe Sorensen, who, belying his Scandinavian heritage, ran a small chile parlor on the corner of Rio Grande and Mountain. Monroe's eccentricities included serving any kind of chile as long as it was green.

Miguel moved the restaurant to Lomas and in 1983 opened a second restaurant on Osuna. A native of Puerto Rico, Miguel came to the United States as a child with his family and received his first culinary training at a Jewish deli in the Bronx. For a time he played minor league ball, eventually finding his way to Albuquerque where he rented a kitchen and opened a snack bar in the old First Security building downtown. When Sorensen wanted to sell, Miguel stepped up to the plate.

Monroe's are true neighborhood gathering places, not tourist restaurants with fancy décor and singing mariachis. The Osuna Monroe's is a bit heavier on the southwestern ambiance with its adobe exterior, tri-level interior, huge kiva fireplace, brick floors, and rustic open-beam construction. The Lomas location was a gas station, and today it is still rather basic except for some wall art and old photos. Miguel's son Matthew is in charge of the Osuna restaurant and Miguel is usually at the helm on Lomas. A hint: the Monroe's on Lomas is next door to the Palms, one of the best Indian art stores in the city—a great lunch and shopping combo.

Developed from recipes originated by Miguel, the food is classic New Mexican, and it is consistently excellent. They manage to tread the fine line in chile preparation. Both red and green have enough heat to satisfy locals without blistering the mouth of an out-of-stater. The service is exceptionally fast and friendly. All the classics are there: chile rellenos, tamales, carne adovada, tacos, and tostadas. They make one of the best green-chile burgers in town, and their seafood enchiladas are legendary. House specialties include huevos rancheros, Mexican pizza, Indian tacos, taco salad, quesadillas, and fajitas. There's a child's menu and a list of "gringo dinners" that includes chicken-fried steak and pork chops. Daily specials are listed on the chalkboard by the entry, and everything may be prepared to go. Monroe's motto is "a day without chile is like a day without sunshine!"

In response to demand, Miguel has made his red and green chile, salsa, and red-chile honey available for purchase in the restaurants or by mail.

Monroe's New Mexican Food, 1520 Lomas Boulevard NW, Albuquerque, 87104; (505) 242-1111; 6051 Osuna Road NE, Albuquerque, 87109; (505) 881-4224; www.monroeschile.com.

El Pinto Restaurant

Shaded by massive cottonwoods and nestled in the North Valley, Albuquerque's most rural neighborhood, El Pinto is your destination of choice if you're looking for New Mexican food served in the atmosphere of Old Mexico. Hidden fountains murmur, and the sounds of a guitar drift through the gardens.

Founded by the Chavez-Griggs family in 1962, El Pinto has grown from a small restaurant to a nine-acre complex of spacious dining rooms, cascading waterfalls, and numerous patios. Open year-round, it is at its best in the warmer months when you can sit outside and enjoy the lovely ambiance. Still featuring the traditional recipes developed by Josephina Chavez-Griggs, her grandsons John and Jim Thomas now head the operation.

Josephina's heirs are doing a fine job. You will find the traditional New Mexican foods: enchiladas, tacos, tostadas, tamales, chile rellenos, burritos, and bowls of lean pork in red chile. The combination plates pair two or three favorites, and if you have a hankering for a variation, say blue tortillas, they will oblige. The house specialty is Chile con Carne Enchiladas, three flat or rolled corn tortillas filled with toothsome shredded pork marinated in fresh red chile and served with rice and beans. Hearty meals such as Chile Ribs, Steak and Enchiladas, and Carne Adovada are available as are some low-fat options, which pair chicken with red chile and steamed, not oil-softened, tortillas.

Their flame-roasted chile is grown exclusively to their specifications and prepared the same way it has been done for 35 years. In autumn, the smell is an intoxicating perfume as it wafts over the valley. Their salsa, which they retail, has won awards in national fiery foods' contests.

El Pinto Restaurant, 10500 4th Street NW, Albuquerque, 87114; (505) 898-1771; www.elpinto.com.

Thai

Thai Crystal

Thai Crystal is a welcome addition to downtown dining. Located on Gold Avenue, the attractive restaurant has a handsome wood-paneled bar and an open, airy dining room with high ceiling, green-gold walls, and an elevated section edged with a temple motif.

Suvadit Chitchakkol (David) is the owner chef, originally from Bangkok but educated in the United States. He has worked under Wolfgang Puck in Newport Beach and served in the kitchens of the *Queen Mary* as well as owning his own restaurant in Redondo Beach, California.

Vegetarian dishes are a specialty during lunch and dinner. Some signature dishes include Satay appetizer, marinated beef or chicken in special curry, charbroiled and served with a peanut sauce and cucumber salad; Larb Kai, a salad blend of ground chicken, mint leaves, onion, chile, and lime juice served with green cabbage; and Tom Kah Fai, a chicken coconut soup. Unusual entrées include Three Mermaids, consisting of crab, squid, and shrimp with chile-shrimp paste in a bean oil sauce with carrots, onions, and bell peppers; Thai Crystal Beef Steak, a barbecue flavored with spicy sauce; Eggplant Thai-Style with egg, chile, mint leaves, and bell peppers; Red Kang Ped Chicken Curry with bamboo shoots, coconut milk, and mint leaves; and that perennial favorite, Pad Thai. If you still have room, check out the delicious house-made coconut ice cream.

Thai Crystal, 109 Gold Avenue SW, Albuquerque, 87102; (505) 244-3344; www.999dine.com.

Vegetarian/Vegan

Annapurna Ayurvedic Cuisine and Chai House

Yashoda Naidoo opened Annapurna Ayurvedic Cuisine and Chai House when she could not find good vegetarian food in Albuquerque, where Ayurvedic food was an unknown concept. The restaurants she created are peaceful, quiet places where the stresses of the world melt away amid soft music and lovingly prepared dishes.

"Contributing to our customers' healing and well-being are our aims," Yashoda says. "We hope to educate, support, and motivate the customer to heal and pursue wellness with good food. We're committed to being the place for healing cuisine."

Specialties include soups and hot dishes such as seasoned steamed vegetables, rice and vegetable combos, *chapattis*, and, of course, authentic chai. A daily lunch special might feature *chapatti*, rice, *mung dal* soup, and a choice of beans or a vegetable; Malaysian stir-fry noodles; *saag* (spinach) or *mataar* (tomato) *paneer* (vegetables, spice, and fresh cheese); vegetable coconut soup; or a south Indian specialty such as Masala Dosa (a rice and vegetable crêpe with spicy vegetable filling), Idli (rice with *urad dal*, soaked, ground into a batter and steamed into cakes), and Sambar Vadai (a spicy vegetable soup served with a cake made from soaked lentils, ground into a paste with spices, made into a patty, and fried). The menu changes daily.

Annapurna Ayurvedic Cuisine and Chai House, 2120 Juan Tabo NE, Albuquerque, 87112; (505) 275-2424; 2201 Silver Street SE, Albuquerque, 87106; (505) 262-2424; www.themenupage.com/annapurna.html.

Vietnamese

May Café

Many years ago, we discovered the May Café while searching for a good restaurant near the State Fairgrounds (now renamed Expo New Mexico). The statue of Paul Bunyan atop the mini-mall where the restaurant is located was just quirky enough to beckon us. The oddity belonged to a previous tenant, but it was such a landmark that the Liem Nguyen, who has owned the May for more than 12 years, decided to keep it.

Although the restaurant offers traditional Vietnamese entrées such as Lemongrass Chicken, most diners go for their Pho, the beef and rice noodle soup, or the Hu Tieu and Mi, the rice and egg noodle soup. The huge bowls are an entire meal with meat, seafood, and noodle of your choice garnished with your choice of Thai basil, bean sprouts, cilantro, and lime wedges. Their Goi Cuon, the delicate Vietnamese spring rolls of noodles, shrimp, lettuce, and basil enveloped in translucent rice wrappers, are another favorite and some of the best we're tasted anywhere.

The décor is basic—tables clustered on two levels with wall hangings of Vietnamese scenes. Lace curtains screen the wall of windows facing the parking lot. The location is convenient for flea market shoppers, fairgoers, and anyone shopping at Ta Lin, the Asian supermarket down the street.

May Café, 111 Louisiana Boulevard SE, Albuquerque, 87108; (505) 265-4448.

Farmers' Markets

Albuquerque Downtown Market, 8th and Central at Robinson Park, Saturdays, 7:00 to 11:00 A.M., July through October, (505) 480-6943 or (505) 243-2230.

Albuquerque Growers' Market, Caravan East Parking Lot, 7605 Central Avenue NE, Saturday and Tuesday, 6:30 to 11:00 A.M., July through November, (505) 869-2369 or (505) 869-5203.

Belen/Valencia County Growers' Market, Anna Becker Park, Hwy 309/ Reinken Avenue, Belen, Friday, 3:00 to 7:00 P.M., mid-July through October, (505) 864-8091.

Bernalillo: High Desert Farmers' Market, 282 Camino del Pueblo, Bernalillo, Fridays, 4:00 to 7:00 P.M., mid-July through October, (505) 896-2230.

Corrales Growers' Market, Recreation Center next to the post office, Corrales, Sundays, 9:00 A.M. to 1:00 P.M., Wednesday, 3:30 to 7:00 P.M., end of April through mid-November, (505) 898-5788.

Village of Los Ranchos Growers' Market, City Hall, 6718 Rio Grande Boulevard NW, Los Ranchos, Saturdays, mid-May to end of October, 7:00 to 11:00 A.M.; Winter Market, November through April, second Saturday of each month, 10:00 A.M. to noon, (505) 898-1624.

South Valley Growers' Association, Cristo del Valle Presbyterian Church, 3907 Isleta Boulevard SW, Albuquerque, Saturday, 7:00 A.M. to noon, mid-May through mid-October, (505) 877-1226.

Specialty Food Stores

B. Riley Fresh Herbs

B. Riley Fresh Herbs was started by accident when founder Dale Porterfield stopped at La Montanita Co-op to sell his garden-grown vegetables and herbs. They had missed a shipment of basil, and when the store eyed his emerald leaves, they bought him out. Realizing that there was a market to be filled, Dale founded the business, which eventually grew to be New Mexico's largest distributor of fresh-cut culinary herbs and gourmet specialty foods. Sadly, Dale succumbed to cancer in 2003, but the torch has been passed to new owner, Dawn Garcia Tran.

If you stop by the warehouse in an out-of-the-way location off Juan Tabo, you can visit the gourmet shop featuring a connoisseur's selection of rare and unusual dried heirloom beans, lentils, peas, limas, rice, imported Italian pastas, grains, chiles, mushrooms, fruits, saffron, seasonings, truffle oil, capers, extra-virgin olive oils, full-bodied vinegars, sauces, goat cheeses, and much, much more. They accept phone orders and will supply you with just what you need whether it is a sprig of thyme or 10 pounds of Tottori 20th Century pears.

B. Riley Fresh Herbs, 670-A Juan Tabo NE, Albuquerque, 87123; (505) 275-0902 or (800) 427-1756; www.brileyfreshherbs.com.

Din Ho

Tucked away in a small strip mall on Montgomery, Din Ho has been supplying Albuquerque with elegant Asian ceramics and foodstuffs since 1981. If you're searching for imported tea sets, cast-iron teapots, serving plates, condiment dishes, or sake sets, you'll find that owner K. Park stocks a top-quality assortment. Those looking for chopsticks will be thrown into a paroxysm of indecision by the extensive selection from utensils for children to elegant lacquered sets.

The store specialty is sushi, and they carry more types of nori than you can count as well as frozen sushi-grade tuna, barbecued eel, and other specialized necessities including pickled ginger and wasabi. In addition, there's rice in its many varieties, canned sauces and condiments, and lots and lots of noodles. Helpful to the linguistically challenged, the shelves are labeled in English so you don't mistake bamboo shoots for lychee nuts.

Din Ho Oriental Market, 6207 Montgomery Boulevard NE, Albuquerque, 87109; (505) 883-2665.

Keller's Farm Store

The Keller family began supplying Albuquerque residents with fresh-off-the-farm beef and fowl more than 50 years ago, and they still raise their own free-range poultry and beef in Pueblo, Colorado, and Moriarty, New Mexico. At Keller's Farm Stores' two locations, you'll discover meats raised humanely on all-natural grains and aged to perfection.

In addition to their premium beef and poultry, Keller's carries an assortment of farm-raised buffalo, elk, quail, rabbit, squab, ostrich, goose, and duckling. Keller's ham, bacon, cold cuts, and sausages are prepared from Old World recipes, with only spices and herbs used for flavorings. Deli items are made fresh daily.

During the holidays, the smokehouse runs 24 hours a day. In the three days before Thanksgiving, 10,000 turkeys are sold, and during Christmas week, more than 10 tons of prime rib roasts are cut. Customers can order complete meals to go, with their choice of meat, sides, and dessert.

Keller's also stocks domestic and imported cheeses and gourmet and natural groceries in addition to fresh pastries, baked goods, and organic produce. A full line of vitamins, herbs, and cosmetics rounds out their offerings.

Keller's Farm Store, 2912 Eubank Boulevard NE, Albuquerque, 87112; (505) 294-1427; Montano Plaza, 6100 Coors Road NW, Ste. H, Albuquerque, 87120; (505) 898-6121.

La Montanita Co-op Natural Foods Market

La Montanita Co-op Natural Foods Market was incorporated in 1976, and for three years was managed largely as a collective. With the growing concerns about the corruption of food sources, the co-op has grown through the years into a two-store, 7,000-member enterprise managed by a nine-person board of directors.

The organization is heavily committed to bringing their associates the highest quality organic produce, antibiotic and hormone-free meats, rBGH-free dairy products, imported and domestic cheeses, and the healthiest grocery, bulk foods, and fresh deli available. You don't have to be a member to shop at La Montanita, but membership has certain privileges such as a monthly newsletter, weekly member-only coupon specials, and member-only discount days. In addition, at year's end refunds are returned to members based on their purchases, and there's a free once-a-week delivery service for seniors, the housebound, and disabled within city limits.

La Montanita Co-op Natural Foods Market, 3500 Central Avenue SE, Albuquerque, 87106; (505) 265-4631; 2400 Rio Grande Boulevard NW, Albuquerque, 87104; (505) 242-8800; www.lamontanita.com.

Nantucket Shoals Seafood Market

There's a fish market in Albuquerque? It's not as bizarre as you might imagine. In 1985 owner Nancy Chavez Berg founded Nantucket Shoals when she figured out that Duke City residents wanted more than what was available in the frozen food section of the supermarket. Originally housed in the same building in which the Artichoke Café resides, the market now sits just a few steps from the Wild Oats on Academy.

An almost blindingly bright and antiseptically clean store with a cheerful seaside motif, Nantucket Shoals receives its shipments three times a week, and if it isn't perfectly fresh, Berg will not stock it. Regular items include clams, oysters, mussels, salmon, halibut in season, tuna, scallops, shrimp, and trout. A circulating tank keeps the latest batch of lobsters ocean fresh.

Fish are all Berg sells, with the exception of some savory butters, homemade frozen chowders, and fish stock. Need salt cod for Portuguese *bacalhau*? Go to Nantucket Shoals. If they don't have exactly what you need, they will order it. Closed Sunday and Monday.

Nantucket Shoals Seafood Market, 5415 Academy Road NE, Albuquerque, 87109; (505) 821-5787.

Ta Lin Supermarket

Not many inland cities the size of Albuquerque can boast of an Asian market as comprehensive as Ta Lin in the Southeast Heights. Owned by the Limary family since the 1970s, the store stocks a mind-bending cultural mélange from China, Japan, Thailand, Korea, India, Pakistan, the Philippines, and other distant ports of call including Latin America and the Middle East. You'll find ethnic foods your local Albertson's doesn't supply. There are aisles of spices, stacks of rice, bins of exotic vegetables, fresh and frozen seafood, and canned goods whose only clue to contents is the picture on the label.

Always a fixture on Louisiana, Ta Lin recently undertook a huge expansion as the anchor store for an International Marketplace on the corner of Louisiana and Central. The new store has 35,000 square feet, more than enough room to relieve its sometimes-congested aisles. Cultural events and cooking classes are in the planning stages for Ta Lin's rebirth.

Ta Lin Supermarket, 230 Louisiana Boulevard SE, Albuquerque, 87108; (505) 268-0206.

Tully's Italian Deli and Meats

Alas, Albuquerque does not have a Little Italy, and basic Italian ingredients are sometimes difficult to find. The situation may be remedied by an excursion to Tully's Italian Deli and Meats. This small deli is jam-packed with a wide selection of domestic and imported meats, cheeses, and specialty items.

The meat counter stocks proscuitto, pancetta, mortadella, salami, house-made sausage, and a variety of veal, beef, and pork cuts. In the freezer, you'll find rabbit, lamb shanks, veal bones, and specialty items.

The cheese selection includes favorites such as Parmegiano-Reggiano, Fontina, fresh mozzarella, ricotta salata, mascarpone, and Locatelli Pecorino-Romano. An assortment of imported pastas, olive oils, and canned goods rounds out the stock.

Tully's Italian Deli and Meats, 1425 San Mateo Boulevard NE, Albuquerque, 87110; (505) 255-5370.

The Chain Gang

Sunflower Market, 10701 Coors Boulevard NW #2, Albuquerque, 87114; (505) 890-7900; www.sunflowermarkets.com. Sunflower is a new chain in Arizona, Colorado, and New Mexico owned by the original founder of Wild Oats.

Vitamin Cottage Natural Grocers, 4420 Wyoming Boulevard NE, Albuquerque, 87111; (505) 292-7300; www.vitamincottage.com.

Whole Foods Market, 5815 Wyoming Boulevard NE, Albuquerque, 87109; (505) 856-0474; www.wholefoods.com.

Wild Oats Natural Marketplace, 2103 Carlisle Boulevard NE, Albuquerque, 87110; (505) 260-1366; 6300 San Mateo Boulevard NE, Ste. A, Albuquerque, 87109; (505) 823-1933; 11015 Menaul Boulevard NE, Albuquerque, 87112; (505) 275-6660; www.wildoats.com.

Wineries

Anasazi Field Winery

Anasazi Field Winery is located on the western edge of the old village of Placitas, between Albuquerque and Santa Fe. The winery is surrounded by orchards watered by a spring-fed irrigation system dating back more than a thousand years to a time the Anasazi people farmed the Placitas Valley.

Vintner Jim Fish and his partners produce dry fruit wines aged in oak for six months to two years. Fruits include raspberry, apricot, peach, apple, plum, blackberry, cranberry, nectarine, wild cherry, domestic cherry, wild mahonia, chokecherry, and currant.

Anasazi Fields is open for tours, tastings, and sales Saturdays and Sundays, March through December, or by appointment. Call for hours.

Anasazi Fields Winery, 26 Camino de los Pueblitos, Placitas, 87043; (505) 867-3062.

Anderson Valley Vineyards

Anderson Valley Vineyards are nestled in Albuquerque's rural North Valley. Founded in 1973 by Maxie and Pattie Anderson, the winery produces vintages such as Chardonnay, Cabernet Sauvignon, White Zinfandel, Johannesburg Riesling, Claret, and some unique specialties such as Balloon Blush and Chile wine. A special event is held each year in conjunction with Albuquerque's International Balloon Festival in October (the largest hot-air balloon festival in the world), and the Balloon Blush wine is released at that time.

Visitors are welcome year-round from noon to 5:30 P.M.

Anderson Valley Vineyards, 4920 Rio Grande Boulevard NW, Albuquerque, 87107; (505) 344-7266.

Bees Brothers Winery

Their wine contains no grapes. Bees Brothers makes mead, one of the world's oldest wines, from fermented honey. Beekeepers Rick Hogan and Bill Smith take good desert honey gathered from alfalfa and wildflowers and convert it into a drink with golden color and many subtle flavors. They produce four styles: Queen's Mead, light with a delicate honey flavor; Spiced Mead, Queen's Mead with five added spices;

Raspberry Mead, a blend of mead and raspberry wine; and Cranberry Mead, a blend of mead and cranberry wine.

The winery isn't open for tastings or tours, but you can purchase the mead at many Albuquerque and Santa Fe wine and liquor stores.

Bees Brothers Winery, 619 Nowicki Lane SW, Albuquerque, 87105; (505) 452-3191; www.beesbrothers.com.

Corrales Winery

Corrales Winery is a newcomer to the New Mexico scene. Situated along the National Scenic and Historic Byway winding through the early Spanish settlement of Corrales, the winery specializes in finely crafting small quantities of rich, delicious red and white wines displaying the fruit flavors of the grapes.

The attractive winery incorporates both Indian and Spanish architecture and overlooks the vineyards and Sandia Mountains. They welcome visitors for tours and tastings Wednesday through Sunday from noon to 5:00 P.M.

Corrales Winery, 6275 Corrales Road, Corrales, 87048; (505) 898-5165; www.corraleswinery.com.

Casa Rondeña

Casa Rondeña is another North Valley winery. Specializing in a fine Bordeaux-style Cabernet Franc, Chardonnay, and the Proprietor's blend of fine whites, the beautiful winery building combines adobe, stone, Moorish tile, and ancient timbers.

Owner John R. Calvin welcomes visitors to the tasting room Thursday through Sunday from 1:00 to 5:00 P.M.

Casa Rondeña Winery, Rondeña Way, 733 Chavez Road NW, Los Ranchos de Albuquerque, 87107; (505) 344-5911; www.casarondena.com.

Gruet Winery

Probably New Mexico's best-known winery, Gruet has received international recognition for its wines: Brut, Blanc de Noirs, Démi-Sec, Blanc de Blancs Vintage Chardonnay, and Pinot Noir. Originally from the Champagne region of France, the Gruet family began making champagne in 1952. In 1984, after a search for the perfect climate and soil conditions to create sparkling wines, Laurent Gruet and Farid Himeur brought their experience in the champagne making tradition to Albuquerque. Currently Gruet produces more than 50,000 cases of wine distributed to 35 states.

The Gruet tasting room is open Monday through Saturday, and tours are scheduled at 2:00 P.M. daily or by appointment.

Gruet Winery, 8400 Pan American Freeway NE, Albuquerque, 87113; (505) 821-0055; www.gruetwinery.com.

Ponderosa Valley Vineyards and Winery

Ponderosa Valley Vineyards and Winery specializes in estate-bottled wines. Since 1993, when this uniquely New Mexican winery was bonded, Henry and Mary Street have been living out their dream of making fine wines on the southern slope of the Jemez Mountains. The vines, planted in 1978, have consistently produced award-winning Riesling wines, and a recent vineyard addition, Pinot Noir, has become their second signature varietal.

The vineyards and winery, 5,800 feet above sea level, are on deep, well-drained volcanic ash deposits, which along with our long, hot days and cool nights provide the ideal conditions to develop the unique wine character.

Visitors are welcome for tastings Tuesday through Saturday 10:00 A.M. to 5:00 P.M., and Sunday noon to 5:00 P.M. Picnics are encouraged during these hours.

Ponderosa Valley Vineyards and Winery, 3171 Highway 290, Ponderosa, 87044; (505) 834-7487; www.ponderosawinery.com.

La Querencia Vineyards and Winery

La querencia means "the place of your heart's desire," and this wine producer takes its place as one of the Land of Enchantment's newest operations. The Brueggeman and Olsen families create award-winning wines with a uniquely New Mexican flavor: Cabernet Franc, Chambourcin, La Luna Azul, a late harvest Vidal Blanc, New Mexico Lemberger, Manzano Red, Valencia White, and others. They now have three and a half acres of vineyards in Bosque Farms, and they manage another two acres in Albuquerque's North Valley.

Visitors are welcome during regular hours and by appointment. Tasting room hours are Saturday and Sunday, 1:00 to 6:00 P.M.

La Querencia Vineyards and Winery, 980 Bosque Farms Boulevard, Bosque Farms, 87068; (505) 869-4637; www.laquerenciawine.com.

Events

The Annual National Fiery Foods & Barbecue Show

March—The Annual National Fiery Foods & Barbecue Show at the Albuquerque Convention Center showcases an astonishing variety of hot and spicy foods on display, including hot sauces, salsas, barbecue sauces, candies, honeys, chips, pestos, nuts, jams, jellies, snacks, soups, salad dressings, mustards, beans, ketchup, and many more. Additionally, some exhibitors offer numerous related, nonfood products including clothing, books, posters, calendars, original art, and kitchenware. On Saturday and Sunday afternoons when the show is open to the public, there are various cooking demonstrations by famous guest chefs.

If possible, plan to get there at noon Saturday to avoid the crush. The show is extremely popular, attracting more than 10,000 attendees at last count.

> The Annual National Fiery Foods & Barbecue Show, Albuquerque Convention Center, Albuquerque, 87102; (505) 873-8680; www.fiery-foods.com.

Herb and Wildlife Festival

May—Every year the Rio Grande Nature Center holds its Herb and Wildlife Festival featuring the sale of plants and various seminars on the culinary and medicinal use of herbs. The Nature Center offers naturalist-led hikes, bosque exploration, exhibits, and hands-on activities.

A highlight of the Nature Center is its glass-walled library over-looking a pond that provides a unique opportunity to view bosque birds and other wildlife in their natural habitat. A speaker system transmits the real sounds of pond life into the room.

> Herb and Wildlife Festival, 2901 Candelaria Road NW, Albuquerque, 87107; (505) 344-7240; www.frgnc.org.

Albuquerque Wine Festival

Memorial Day Weekend—This holiday weekend is the ideal time to come to the famous Balloon Fiesta grounds in Albuquerque for a wine festival extraordinaire. Located on lush green grass next to the golf course, the festival allows you to browse through handcrafted art, listen to upbeat music, and, best of all, taste all the great wines of New Mexico.

> Albuquerque Wine Festival, New Mexico Golf Academy at Balloon Fiesta Park, Albuquerque; (866) 494-6366 or (505) 834-0101; www.nmwine.com.

New Mexico Wine Festival at Bernalillo

Labor Day Weekend—One of five special three-day festivals sponsored by the New Mexico Wine Growers Association brings together more than 25 wineries from across New Mexico. Tastings, live entertainment, gourmet food, and fun are the order of the day. An arts show and a contingent of craftspeople and vendors of agricultural products adds to the festivities.

This is your chance to sample a variety of vintages and speak with the vintners themselves. Wine is available for purchase by the glass, bottle, or case. The expected attendance is more than 25,000.

> New Mexico Wine Festival, Loretto Park, Bernalillo; (800) 866-494; www.nmwine.com.

Annual Apple Festival

October—For more than a decade, Manzano Mountain Retreat has been the site of an annual Apple Festival, which offers a live country-western band, a dance, apple baked goods, horseshoes, sack races, and a barbecue. They are one of New Mexico's largest apple producers with more than 32 varieties of apples.

> Annual Apple Festival, Manzano Mountain Retreat, 210 County Road, A003, Cedarvale, 87009; (505) 384-4467; www.manzanoretreat.com.

Recipes

Chiles Rellenos de Queso

Courtesy of Jane Butel
Reprinted by permission of *Jane Butel's Southwestern Kitchen*
HPBooks, a division of Penguin Group (USA) Inc.

4–6 servings

12 large, mild green chiles, parched and peeled with stems on, or you
can use three 8-oz. cans of whole green chiles
8 oz. Monterey Jack cheese, cut into 12 long, narrow strips
Cornmeal batter (see recipe below)
Vegetable oil for frying
Red-chile sauce (see recipe below)

1. Insert cheese strips into chiles, cutting a small opening just below the crown on the parched chiles or using the small slit that was cut for stemming the canned chiles. Make sure that the cheese strips do not burst the chiles or overfill them. Drain chiles thoroughly on paper towels to ensure that the batter will coat them well. Prepare batter.

2. Preheat 3 to 4 inches of oil to 375° F in a deep, heavy skillet, large saucepan, or deep fat fryer, using a deep-fat thermometer for accurate temperature. Dip the stuffed chiles in the batter. Place in hot oil and fry until golden. Tongs work best to hold and turn them. Drain well on paper towels. Serve piping hot with chile sauce.

Cornmeal Batter
1 C. flour
1 tsp. baking powder
$^1/_2$ tsp. salt
$^3/_4$ C. cornmeal—blue, white, or yellow (Jane prefers the blue)
1 C. milk
2 eggs

In a medium-size bowl, combine flour, baking powder, salt, and cornmeal. Blend the milk and eggs, then add to the dry ingredients. Mix until smooth. If necessary, add a little more milk to achieve a smooth batter that will adhere to the chiles. Makes enough batter for 12 chiles.

Red-Chile Sauce
(This is the basic red-chile sauce used to create enchiladas and to serve over burritos, chile rellenos, tamales, and chimichangas)
2 Tbsp. butter, lard, or bacon drippings
2 Tbsp. all-purpose flour
$^1/_4$ C. ground mild red chile
$^1/_4$ C. ground hot red chile
2 C. beef stock or water
1 garlic clove, crushed
Pinch of ground Mexican oregano
Pinch of ground cumin
$^3/_4$ tsp. salt (if not using stock)

1. Melt butter, lard, or bacon drippings in a medium-size saucepan over low heat. Add flour and stir until smooth and slightly golden.

2. Remove pan from heat and add ground chile. Return to heat and gradually stir in stock. Add garlic, oregano, cumin, and salt, if using, and cook, stirring, for about 10 minutes. Simmer at least 5 more minutes for flavors to blend.

Duck Confit

Courtesy of Jennifer James
Jennifer James Contemporary Cuisine and Graze

Spice Mix
1 C. ground cumin
1 C. ground coriander
1 C. ground cinnamon
6 Tbsp. ground allspice
4 Tbsp. ground clove
5 Tbsp. ground ginger
5 Tbsp. ground nutmeg
6 Tbsp. ground thyme
9 bay leaves, ground

Additional ingredients
1 duck
Sliced onion
Garlic cloves
Fresh thyme
Rendered duck fat

Rub duck with spice and layer with sliced onion, garlic cloves, and fresh thyme. Refrigerate and let rest for three days. Remove onion, garlic, and fresh thyme, cover with rendered duck fat, and roast at 300° F for three hours. Store refrigerated in duck fat.

Cream of Artichoke Soup

Courtesy of Pat Keene
Artichoke Café

12 servings

1 medium yellow onion, diced
1 medium red onion, diced

1 tsp. fresh garlic, minced
$^1/_2$ lb. salted butter
1 gallon chicken stock
$^1/_2$ C. heavy cream
5 lbs. artichoke hearts canned in brine
1 Tbsp. fresh tarragon leaves, minced
salt and pepper

Sauté the first 3 ingredients in butter until soft. Add stock and cream. Bring to simmer. Add artichoke hearts, tarragon, and salt and pepper to taste. Simmer for 25 minutes. Prepare roux.

Roux
4 oz. butter
$^1/_4$ C. flour

Melt butter and add flour; cook stirring constantly to form a paste that smells like cooked pie dough. Do not let it burn and smooth all lumps with a whisk. Add $^1/_2$ C. roux to thicken simmering soup. Be careful not to scorch it, stirring constantly until thickened.

Santa Fe Farmers' Market

Cloud Cliff Bakery

Las Golondrinas

Spanish Table

SANTA FE:
THE CITY DIFFERENT

Why is Santa Fe the City Different? The answer depends on the individual's perception. If you're a visitor, it's quintessential New Mexico with its homogenous Territorial or Pueblo Revival architecture, its verdant plaza, and its patient Indians selling crafts and jewelry under the portico of the Palace of the Governors. It's a place to enjoy the world-famous restaurants, search the galleries for the perfect piece of southwestern art, or check out the many and varied museums.

Santa Fe is the capital city. To state office workers, it is a place to keep the wheels of government turning. The many state office buildings bustle with activity, and once a year the legislators descend upon the town to meet in the Round House, the capitol building built in the shape of an Indian kiva.

To the average resident, it is a home, which year by year grows more precious due to escalating real estate and living costs. To the art community, it's a place of nurture where it's possible to enjoy the company of kindred spirits. There's a joke that goes, "In Santa Fe, a gas station first becomes a restaurant and then a gallery."

The impressive setting at the foot of the Sangre de Cristo Mountains, the high, dry climate, and the opportunities for outdoor recreation are constants. The city is old. In 1608, Don Pedro de Peralta succeeded Don Juan de Oñate as governor of New Mexico, and the following year he moved the colony's capital from San Gabriel to the site of an abandoned Indian pueblo at the foot of the mountains. He named the place La Villa Real de Santa Fé, and most historians date its founding at 1610. During the Pueblo Revolt of 1680, the Indians chased the Spanish south, but in 1692, the Spanish returned and reclaimed control of Santa Fe with hardly a struggle.

Today Santa Fe is a modern city, its adobe and picturesque beginnings notwithstanding. The historic center retains its charm, but a modern pulse beats in the commercial areas on the outskirts where you'll find malls and Burger Doodles just like in any city. Parking around the plaza can be a problem, especially when the legislature is in session or when crowds show up for special events such as the Indian or Spanish Markets. Your best advice is to secure a map or visitors guide before venturing forth. City parking lots are clearly marked and are definitely preferable to attempting on-street parking. Our favorite is the covered garage on Sandoval and San Francisco, only two blocks from the plaza.

Visitor Information Centers are located at the Santa Fe Convention and Visitors Bureau, Sweeney Center, 201 West Marcy Street, Santa Fe, 87501; (505) 955-6200; Santa Fe Visitors Center, Santa Fe Premium Outlets, 8380 Cerrillos Road, Santa Fe; New Mexico Department of Tourism, Santa Fe Welcome Center, Lamy Building, 491 Old Santa Fe Trail, Santa Fe, 87501; (800) 545-2040 or (505) 827-7336; and La Bajada Visitor Information Center, Interstate 25, 17 miles south of Santa Fe; (505) 424-0823.

Bakeries

The Chocolate Maven Bakery & Café

The Chocolate Maven Bakery & Café is as far from Santa Fe style as it's possible to come. Hunkered in next to a warehouse on San Mateo, the industrial exterior actually hides a cozy café with daffodil yellow walls spiced with the work of local artists. The bakery is visible behind a bank of windows at the back, and while you enjoy your breakfast or lunch, you can watch the bakers at work, rolling out croissants or popping their wonderful brownies into the oven.

The Chocolate Maven has been a Santa Fe landmark for 25 years. Originally owned by writer Judyth Hill and located on Guadalupe Street, the Maven had a following of writers, artists, and performers who came for the brownies and stayed for the stimulating intellectual interchange. The business was sold in 1990 to Mandy Clark, who in turn passed it on to the present owners, Daram Andrew Segal and his wife, Guru Kiren Ramos. They had been searching to expand their business, Love and Company Bakers, from its modest beginnings in a converted garage in Española.

With new blood, the Maven has flourished, instituting lunch service in 1999 under the direction of executive chef Ariel Harrison. In the fall of 2001 they added breakfast and brunch. For breakfast you have a choice of free-range eggs, rosemary skillet potatoes, Belgian waffles with peach compote, and three kinds of pancakes with pure Vermont maple syrup. For lunch, your selection includes soups, salads, sandwiches, pizza, and daily gourmet specials. Baked goods are available for takeout. Don't pass up the opportunity to grab a sack of their King Harold Ginger Snaps. They're positively addictive.

The Chocolate Maven Bakery & Café, 821 West San Mateo, Santa Fe, 87505; (505) 984-1980; www.chocolatemaven.com.

Cloud Cliff Bakery and Café

Santa Fe is fortunate to have Cloud Cliff Bakery and Café, one of several top-notch artisanal bakeries. Cloud Cliff Bakery, Café, and Artspace began in 1984 when Willem Malten took over the Better Bunz Bakery, founded by Pat Krug in the barrio of Santa Fe. In 1985, the bakery changed its name to Cloud Cliff, moved to a larger space closer to the center of the town, and opened up a small coffeehouse and a pizza counter.

Cloud Cliff now supplies 40 retailers in northern New Mexico, including such varied outlets as Whole Foods and Costco. Their bakers turn out a full line including the Nativo brand, which denotes not just its organic ingredients but also the local character of the product. Other specialties include Levant whole-wheat and white, French peasant, rye, amaranth, challah, spelt, millet, and potato-sesame loaves. Holidays mean pastries such as stollen and *lebkuchen*.

If you come for the bread, stay for the food, which Willem styles nouvelle cuisine, an amalgam of New Mexican and international cuisine. He trained with Alice Waters at Chez Panisse in Berkeley and at Tassajara and Greens in San Francisco.

You can order wraps for on-the-go consumption, or you can sit right down at the spacious café and have a great bowl of soup (varieties change daily), black bean chili from a Tassajara recipe, a salad of Santa Fe farmers' market greens, or a sandwich on house ciabatta bread. The "World Cooking" menu lists yummy entrées including Stir Fry, Ancho Chile Salmon, Organic Lamb and Quinoa in a light lemon zest curry sauce, Fajitas, or Vegetarian's Delight: papas, beans, and red wehani rice. Every kind of coffee drink and tea is available, and there is a children's menu.

Cloud Cliff Bakery and Café, 1805 2nd Street, Santa Fe, 87505; (505) 983-6254; www.cloudcliff.com.

The French Pastry Shop

In order to be on the plaza before dawn during Indian Market, we always rise in the wee small hours of the night for the drive to Santa Fe. The pain of such an ungodly hour is always assuaged by the knowledge that a hot cup of coffee and an apple tart are waiting at the French

Pastry Shop in La Fonda Hotel. With apples cartwheeled in sweet cinnamon glory over the buttery crust, which flakes at the touch of a fork, the tart welcomes us to the morning.

The shop is a combination of bistro and retail bakery specializing in "Viennoiserie." Owner George Zadeyan is an intense, wiry Frenchman who immigrated to the States from a town near Marseille with his two brothers. George exudes energy as he bustles around the cozy shop with its huge brick fireplace. Every morning the cases are filled with éclairs, napoleons, fruit tarts, Montmartres, Saint Michels, and on weekends, rum baba. All are made fresh daily by head baker Hector Mendoza, who learned his trade at the feet of a series of French master bakers who preceded him. The recipes have not changed since the shop's opening in 1974.

The French Pastry Shop is not just a place to pamper your sweet tooth, although there isn't a better place to indulge. They serve a selection of soup, salads, sandwiches, and crêpes in addition to their pastries. You'd expect to find *croque monsieur* and *croque madame*, French onion soup, salad Niçoise, and quiche Lorraine, and you wouldn't be disappointed. Don't neglect the wonderful fruit crêpes with fillings of peach, apricot, cherry, strawberry, blueberry, or banana, topped with real whipped cream. The menu is constant from its 6:15 A.M. opening to the 5:00 P.M. closing.

The French Pastry Shop, 100 East San Francisco Street in the La Fonda Hotel, Santa Fe, 87501; (505) 983-6697.

Sage Bakehouse

Sage Bakehouse produces artisanal breads that are distributed to fine restaurants from Taos to Albuquerque. They operate a very small retail outlet and café on Cerrillos where you may pick up a loaf fresh out of their ovens or dine on a bowl of soup, a slice of quiche, or a sandwich made with their nonpareil bread. Pastries, cookies, brownies, and both pear-almond and apple tarts are also available.

Doughs are made from carefully milled organic grains, filtered water, and sea salt. Almost all breads are made with a wild yeast starter using a slow, cool rise. The French ovens bake 500 pounds of dough at a time directly on the oven deck. This creates a crust both crackled and chewy.

The list of breads includes their farm bread, an elemental essential bread characterized by its dark, caramel crust and chewy interior texture; *pane paisano*, a pillowy version of Italian country bread; sourdough, a bit tangier and chewier than the typical Bay Area offering; whole-wheat farm, a heartier version of the farm bread; calamata olive; chipotle-caciotta, made with chipotle peppers, roasted corn, and handmade caciotta cheese; pecan-raisin, a dense loaf filled with more than one-third pound of select raisins and pecans; a traditional Jewish rye with caraway seeds; and on Saturday, cinnamon-raisin.

Owners Andree Falls and Amy Cox post their philosophy on the bakery wall: "Like wine, bread reflects both its regional soil and the character of the people who make it. Bread is the embodiment of a culture, a people, a way of life. Thousands of years and an infinite number of loaves since its invention, bread is still the staff of life itself."

Sage Bakehouse, 535 Cerrillos Road, Santa Fe, 87501; (505) 820-7243.

Breweries and Brewpubs

Chama River Brewing Co.

See write-up on page 7, Albuquerque section.

Chama River Brewing Co., 4056 Cerrillos Road, Santa Fe, 87507; (505) 438-1800; Downtown Café, 133 Water Street, Santa Fe, 87501; (505) 984-1800; www.bluecorncafe.com.

Santa Fe Brewing Company

The Santa Fe Brewing Company is New Mexico's oldest microbrewery. Founded in 1988 by Mike Levis and transferred to a partnership in 1996, it is now owned by Brian Lock, who uses Old World brewing methods and ingredients to produce English ales that have become local favorites. They use top-quality ingredients including the finest domestic and English malts and whole-flower hops. All beers are bottle-conditioned, a process in which the beer undergoes a secondary fermentation in the bottle. The additional fermentation creates the carbonation and gives the beers a rich, complex taste. This method of bottling leaves a fine yeast in the bottom of the bottle, which Lock says is your proof that it has been properly conditioned.

Their Santa Fe Wheat is a full-bodied, German-style wheat beer with a fruity nose and smooth finish, containing hints of clove and spice. It is brewed with more than 60 percent wheat malt and fermented with a Bavarian yeast strain. The Santa Fe Pale Ale is an English-style pale ale with a depth and complexity associated with traditional English brewing. It has a malty nose, rich taste, and subtle yet tangy hop finish. The Santa Fe Nut Brown Ale is a full-flavored English brown ale. Its malty flavor is balanced with the delicate roasted taste of chocolate malt. This beer has a clean, smooth finish, yet it is big enough to stand up to even the spiciest of foods. The popular Chicken Killer Barley Wine is an

English-style strong ale. At nearly 10 percent alcohol, it's malty profile and subtle hop character lends itself well to discreet sipping, rather than slapdash intake.

Special beers including Fiesta IPA, Stout, Porter, Dunkelweisen, and Sangre de Frambuese are brewed seasonally.

The Santa Fe Brewing Company's tasting room is open Wednesday through Saturday, 4:00 P.M. to close.

Santa Fe Brewing Company, 18 SR 14 East Frontage Road, Santa Fe, 87507; (505) 424-3333; www.santafebrewing.com.

Second Street Brewery

Second Street Brewery is the type of neighborhood pub that both locals and visitors can call their own. An unpretentious gathering place serving pub grub and libations, the business was begun by a home brewer and a family of winemakers.

Beer master Rod Tweet produces four beers at the 2nd Street location. Their Extra Special Bitter (ESB) is a robust beer with a caramel, nutty palette and fruity profile from their yeast. It's bitter hopped just enough to balance the sweetness and hopped again in the kettle and during conditioning. The India Pale Ale (IPA) is strong and malty but with a dry finish. Assertively bittered, the beer is late hopped in the kettle and dry hopped with Cascade and Crystal hops. Second Street's Golden Ale is very pale in color and has a pleasant malt profile balanced by the spicy and refreshing additions of Czech, Saaz, and other hops. The Cream Stout is a mid-gravity ale inspired by the sweeter "London style" stouts. Chocolate and caramel notes dominate with roasted flavors. Hops provide the balance.

In addition, they produce a roster of seasonal beers: Oktoberfest, Festivus, Bavarian Pilsner, Bavarian Hefewiezen, and Maibock, to name a few.

Second Street Brewery, 1814 2nd Street at Railroad Tracks, Santa Fe, 87505; (505) 982-1160.

Chocolatiers

The Chocolate Smith

The Chocolate Smith sells all varieties of chocolate as long as it's dark. Owners Clif Perry and Chris White only craft what they love, and that does not include the milk or white varieties. Cliff has designed, built, and operated retail chocolate shops in Denver and Vail, Colorado, and most recently in Port Townsend, Washington. Chris, a native Vermonter, is a lifelong chocolate enthusiast and entrepreneur. Between the two owners, there are more than 20 years of chocolate manufacturing experience.

The Smith's confections are handwrought in small batches. You probably won't find your traditional vanilla cream, but you will discover some delectable alternatives such as goat cheese truffles, pistachio green and red-chile bark, or chocolate-covered cherries first marinated in port wine. Their one concession to non-dark chocolate is the lemon lavender white chocolate bark with almonds. Check out their signature item, sinfully rich chocolate pâté, organic chocolate flavored with Irish cream and enrobed in Dutch cheese wax. It looks like Gouda on the shelf.

> The Chocolate Smith, 1807 2nd Street, #31, Santa Fe, 87505; (505) 473-2111; www.chocolatesmith.com.

Todos Santos Chocolates and Confections

If you are searching for the unusual, Todos Santos Chocolates and Confections is a must. Tucked away in an obscure corner of Sena Plaza Courtyard, the tiny shop is jam-packed with the unusual: chocolates covered in edible gold or silver leaf and portraying Buddhas, *milagros*, saints, and even a (blush) scene from the *Kama Sutra*. Owner Hayward Simoneaux calls the work "edible folk art." Yes, he also has the more mundane truffles, toffee, brittle, and seasonal holiday candies.

Originally from New Orleans, Simoneaux is self-taught. He began his creative passion by collecting old chocolate molds, learned to make his own, and opened Todos Santos in 1999. He uses only the best quality butter, cream, and Valrhona chocolate from France. Drop in and find something special, perhaps one of those candy cigarettes you remember from your childhood.

> Todos Santos Chocolate and Confections, 125 East Palace Avenue, Santa Fe, 87501; (505) 982-3855.

Coffee Roaster

Las Chivas Coffee Roasters

Santa Fe is not Seattle, but people in New Mexico can be notoriously fussy about their coffee. Most restaurants have received the message, but when you're on your own, trek over to one of the two Las Chivas Coffee Roasters, where you can grab a cup of joe or a pound of beans, ground or whole.

The selection is truly international with beans from the Americas, the Caribbean, Africa, the Middle and Near East, Indonesia, and the Pacific. Some of the world's most famous coffee vintages cross their counters, including several estate selections. You'll find Jamaican Blue Mountain, Kona, Zimbabwe La Lucie Estate, Puerto Rico Yauco Select, Costa Rica La Minita, and more.

There's a large selection of blends and dark roasts to suit almost every palate, and if you absolutely must have flavored blends, they use the finest European-style embellishments to add to their fully developed roast of Colombian beans.

Las Chivas Coffee Roaster, the Agora Center, 7 Avenida Vista Grande, Santa Fe, 87508; Plaza Entrada, 3003 South St. Francis Drive, Santa Fe, 87505.

Cooking Schools

Cookworks

Three stores on South Guadalupe with culinary themes operate under the Cookworks name. One sells equipment, another gourmet groceries, and a third, tableware (see write-up under "Cookware"). At the rear of the equipment store, a demonstration kitchen provides a platform for classes with top local and regional chefs such as Eric DiStefano from Geronimo's and Martin Rios from the Old House. Although not hands-on lessons, the learning experience is personal, with great interaction between chef and students in the intimate setting. Food prepared during the occasion is served to the students at the conclusion of the class, frequently paired with wines.

Classes generally run in the evening for three hours, and new schedules are developed quarterly.

Cookworks, 322 South Guadalupe Street, Santa Fe, 87501; (505) 988-7676.

Las Cosas Kitchen Shoppe and Cooking School

Las Cosas Kitchen Shoppe and Cooking School in the DeVargas Center has a wide variety of programs. At last count, they offered 25 hands-on two and a half hour courses ranging from Oaxacan moles and *pepianes* to a soups and stocks workshop.

School director John Vollertsen and Chef Emily Swantner concentrate on technique and world cuisine, leaving the southwestern recipes to Curtis's downtown school. John, who combines gigs as an actor with his culinary duties, is an exuberant and amusing host, mixing humor with lessons on how to roll a tamale. He keeps the energy high in the limited confines of the store's kitchen, where participants pair up to do a share of the preparation. Occasionally guest chefs such as Pranzo's Jeff Copeland and Joseph Wende of Joseph's Table in Taos make an appearance. Special classes for the holiday are popular with topics including A Dickens's Christmas and Go Stuff a Turkey.

Las Cosas Kitchen Shoppe and Cooking School, 181 Paseo de Peralta, DeVargas Center, Santa Fe, 87501; (877) 229-7184 or (505) 988-3394; www.lascosascooking.com.

Santa Fe School of Cooking and Market

Don't know a *pasilla* from a poblano? Confused about chiles, tortillas, and tamales? Susan Curtis's Santa Fe School of Cooking is the ticket to the secrets of New Mexican cuisine. Located on the upper level of the Plaza Mercado, the sunny classroom has an exhibition kitchen where top chefs share their secrets to an appreciative audience from all points of the globe. You'll find James Campbell Caruso, executive chef for El Farol; Steve Cooper, cooking instructor at Santa Fe Community College; Rocky Durham, former executive chef for the Santa Fe chain in the United Kingdom; Lois Ellen Frank, author of *Native American Cooking: Foods of the Southwest Indian Nations*; Daniel Hoyer, former sous chef at the Coyote Café and chef at La Traviata; Kathi Long, expert in regional cooking of Mexico; Eddie Lyons, from the Pink Adobe; Allen Smith, a former teacher at Peter Kump's New York Cooking School; and Carmen Rodriguez of the Santa Fe Courtyard Marriot.

In a scurry of activity, the instructors prepare many recipes in the two-hour class, all the while maintaining a steady stream of hints, tips, and coaching. At the end of the demonstration, lunch of the morning's labors is served. After lunch, people wander through the school store, which carries a variety of cookware, cookbooks, spice mixes, chiles, salsas, and other regional and local products. You'll discover hard-to-find items such as La Chamba black micaceous clay pottery from Colombia, Nielsen-Massey vanilla, Anasazi beans, and chipotle en adobo.

Susan Curtis is the owner and director of the school, which she founded in 1989 after a career in restaurant consulting for a chain of upscale southwestern restaurants in the United Kingdom. Daughter Nicole Curtis Ammerman directs all retail, inventory, customer service, and staff activities at the school, as well as overseeing daily operations.

Their selection of classes is encyclopedic, ranging from Traditional New Mexican to Southwest Lasagna. Some participation classes are available.

Santa Fe School of Cooking and Market, 116 West San Francisco Street, Santa Fe, 87501; (505) 983-4511; www.santafeschoolofcooking.com.

Cookware

CULINARY
NEW MEXICO

Cookworks

Cookworks is the creation of Chuck Kehoe, who makes his home in San Francisco and has stores in Dallas and Miami in addition to Santa Fe. His concept was to provide a different shopping environment for the City Different, and he has succeeded handsomely. Cookworks is comprised of three separate stores, one for equipment, one for gourmet groceries, and one for tableware. They line the west side of South Guadalupe Street like the beds of the three bears.

The enterprise at 318 is an adobe building with Territorial styling. The interior shines like a jewel with displays of Simon Pearce glass, Castillo silver from Taxco, Provence ceramics, French porcelain, and imported linen from Germany, France, Italy, and Latvia. The air carries a sweet perfume from a selection of scented candles and natural bath and body products, and a rack of international travel coffee-table books tempts the browser.

At 316 Guadalupe, the brick-fronted stone building that once held a warehouse is now the gourmet grocery. Just the aroma emanating from the cheese board with its samples will make you hungry. They carry a wide variety of items you won't find elsewhere: Teuscher chocolates, Fauchon jams and jellies, Petrossian Paris caviar and fois gras, and imported cheeses and pastas, plus canned specialty items, teas, and coffees.

The third store at 322 Guadalupe has an adobe front with arched windows outlined in brick. Cooking equipment is their stock and trade, and you'll find displays of All-Clad and Le Creuset pots, knives from the top manufacturers, small electronics such as food processors and blenders, bakeware, and a wide selection of kitchen gadgets. This store is where the cooking classes are held.

Cookworks, 316 South Guadalupe Street, 318 South Guadalupe Street, 322 South Guadalupe Street, Santa Fe, 87501; (505) 988-7676.

Las Cosas Kitchen Shoppe and Cooking School

Las Cosas occupies two stores within the DeVargas Mall on the north side of town. Owners Mike and Karen Walker stock the equipment store with a variety of name-brand cookware including Kuhn Rikon pressure cookers; Le Creuset, Emerilware, and Cuisinart pans; Rösle implements; Asian woks; Spanish paella pans; Le Forme bakeware; Pillivuyt porcelain; many kitchen gadgets; Chantal and Emil Henry earthenware; and J. A. Henckels, Global, and Wüsthof knives.

The "small electrics" section displays juicers, toasters, mixers, blenders, waffle irons, bread machines, and more. A special housekeeping section stocks specialty items such as irons, ironing boards, brooms, mops, and cleaning supplies. In the cookbook area, you'll find a big selection of books not only on New Mexican cuisine but racks of domestic and international favorites.

The second store is only a few steps away in the mall. It is devoted to tableware with a small section stocking gourmet grocery items such as Dean and Deluca spices, Boucheries frozen entrées, Stonewall Kitchen jams, and Good Wife hors d'oeuvres. The tabletops display Wedgwood Grand Gourmet china, Vietri Italian earthenware, Riedel glass, and other top-of-the line goods. In addition, you can pick up your favorite Joseph Schmidt chocolates or a bottle of Thymes Basil Body Lotion.

Las Cosas Kitchen Shoppe and Cooking School, 181 Paseo de Peralta, DeVargas Center, Santa Fe, 87501; (505) 988-3394; www.lascosascooking.com.

Cutlery of Santa Fe

Cutlery of Santa Fe is a small shop with a big selection of all things relating to cutlery: kitchen knives, sharpeners, Arkansas stones, corkscrews, carving sets, salad servers, steak sets, and every variety of pocketknives known to man. Alan Van Pelt and his partner, Leslie Van Pelt, pride themselves in personal service, knowledge of their products, and depth of experience, which adds up to 26 years in the present location.

Good cooks value their knives and know there's no substitute for quality. Quality is the byword at the Cutlery with a broad selection of knives by R. H. Forshner, Global, Sabatier, J. A. Henckels, and Wüsthof. Tell the Van Pelts what you require, and they can supply you with anything from a paring knife to an Asian *santoku*.

In addition to the culinary line, you'll find beautiful inlaid pocketknives from a local artist, Laguiole knives and corkscrews, and knives by Swiss Army and Victorinox.

Cutlery of Santa Fe, 107 Old Santa Fe Trail (La Fonda storefront), Santa Fe, 87501; (505) 982-3262; www.cutleryofsantafe.com.

Dining

CULINARY
NEW MEXICO

315

You may think 315 is an unusual name for a bistro, but when you realize it's located at 315 Old Santa Fe Trail, the mystery is solved. The best description of the operation is a small restaurant with big food. Chef Louis Moskow manages to pack two dining rooms and a wine bar into the confines of an old adobe home. More space becomes available when the patio opens in warm weather.

Chef Moskow started his culinary career while still a teenager and, after graduating from the Culinary Institute of America in Hyde Park, went on to study extensively in Germany and Italy. In his return to the States, he worked in New Orleans with Emeril Lagasse at the Commander's Palace and in New York with notables such as Alfred Portale at the Gotham Bar and Grill and David Burke at the Park Avenue Café. He says, "I really wanted to be an artist but discovered I had no talent. Instead, I turned those urges to the creation of good food."

Louis's menus change seasonally, and there are nightly specials. Some favorite starters are Country Pâté with pistachios and green peppercorns, Squash Blossom Beignets with goat cheese fondue and tomato coulis, and Baby Arugula Salad with teardrop tomatoes and fresh mozzarella *bocaccini*. Signature entrées are the plump Black Mussels in white wine, lemon, parsley, and tomatoes with club fries (some of the finest we've tried), the Duck Confit with potato galette, ribbon vegetables, and dried cherry sauce, and the Basil Wrapped Shrimp with apricot chutney and curry sauce. Don't neglect the dessert offerings. You'll discover classics such as crème brûlée, flourless chocolate cake, profiteroles, and the signature pot du crème.

Chef Louis has been searching fruitlessly for expanded restaurant quarters for several years. Commercial real estate in Santa Fe is very expensive. He intends to stay in Santa Fe, but if you'd like to try his modern American bistro cuisine, you should check to determine if he is still at the same location.

The 315 Wine Bar is open Thursday through Sunday and features 20 wines by the glass and more than 250 vintages from France, Italy, Germany, Spain, South America, Australia, and the United States. There's a tasting menu with food specially prepared to accompany wines in cruvinet, a system used for effectively preserving and dispensing fine varietal wines by the glass.

Lunch is served Thursday through Saturday and dinner daily.

315, 315 Old Santa Fe Trail, Santa Fe, 87501; (505) 986-9190; www.315santafe.com.

Anasazi Restaurant

Chef Tom Kerpon brings his special brand of contemporary southwestern cuisine to the Anasazi Restaurant, located at the Inn of the Anasazi. Tom's menus are based on the freshest natural ingredients and locally grown organic produce. The menu changes seasonally and might include such starters as the chilled Maine Lobster Salad with tangerine vinaigrette, a dainty half-sized cold-water lobster tail on an immaculately fresh bed of baby greens swathed with a tangy citrus-dominated dressing. Or go native with the Navajo Flat Bread with Fire-Roasted Peppers and a Black Olive Caponata Relish.

The Anasazi specializes in grilled and roasted entrées, and the selection includes seafood, poultry, beef, lamb, game, and vegetarian specials. You might enjoy the Grilled Colorado Lamb Rack with minted démiglace, roasted garlic Yukon Gold potatoes, and sun-dried tomato salsa or the coriander-crusted Venison Medallions with ancho-apricot démiglace, Peruvian purple potatoes, and morel mushrooms. The Rosemary-Garlic Roasted Chicken with natural jus, tomato-leek quinoa, and green beans is perfect for anyone overdosed on enchiladas and chile.

Save room for dessert. Pastry chef Donna Rodriguez makes luscious tirámisu and crème brûlée as well as turning out house-made ice creams and sorbets. Served in a praline shell with fresh berry garnish and raspberry coulis, her trio of Margarita sorbets are the perfect ending to a big meal.

The restaurant is beautiful: softly lit and dominated by earth elements, which evoke a sense of timeless tranquility. Rock walls patterned on the masonry of Chaco Canyon blend into smooth plaster walls emblazoned with ancient petroglyphs. Fires flicker softly in the kiva fireplace, and Native American weavings and supple leather-covered chairs blend with vigas and *latillas* to create a subdued, romantic atmosphere. They are open for breakfast, lunch, and dinner daily.

Anasazi Restaurant, 113 Washington Avenue, Santa Fe, 87501; (505) 988-3236.

Café Pasqual's

A Santa Fe tradition is breakfast or weekend brunch at Café Pasqual's, a little corner restaurant named after the patron saint of the kitchen. In the A.M., it's a bustling bistro with sunlight streaming in the generous windows and both visitors and locals filling the tables or congregating at the common board. In the evening, its ambiance changes from casual to sedate with subdued lighting and romantic dining *à deux*. The décor is Old Mexico, with walls lined in colorful tiles and murals by famed Oaxacan artist Leovigildo Martinez, whose work is reminiscent of Chagall with a surrealistic south-of-the-border twist.

The food is fabulous, rich in color and flavor, a fortuitous combination of culinary traditions of New Mexico, Old Mexico, and Asia. In 1999, they received the James Beard Award for a "timeless, grassroots restaurant that serves memorable food and is strongly embedded in the fabric of the community."

Menus are daunting. Choosing is hard. For breakfast do you have the Smoked Trout Hash, a potato cake with smoked trout, two poached eggs, and *tomatillo d'arbol* salsa, or the Huevos Motululeños, the Yucatan breakfast of two over-easy eggs on corn tortillas with black beans topped with sautéed bananas, feta cheese, peas, jalapeño, and green-chile salsa? Or you can wimp out with a lovely omelet, whole-wheat pancakes, or French toast made with their honey whole-wheat bread.

Lunch features the soup of the day, salads, and local favorites such as their Grilled Salmon Burrito and the Free-Range Organic Chicken Mole Enchiladas.

Dinner gets serious with starters including Japanese Persimmon, Shaved Fennel, and Pecorino-Romano on French Greens tossed in walnut oil vinaigrette or Warm Brie and Whole Roasted Garlic with a salsa of roasted tomato-jalapeño and tomatillo. For a main course, try the Thai Green Curry with red potatoes, carrots, Japanese eggplant, tomatoes, shitake mushrooms, zucchini, spinach, and jasmine rice. For a couple extra bucks you can add organic tofu or Niman Ranch filet mignon.

No matter what you select, you may be assured that owner and chef Katharine Kagel serves only organic chicken, naturally raised beef and pork, and fresh, seasonal, organic produce. In addition to being an innovative chef, Katharine is a talented artist who owns a nearby gallery, where her work is featured along with artists from the West and around the world.

Café Pasqual's, 121 Don Gaspar, Santa Fe, 87501; (505) 983-9340; www.pasquals.com.

The Compound

The Compound is everyone's idea of what the perfect Santa Fe restaurant should be. Located in its own preserve off Canyon Road, the Compound is private, well designed, and ultimately stylish. The property has a rich history. Before becoming a restaurant, it was part of a group of houses on Canyon Road known as the McComb Compound. Glitterati from stage and screen, prominent industrialists, and figures of international society could rent a home in the complex and be assured of their privacy.

Eventually, Will and Barbara Houghton acquired the main house and decided to convert it into a restaurant. For a designer, they went to Alexander Girard, who is best remembered for donating his enormous collection of more than 106,000 items to Santa Fe's Museum of International Folk Art.

Owner and chef Mark Kiffin does justice to the Compound's pedigree by creating a seasonal, contemporary American menu combining the culinary influences of the Mediterranean with those of the New World. Chef Kiffin, a native of Colorado, graduated from the Culinary Institute of America in 1982. Before coming to the Compound, Kiffin served as corporate executive chef for Star Concepts, parent company of Dallas's Star Canyon and AquaKnox restaurants, where he worked directly with chef and owner Stephan Pyles. In 1990, he collaborated with Mark Miller at the Santa Fe–based flagship Coyote Café and later Coyote Café MGM Grand in Las Vegas. He also worked as consulting chef for the opening of Miller's Red Sage in Washington, D.C.

In 2001 Mark was invited to participate in the Master Guest Chefs series at the James Beard House in New York City, and he is one of only 25 chefs invited from around the world to cook at the James Beard Foundation Awards reception.

What are some of the dishes Mark has made memorable? Classic starters include Sweetbreads and Foie Gras with cèpes, cayenne, and Spanish sherry; Trevisio and Endive Salad with Spanish onion, Cabrales cheese, and walnut oil; and Tuna Tartare topped with Ostra caviar and preserved lemon. Two of his entrées near cult status: Buttermilk Roasted Chicken with creamed spinach and foie gras pan gravy and the Grilled Beef Tenderloin with Italian cèpe O'Brien potatoes and foie gras hollandaise. Mark's dessert menu is extensive with standards such as Liquid Chocolate Cake and new takes on old recipes including his Caramelized Pineapple Upside Down Cake with crème fraîche, lime, and fresh mint. For the kid in all of us, there's even a plate of freshly baked cookies accompanied by, what else, a glass of milk.

Under Mark's guidance, the old is new again. He has rejuvenated and renewed the Compound with its modern menu, a knowledgeable and attentive staff, and an inviting, elegant setting.

The Compound, 653 Canyon Road, Santa Fe, 87500; (505) 982-4353; www.compoundrestaurant.com.

Coyote Café

No discussion of Santa Fe restaurants would be complete without the mention of Mark Miller's Coyote Café. For more than two decades, Miller has been creatively revolutionizing modern southwestern cuisine. As much an academic as a chef, he has succeeded by getting in on the ground floor of a number of culinary trends that have passed into general acceptance. Beginning his career in Berkeley, he was among the first to use wood mesquite in grilling and to bring the tastes of Latin America and the Caribbean to his dishes.

When he moved to Santa Fe in 1987, he already was established as one of the founders of American regional cuisine. He has authored 10 cookbooks, all centered on the elements, preparation, and history of southwestern cuisine. He has his own line of southwest foods, Coyote Cocina, and he has expanded his restaurant empire to Las Vegas, Washington, D.C., and Sydney, Australia. Miller has received the James Beard Award for the Best Chef of the Southwest. The Coyote Café was voted "Most Popular" by Zagat Guide and is the winner of the DiRona Award.

An amalgam of three restaurants, the café proper opens for lunch and dinner; Cottonwoods, open daily for lunch, is situated on the first floor below the café; and the Cantina, the rooftop, open-air restaurant, features authentic Mexican cuisine in a casual relaxed atmosphere during the summer months. All bear Miller's indelible stamp of brilliance.

Will you find the everyday tamales and enchiladas at the Coyote? Certainly not! Your appetizer might be Moroccan Spiced Apple Consommé with a confit of chicken, foie gras terrine, and Pedro Ximenz Sherry or the Wild Boar Tamale with *huitlacoche* sauce. Your choice of entrées could be Mark's famous Classic Wood Grilled "Cowboy Cut" Dry-Aged Angus Beef Ribeye or the Filet of Tea-Smoked Salmon, slow roasted with fennel and star anise. The restaurant has been described as a feast for the mind, eye, and palate. The décor is warm and understated. Although their motto is "food to make you howl," you'll not find an overdone exhibition of Santa Fe style.

Cottonwoods concentrates more on traditional Mexican flavors with appetizers such as Queso Fundido, a fondue of house-made chorizo and Mexican cheese, or the Sopa Azteca, tortilla soup with chile *pasilla*, avocado, and Mexican *crema*. The tacos are special. Taco al Pastor is a soft corn tortilla stuffed with spit-roasted pork with pineapple and served with tomatillo avocado and tomatillo *arbol* salsa and *frijoles charros*. Baja Fish Tacos are filled with red chile–rubbed fresh denizens of the deep, topped with angel hair cabbage slaw. There's Miller's Ensalada Caesar as well as a selection of tortas and tostadas.

When the warm weather rolls around, the rooftop Cantina is extremely popular for lunch and after-work libations. Their menu mirrors Cottonwoods's to some degree, with the addition of a greater selection of tortas, burritos, enchiladas, ribs, and an Oaxaco Mole and Shrimp served in the style of Veracruz.

Whichever Coyote Café restaurant you choose, your palate is sure to experience an adventure. This is not your *abuela*'s cooking.

Coyote Café, 132 West Water Street, Santa Fe, 87501; (505) 983-1615; www.coyote-cafe.com.

Geronimo

Are words sufficient to describe Geronimo? From its elegant, contemporary interior to its nonpareil cuisine, Geronimo ranks among the very best New Mexico has to offer. Owners Cliff Skoglund and Chris Harvey knew what they were doing when they hired Eric DiStefano to head the kitchen at the 250-year-old hacienda on Canyon Road.

DiStefano was born and raised in Hershey, Pennsylvania, and developed a passion for food at his mother's table. He began his career with a five-year apprenticeship at the Hotel Hershey under the mentorship of Heinz Hautle and Rory Reno. From the Hershey he went on to work at the Breakers in Palm Beach, Florida, and the Registry Resort in Scottsdale, Arizona. Returning to Pennsylvania, he was appointed chef de cuisine at the Hotel Hershey.

DiStefano was lured west to work for the Hacienda del Cerezo, a high-end inn, but when he heard Cliff Skoglund of Geronimo was searching for a chef, he accepted his proposal. The rest is history.

Describing his cuisine as "global fusion," Chef Eric is passionate about food and is considered a visionary in his ability to blend flavors and combine different types of food in unusual, creative ways. The base of his technique is French, but the distinct culinary influences of Asia, the Southwest, and his own Italian roots mingle to bring taste to new levels.

Geronimo's menu starts with the prix fixe chef's selection of first course, entrée, and dessert with paired wines. If you'd prefer another combination, a full menu follows. For a first course, you might select the Seared Sonoma Foie Gras with a warm baby Fuji apple "pie," grape must, and a salad of crispy bacon and chicory or the Warm Olive Oil Marinated Tomato Tart with fresh thyme and Tuscan olive oil–infused goat cheese, smoked salmon, and Taos egg salad.

For a main course, you then choose from entrées such as Seared Diver Scallops on a bed of julienned smoked Lancaster County pork loin and leeks with a fresh red pepper coulis and micro green salad or the Peppery Elk Tenderloin with applewood smoked bacon, roasted garlic, fork-mashed Yukon Gold potatoes, and a creamy brandied mushroom sauce.

Wine is available by the glass, the bottle, and the half bottle, and you'll find some of the world's best vintages in Geronimo's cellars. Sommelier Paul Montoya is the man to trust when selecting a wine to accompany your meal.

The lunch menu echoes the dinner offerings. You'll discover first courses such as the Sautéed Maryland Blue Crab Cake with red pepper on a bed of leeks, spicy Asian salad, and Tobiko butter sauce. For an entrée, you couldn't go wrong with the plump Washington State Black Mussels braised in a spicy Chardonnay clam broth with carrot pappardelle pasta, zucchini, and grilled focaccia.

Desserts run from the deceptively simple house-made ice creams to the extravagant Black Mission Fig and Macadamia Nut Baklava with a warm eggnog fig sauce.

Restaurant décor is classic simplicity with white plaster walls punctuated by pale, abstract art. Food takes center stage here. The building is old, having been built in 1753 by a Spanish farmer named Geronimo Lopez. The house and land passed from owner to owner until in 1990 Cliff Skoglund purchased the place, opened a restaurant, and named it after the original owner.

Whenever you visit Geronimo, you know you are in for a quality experience. Lunch is served Tuesday through Saturday, and dinner nightly.

Geronimo, 724 Canyon Road, Santa Fe, 87501; (505) 982-1500; www.geronimorestaurant.com.

O'Keeffe Café

If you visited Santa Fe when the O'Keeffe Café first opened, you are in for a wonderful surprise. Instead of a ho-hum eating place serving $10 lunches to museumgoers, the café, under the direction of Michael O'Reilly, has morphed into a gorgeous, sophisticated restaurant with food and wine to match.

The 150-year-old Territorial home, which served as barracks for Union officers during the Civil War, may be old Santa Fe on the outside, but on the inside it is modern. Large black-and-white photos of O'Keeffe in her kitchen hang on the stone-colored walls. The lipstick red banquettes and chairs combine with the subdued colors to create an unusual and striking contrast. The red theme is carried to the hostess station, which is adorned with two dozen red, long-stemmed roses, and each sparkling white–clothed table has one red rose in a crystal vase. The result is simple and urbane.

O'Reilly spent 20 years importing French wines to the States and then exporting Napa Valley wine to 100 countries. He retired to Santa Fe, got bored, and took on a new challenge. His extensive wine list is five pages long, and the vintages are chosen from the world's top 2 percent as rated by wine experts.

Executive chef Tony Lewis is a graduate of Johnson and Wales, and Bethlyn Rider, sous chef, attended the Culinary Institute of America in Hyde Park, New York. They select local produce whenever possible. Their lamb is from Tierra Amarilla, where Antonio Manzanares raises organic churro sheep, the breed brought to the Americas by the conquistadors. The organic chicken is raised without growth hormones in Socorro. The bovine growth hormone–free rib eye steaks come from Niman Ranch in California, the domestic elk loin from the Colorado Rockies, and the organic goat cheese from Nancy Coonridge in Pie Town, New Mexico. Those beautiful roses are grown in a pesticide-free geothermal greenhouse in Animas in southwestern New Mexico.

The dinner menu features starters such as Potato Gnocchi with White Truffles or the Tapas de la Tierra y el Mar, a selection of house-smoked duck wontons, wasabi-crusted sea scallops, seaweed salad, an organic polenta torta, stuffed shrimp with pine nut pesto, and organic buffalo mousseline.

For an entrée you might choose the Smoked Hudson Valley Muscovy Duck Breast with a dried green grape risotto and almond cream or the excellent Smoked Bacon–Wrapped Monkfish Fillet in Dijon cream sauce with roasted vegetables and organic quinoa.

Lighter dishes adorn the lunch menu including Crab Cakes with Chipotle Aioli or a salad of Warm Lobster over Tossed Baby Greens with avocado, dressed with a champagne-tarragon-truffle oil vinaigrette. Maybe you'd prefer a cup of their creamy Sweet Potato Velouté with Vermont maple syrup and pine nuts that you can pair with half a roast beef sandwich with smoked garlic and horseradish blue cheese mousse.

For a special occasion, order the chefs' tasting menu, which starts with an *amuse bouche* and proceeds through five courses with wine. There's also a three-course prix fixe dinner nightly from 5:30 to 7:00 P.M. with soup, your choice of entrée, and dessert.

O'Keeffe Café, 217 Johnson Street, Santa Fe, 87501; (505) 946-1065; www.okeeffecafe.com.

The Old House at the Eldorado Hotel

Not too many true culinary whiz kids grace our kitchens, so it is a pleasure to know Martin Rios. With his tremendous enthusiasm and creativity, Rios, of the Eldorado Hotel's Old House Restaurant, can take his place among the top-ranked chefs in America. For Rios, cooking is not just a profession, it is a calling. And in the sometimes catty world of famous chefs, he is roundly respected for both his skill and dedication.

A native of Guadalajara, Chef Martin's first instructor was his mother, Guadalupe. As a child, he hung out at her restaurant and accompanied her to market, where he learned the importance of good ingredients. He started in the business in a Santa Fe kitchen in the humble role of dishwasher, gradually working his way up to executive sous chef. Moving to the Eldorado Hotel in 1986, he held positions as kitchen and banquet supervisor and in 1992 as executive chef for the Old House.

Then he left Santa Fe for five years, working in kitchens of David Burke at the Park Avenue Café in New York and at the five-star Short Hills Hilton in New Jersey. During this time, he found time to attend the Culinary Institute of America.

During a visit to France, he worked in the kitchen of Michelin Three-Star Chef Georges Blanc in Vonnas, France, and with the World

Pastry Champion Jean Marc Guillot. It was a seminal time in the foundation of his art.

In 1997 he was approached by the Eldorado to take over their fine dining restaurant, and he agreed with the provision that he would do dinner only in order to concentrate on making the Old House more than a hotel restaurant. In 2000, he was named "Chef of the Year" by both the New Mexico Restaurant Association and the Santa Fe Restaurant Association, and he is the first chef from New Mexico to be awarded the Robert Mondavi Culinary Award of Excellence.

When queried about his cuisine, Rios says, "My technique is heavily French, although modified. I keep things simple by respecting flavors and utilizing ingredients in the best way I know how. "

His ingredients are a listing of the best in meat, seafood, and produce. Goat cheese is from New Mexico's Sweetwood Farms, and the certified–organic pastured chicken is from Socorro's Pollo Real. Lobster is shipped in fresh from Maine, and Dungeness crab from Seattle.

Starters in the Old House's gracious dining room might include the Ahi Tuna Tartare with pickled jalapeño, avocado mousseline, and mango-ginger salad with tobiko and red curry-coconut vinaigrette or the Glazed Semi-Boneless Quail served with a puree of cannellini beans, seasonal vegetables, and apple cider–peppercorn sauce. A selection of entrées could include the Pan-Seared Diver Sea Scallops with creamy risotto, Spanish Serrano ham, foie gras, and Spanish Xeres sherry or the heavenly Mustard and Pepper Crusted Lamb Rack with Yukon potato–goat cheese soufflé, spinach, and thyme-olive lamb jus.

If you've still got room, the dessert menu will tempt you with delicacies such as Milk Chocolate and Gingerbread Pudding bathed in cappuccino sabayon and raspberry puree topped with maple-macadamia ice cream or an elegant Pistachio Croquant Napoleon with lemon–white chocolate mousse, cassis sorbet, and Meyer lemon gelée.

The Old House at the Eldorado Hotel, 309 West San Francisco Street, Santa Fe, 87501; (800) 286-6755 or (505) 988-4455; www.eldoradohotel.com.

Paul's Restaurant of Santa Fe

We'll let you in on a little secret: Paul's Restaurant of Santa Fe has consistently won awards such as "The Best of Santa Fe" for many years, but its fame hasn't gotten beyond the town cognoscenti. We discovered it because we love folk art and make countless pilgrimages to the city's Museum of International Folk Art. We had to try a restaurant with its décor based on the whimsical, playful characters inhabiting the world's artistic fantasies.

Much of Paul's folk art comes from a small gallery just around the corner. You'll find Navajo carved chickens, Haitian voodoo flags, carved heads from Guatemala, and beaded alligators from Africa. The small bistro has eye-catchers everywhere you turn.

Owner and chef Paul Hunsicker opened Paul's in 1989 after stints chefing in Connecticut and at the Nectarine in Santa Fe. He is always on hand to greet customers, prepare their orders, and check on the service. He is a very busy man, but his personal attention to detail shows in the food.

His menu is classic bistro. A dinner starter might be his signature Stuffed Pumpkin Bread with pine nuts, corn, and green chile, served with queso blanco, red-chile sauce, and caramelized apple. The Red-Chile Duck Wontons in a soy ginger sauce would be a lighter choice. Popular entrées include his Baked Salmon with a pecan-herb crust and sorrel sauce or the Mediterranean Lamb with eggplant, olives, mushrooms, and roasted peppers.

The lunch menu features several scaled-down versions of the evening fare. During a recent meal, we feasted on Grilled Polenta over a bed of spinach, onion, roasted peppers, and mushrooms in a tomato-cilantro sauce. There are sandwiches for both vegetarians and carnivores as well as one or two salads including the deceptively simple Caesar Salad Romaine with an anchovy dressing and red-chile croutons. Leave room for the fabulous award-winning cheesecake brûlée.

Lunch is served Monday through Saturday and dinner nightly.

Paul's Restaurant of Santa Fe, 72 West Marcy Street, Santa Fe, 87501; (505) 982-8738; www.paulsofsantafe.com.

Il Piatto Cucina Italiana

Where can you get fine Italian cuisine in Santa Fe? Il Piatto Cucina Italiana is the place to head. A popular, moderately priced bistro, Il Piatto is owned by Chef Matt Yohalem. A graduate of Johnson and Wales Culinary Arts program, Yohalem has worked in such renowned restaurants as Le Cirque and Union Square Café in New York, Santa Fe's Coyote Café, and Commander's Palace in New Orleans. He also owns Belle Forche Criolle Restaurant and Bar in New Orleans's historic French Quarter. His Santa Fe chef de cuisine is Tim Butterly.

With a menu changing seasonally, you might find starters such as Grilled Calamari with shaved fennel salad and aioli, Bruschetta with house-cured salmon and herbed mascarpone, or a salad of mixed greens with apples, walnuts, and Gorgonzola. Of course, pasta is represented, but it's not your common linguine. Try the Pappardelle with braised duckling, caramelized onions, and mascarpone-duck jus or the Sautéed Calamari with lemon, garlic, and red pepper over spaghetti. More substantial entrées include Pancetta-Wrapped Trout with grilled polenta and wild mushrooms or the Roasted Garlic and Basil Stuffed Duck Breast with toasted almonds.

Open for dinner seven nights and lunch Monday through Friday, the 75-seat restaurant is frequently packed. Traffic is better accommodated when the weather warms and the patio opens.

Il Piatto Cucina Italiana, 95 West Marcy Street, Santa Fe, 87501; (505) 984-1091; www.ilpiattorestaurant.com.

La Plazuela at La Fonda

La Fonda Hotel is a landmark, built in 1920 and one of the original Harvey Houses, a chain of fine hotels serving the Atchison, Topeka, and Santa Fe Railroad. The massive adobe still stands on the corner of East San Francisco Street and the Plaza. At the heart of the hotel, La Plazuela is enclosed in a beautiful indoor courtyard with soaring ceilings, ornately carved furniture by local artisans, folk art murals, and windows painted with flowers, chiles, and birds by hotel artist Ernest Martinez.

Chef Lane Warner is a graduate of the Culinary Institute of America and worked in Indiana before coming to Santa Fe, where he was executive sous chef under Maurice Zeck before being promoted to executive chef in 1999. He has perfected his own spin on Nuevo Latino cuisine, fusing flavor and color with ingredients such as sweet potatoes, corn, jicama, banana leaves, *asadero* cheese, chiles, citrus, and tropical fruits.

"Neuvo Latino food reflects the spirited cultures of South America. It is elegant with an exotic flair," Warner says. "I live by the 'simpler is better' philosophy. If done well, uncomplicated dishes can be the most exquisite. Using techniques of authentic Latin cuisine, good, fresh ingredients should stand on their own."

Entremets at La Plazuela might start with Callos de Hacha, pan-seared jumbo sea scallops wrapped in *jamón serrano* and served with orange blossom honey and white truffle butter sauce. Follow this by Ensalada de Cangrejo, Peekytoe crabmeat with frisée, endive, sliced grapes, and toasted almonds, topped with chunky papaya vinaigrette. For an entrée you might choose Filet con Chipotle, a char-grilled filet mignon served with chipotle infused démi-glace, roasted garlic mashed potatoes, and fresh seasonal vegetables, or for a vegetarian, Plato de Legumbres a la Plancha, a grilled vegetable plate consisting of a portobello mushroom, red and yellow bell peppers, leeks, eggplant, jicama, and the polenta of the day with a carrot-rosemary sauce and balsamic reduction. Desserts range from a Mexican Chocolate Streusel with roasted banana ice cream to their rendition of cheesecake topped with Mexican chocolate mousse and caramel sauce.

La Plazuela serves breakfast, lunch, and dinner daily. Its lunch menu is lighter and consists of scaled-down versions of many of the dinner starters plus a selection of soups, salads, and sandwiches. A child's menu is available.

La Plazuela at La Fonda, 100 East San Francisco Street, Santa Fe, 87501; (505) 982-5511; www.lafondasantafe.com.

Santacafé

When the dizzying proliferation of Santa Fe restaurants has you in a quandary, there's one place you can go that never disappoints. Santacafé, under the direction of owners Judy Ebbinhaus and Bobby Morrean, has discovered the secret of consistently excellent food and service.

Morrean came up in the kitchen hierarchy the hard way, starting as dishwasher at 12 and progressing to busboy, waiter, and finally owner. He knows the proven dishes his customers expect, and he makes no bones about telling the chef "don't fuss with it." Once he hired an up-and-coming star chef only to discover he didn't want to take direction. Bobby advised him to get his own kitchen, and they parted company. Current executive chef David Sellers was privy to this exchange, and he knows enough not to mess with Santacafé classics such as their wonderful Crispy Calamari with Four Chile Dipping Sauce, the Red-Chile Onion Rings with Judy's catsup, or the Roasted Duck Spring Rolls with Southwestern Ponzu.

Part of the restaurant's attraction is its location in half a restored and remodeled house originally built in 1857 and 1862 by Padre Gallegos. Gallegos was a colorful and controversial priest and politician who was defrocked by Bishop Lamy in 1852. Built around an interior patio used for summer dining, the old Territorial adobe is divided into four dining rooms and a bar. The décor is simple, with white walls, white shutters, and subdued lighting. Most rooms have a kiva fireplace, above which hangs a pair of elk antlers, bedecked during the holidays with Christmas balls.

The menu has a decided southwestern slant with some international influences. For starters, you could order the Hoisin and Habañero Glazed Baby Back Ribs with pineapple slaw or the New Mexico Squash Blossom Beignets with sun-dried tomatoes and English peas. The Roasted Poblano Chile Relleno with three mushroom quinoa and chipotle cream is a variation on an old favorite, while the Grilled Veal T-Bone with mushrooms, Marsala, rosemary, and cream bespeaks a European flavor. If you're not condemned to a low-carb diet, you'll enjoy their bread basket, which has a selection of house-made delights including their garbanzo flour flatbread or the green-chile loaf.

At lunch, the emphasis is on salads, such as the Baby Spinach Niçoise with rare-seared tuna and garlic-caper vinaigrette or the yummy Chicken Confit Enchiladas with peppy Chimayo red chile and black bean salsa. The classic calamari and spring rolls are available any time, and Santacafé is one of the few restaurants serving an artisanal cheese plate. The extensive wine list fills many pages and features Domaine Chandon wines by the bottle or glass.

Open for lunch Monday through Saturday, summer Sunday brunch, and dinner nightly.

Santacafé, 231 Washington Avenue, Santa Fe, 87501; (505) 984-1788; www.santacafe.com.

Trattoria Nostrani

Trattoria Nostrani is an Italian bistro transplanted to Santa Fe. Owner and executive chef Eric Stapelman trained in classical French cuisine under Chef Richard Price at Manhattan's East West Restaurant as well as undergoing training in Kaiseki, formal Japanese cuisine born as an adjunct to the tea ceremony. His restaurant Zucca was listed among the top 50 in New York during the 1980s.

Now happily ensconced in the City Different, he and partner/chef Nelli Maltezos have turned their talents into presenting a country Italian dining experience to palates fried by too many chiles. They make a good pair. Maltezos began her culinary career at Charlie Trotter's Restaurant in Chicago where she spent two and a half years honing her skills, eventually becoming Trotter's assistant sous chef. After moving to Manhattan in 1994, she and Stapelman collaborated at Zucca before the talented duo moved to Santa Fe and opened their own restaurant.

Trattoria Nostrani is set in a historic Territorial-style home, and dinner is served in four simple but elegant dining rooms with comfortable banquettes and 1950s Thonet chairs.

The menu is northern Italian and changes seasonally. For antipasto you might choose the Bresaola, air-dried beef with fried ciopollini onions, mâche, and Parmesan dressing, or Corstata Al Gorgonzola, a cheese tart with black olives and caramelized onion. Typical *primo* might include bistro favorites such as Pappardelle Alla Pisana, pasta with pancetta, mushrooms, and duck liver sauce, or Risotto Del Granchio, jumbo lump blue crabmeat risotto. *Secondi* could be Cacciucco, a Livornese shellfish stew with shrimp, clams, mussels, baby octopus, and calamari, or that perennial favorite, Osso Buco, served with farro and rapini.

One of Chef Eric's greatest prides is his extensive wine list, which he says is the most comprehensive in New Mexico with a catalog of 350 vintages. He has earned three *Wine Spectator* "Awards of Excellence."

A word of caution, the exterior sign is very discreet, so look for their trademark red rooster. There is a small parking lot in front, but if it fills, on-the-street parking seems no problem in the evening.

Trattoria Nostrani, 304 Johnson Street, Santa Fe, 87501; (505) 983-3800; www.trattorianostrani.net.

When Haute Cuisine Pales

You'd think from our report that visitors to Santa Fe dine exclusively on ambrosia and hummingbird's tongues. There comes a time when a simple, inexpensive meal is best, and the following places provide just that.

Bobcat Bite

For what is arguably the best hamburger in or around Santa Fe, take the Old Las Vegas Highway north and keep your eye peeled for the Bobcat Bite Restaurant. Once a trading post, then a gun shop, and now a simple roadside restaurant, the Bobcat's menu concentrates on *big* nine-ounce burgers cooked the way you like them. If you insist, there are other alternatives, including pork chops, ham steak, NY strip, or rib eye. Décor is minimal: five small tables in a one-room cabin with dark vigas and linoleum floors. The hours are unusual. They're open only Wednesday through Saturday from 11:00 A.M. to 8:00 P.M.

Bobcat Bite, Las Vegas Highway, Santa Fe (no zip); (505) 983-5319.

The Guadalupe Café

The Guadalupe Café is the place to go if you're after traditional southwestern food. The little adobe cottage across from the New Mexico Information Center caters to the enchilada and beans crowd, and they do it very well. Owners Leonard and Isabelle Koomoa have been restaurateurs for more than 25 years, launching their first café on Guadalupe Street in 1975.

Open for breakfast, lunch, and dinner daily, their midday business is so popular you might find yourself waiting in line for a table. There's a series of small rooms adorned with oils on loan from the Thomas Moxley Gallery, gracious *bancos*, and a kiva fireplace. During clement weather, an attractive outside patio provides alternate seating.

The breakfast menu covers two pages and runs the gamut from two eggs any style to a Florentine Egg Roll, a monster serving of chopped spinach blended with feta cheese and scrambled eggs, rolled in a whole-wheat flour tortilla, and oven fired with chile and cheese. This is guaranteed to light your fire for the day.

And while we're on the subject of fire, be advised their red chile is *hot*. They do warn you, stating, "Our chile is traditionally hot and our plates require time to prepare. Being a key ingredient, we will not prepare these plates without chile. Samples ... are available upon request." If you're timid, there are plenty of selections without the incendiary ingredient.

Lunch and dinner are similar with old favorites such as burritos, enchiladas, chimichangas, and flautas, but you also can order more-upscale variations, for example Roasted Poblano Chile Stuffed with Shrimp or Camarones de Guadalupe, shrimp sautéed in white wine spiced with garlic and crushed red chile peppers, served with a rolled Anasazi bean, blue-corn, and cheese enchilada and garnished with guacamole. All dishes are made to order from scratch.

**Guadalupe Café, 422 Old Santa Fe Trail, Santa Fe, 87501;
(505) 982-9762.**

India Palace

If you're into East Indian cuisine, Indian Palace Restaurant has two locations, one at Don Gaspar and Water Street, the second on Las Vegas Highway at Sunrise General Store, not far from the Bobcat. Both restaurants are owned by Nitin Bhatka and are not associated with Albuquerque's India Palace or India House on Cerillos. The daily buffet with seven dishes including saffron rice, tandoori chicken, meatballs, three vegetables, and a selection of relishes is fresh and delicious, or you can order off the extensive menu. They serve the best chai I've ever tasted.

> India Palace, 227 Don Gaspar, Santa Fe, 87501; (505) 986-5859; India Palace at the Sunrise General Store, 52 Las Vegas Highway, Santa Fe, 87505; (505) 982-6705.

Jinja Asia Café

Jinja Asia Café, at the north end of the DeVargas Mall, prepares tasty stir fries, spring rolls and lettuce wraps, sweet and sour salads, wok bowls, noodle soups, and "large plates," such as Kung Pao Chicken and Rice Paper Salmon. Service is snappy, and you can order to go. Your selection is directly relayed by computer to the kitchen where the action is. There are no paper lanterns or coiled dragons. Walls are shaded in tones of mustard and rust and adorned with travel posters and photos of Asian scenes. Most prices are less than $10.

> Jinja Asia Café, 510 North Guadalupe, Santa Fe, 87501; (505) 982-4321.

The San Marcos Café

The San Marcos Café is a couple miles out of town on the old Turquoise Trail. You've probably passed by several times thinking it solely a feed and supply store. Tucked into the front of the building, the café is open for breakfast and lunch. Owner Susan MacDonnell serves an eclectic cuisine—mostly New Mexican but peppered with daily specials such as Lamb Madeira with pasta. There's always a couple of made-from-scratch soups, a quiche of the day, and a fiery green-chile stew. Save room for their bourbon apple pie. It's a sell-out favorite.

> San Marcos Café, 3877 NM Highway 14, Santa Fe, 87508; (505) 471-9298.

Tortilla Flats

A good, basic New Mexican restaurant with no pretensions to nouvelle cuisine, Tortilla Flats has fed hungry Santa Fe families and knowledgeable visitors since 1986. The Macias brothers have crafted their recipes to appeal to the general palate, not too bland and not too spicy. All their chile sauces are vegetarian, as are many of the dishes. Portions are generous. You'll discover all the usual players: enchiladas, burritos, quesadillas, and fajitas, as well as daily specials such as Pork Chop Adovada, a marinated center cut slow baked in a red-chile caribe.

Tortilla Flats, 3139 Cerrillos Road, Santa Fe, 87507; (505) 471-8685; www.tortillaflatsofsantafe.com.

Out of Town

The Restaurant at Rancho de San Juan

Since Santa Fe has so many excellent places to eat, why would you drive 36 miles to dine? The answer is the Restaurant at Rancho de San Juan, a Relais and Chateaux property. Voted as one of the "Top 25 Inns with Great Chefs in North America" by *Condé Nast Traveller*, Rancho de San Juan's restaurant offers a prime dining experience.

The inn is nestled in the foothills of the Black Mesa Land Grant and overlooks the Ojo Caliente River Valley with views of mesas and the Jemez Mountains in the distance. The inn itself, with its casitas and spa services, is a luxurious getaway, but you don't have to be a guest to enjoy the exquisite prix fixe four-course dinners prepared by Executive Chef Chris Roche.

The inn's cuisine is "world eclectic." One evening you might encounter a starter of Roasted Oysters on the Half Shell with Parmesan and herb crust or Oyster Mushroom, Roasted Shallots, and Crisped Avocado Napoleons with piquillo pepper rouille. From a choice of three entrées, you'd find Applewood Smoked Bacon–Wrapped Filet Mignon with wild mushroom démi-glace, sautéed spinach, and chive mashed potatoes; Jamon Serrano–Wrapped Diver Scallops with sautéed polenta, snow peas, scallion oil, and red pepper essence; or a vegetarian special such as Rancho Polenta Lasagna with piquillo pepper coulis and sautéed crimini mushrooms. Salad could be Watercress Frisee and Fresh Fennel with lemon vinaigrette and yellow tomatoes, and for dessert, you'd have a choice of Red Wine Poached Black Mission Figs with whipped goat cheese and pistachio baklava, the chef's house-made sorbets, or a selection of artisan cheeses. The menu is available with or without wine recommendations. Another alternative is the Chef's Table, a six- or seven-course dinner served in a special dining room with kitchen view.

David G. Heath and John H. Johnson III, who until this year was not only innkeeper but also executive chef, a position he's recently delegated to Chef Roche, own Rancho de San Juan. The dining rooms are pleasing to the eye with original artwork from the inn's private collection by prominent artists such as Tony Abeyta and Gregory Lomayesvi. You'll dine on imported Frette linens set with family sterling and Riedel crystal. In summer, cocktails are served on the sunset terrace or in winter in the cozy Kachina Bar.

The inn closes for the month of January and reopens the first Tuesday of February. Dinner is served Tuesday through Saturday with seatings at 6:00, 7:00, and 8:00 P.M. Tables do not turn over and are yours for the evening.

The Restaurant at Rancho de San Juan, U.S. Highway 285, Mile Marker 340 (between Española and Ojo Caliente), Española, 87532; (505) 753-6818; www.ranchodesanjuan.com.

Farmers' Markets

Española Farmers' Market, Española Plaza, Calle Don Diego, behind Bond House, Mondays, noon to dusk, June through October, (505) 685-4842.

Santa Fe Rail Yard Farmers' Market, Rail Yard at Guadalupe and Cerrillos, Saturdays and Tuesdays, 7:00 A.M. to noon, April through November; Winter Market, El Museo Cultural at the Rail Yard, Saturdays, 7:00 A.M. to noon, November through March, (505) 983-4098.

Santa Fe Rodeo Fairgrounds Farmers' Market, Rodeo Grounds, Thursdays, 3:00 to 7:00 P.M., July through end of September, (505) 983-4098, ext. 15.

Specialty Food Stores

The Marketplace Natural Grocery

The Marketplace, founded in 1982, is Santa Fe's locally owned natural grocery. Proprietor Jill Markstein features natural and organic produce, organic dairy products, local and organic meats, and poultry, fresh seafood, organic coffee and tea, fresh local breads, pastries, pies and cakes, bulk herbs, spices, grains and nuts, vitamins and supplements, and more.

Check out their deli for breakfast, lunch, or dinner. They have a wide variety of freshly made dishes from creative ethnic recipes to some of your old favorites. If you're planning an outdoor adventure, they do bag or box lunches to order.

Their mission statement is "to offer high-quality natural foods and other products at reasonable prices, to provide excellent customer service, to serve as an informational resource, and to contribute to and support the well-being of the local community and the Earth."

The Marketplace Natural Grocery, 627 West Alameda Street, Santa Fe, 87501; (505) 984-2852; www.themarketplaceng.com.

The Spanish Table

The Spanish Table is a nifty little store on Guadalupe, just a couple of blocks north of Cookworks. With its colorful Spanish and Portuguese ceramics, its bountiful books and cookbooks, its hard-to-find ingredients such as Arbequina olives or Marcona almonds, and its cold case of Spanish-style cured meats and cheeses, it's a wonderful place to spend part of an afternoon browsing.

The cookware comes in all shapes and sizes from a *cazuela* serving two to a paella pan a yard in diameter. There are hand-painted serving dishes, plates, pitchers, and bowls. A clever item is the olive dish with two bowls, one for the olives, and the other for the pits.

If you're searching for a gift book for a child, how about *El Gato Ensombrerado—Cat in the Hat* in Spanish? Love flamenco or fado music? They have a big selection of CDs from which to choose.

Owner Steve Winston, a retired customs officer, has other stores in Seattle, his home, and Berkeley, California. Although he's seldom in residence in Santa Fe, his store manager, soft-spoken Karen Squires, will be more than happy to help you with your selections. If you live in one of the three areas where the stores are located, you may request their quarterly newsletter packed with recipes, new products, books, and music. Outside those areas, the newsletters are available for a fee.

The Spanish Table, 109 North Guadalupe Street, Santa Fe, 87501; (505) 986-0243; www.spanishtable.com.

The Chain Gang

Whole Foods Market, 753 Cerrillos Road, 87501; (505) 992-1700; www.wholefoods.com.

Wild Oats Natural Marketplace, 1090 S Saint Francis Drive, Santa Fe, 87501; (505) 983-5333; www.wildoats.com.

Vitamin Cottage Natural Grocers, 3328 Cerrillos Road, 87507; (505) 474-0111; www.vitamincottage.com.

Wineries

Balagna Winery

The tasting room of former Los Alamos nuclear chemist John Balagna's winery possesses a splendid overlook of the White Rock Canyon of the Rio Grande and the Sangre de Cristo Mountains.

Wines produced here are all from New Mexico grapes. They include Chardonnay, Riesling, Zinfandel, and blends such as Celeste Blaco, Dago Red, and Italian varietals. A best seller and a souvenir of the atomic city, La Bomba Grande wine commemorates the 50th anniversary of the first nuclear bomb.

Open daily for tours, tasting, and sales from noon to 6:00 P.M.
Balagna Winery, 223 Rio Bravo Drive, Los Alamos (White Rock), 87544; (505) 672-3678.

Santa Fe Vineyards

Santa Fe Vineyards produces 10 wines including Chardonnay, Cabernet, White Zinfandel, and Indian Market White. The winemaking facility, gift shop, picnic area, and tasting room are located 20 miles north of Santa Fe, just off Highway 285, and are open daily.

A second tasting room is located in the Amado Peña Gallery at 235 Don Gaspar (corner of Alameda and Don Gaspar) in Santa Fe. Visitors are welcomed daily at the winery and at the Santa Fe tasting room.
Santa Fe Vineyards, RR 1 #216, Española, 87532; (505) 753-8100.

Events

ArtFeast

February—To celebrate the world-class art galleries and world-famous restaurants of the region, the Santa Fe Gallery Association presents a series of events blending the best of Santa Fe's aesthetic and epicurean offerings. The highlight of the ArtFeast is the Edible Art tour in which 25 galleries and restaurants team up to offer edibles and art. Special exhibitions, a panel discussion on art, and an international dinner are also planned. All proceeds are disbursed to teachers in the Santa Fe public schools for the purchase of art supplies.

> ArtFeast, P.O. Box 9245, Santa Fe, 87504; (505) 982-1648 or (505) 988-2515; www.santafegalleries.net.

Taste of Santa Fe

First Tuesday in May—Please your palate by attending the annual Taste of Santa Fe at Sweeney Center. The creations of more than 25 premiere Santa Fe chefs are available for sampling, and there is an auction and live music. A project of the Museum of New Mexico Foundation, it supports the Palace of the Governors, which benefits from the evening's proceeds. Participating restaurants in past years include Il Piatto, La Fonda, Inn of the Anasazi, Bishop's Lodge, and El Farol, to name a few.

> Taste of Santa Fe, 201 West Marcy Street, Santa Fe, 87501; (505) 982-6366; www.museumfoundation.org.

Santa Fe Wine Festival

Fourth of July Weekend—Presented by the New Mexico Wine Growers and El Rancho de las Golondrinas, a living museum 15 miles south of the city, the annual wine festival combines wine tastings, arts and crafts, food, music, and entertainment. The village is in full operation with costumed villagers re-creating life in old New Mexico at a Spanish colonial ranch from the 18th century.

> The Santa Fe Wine Festival, El Rancho de las Golondrinas, 334 Los Pinos Road, 87507; (505) 471-2261; www.golondrinas.org.

Santa Fe Wine and Chile Fiesta

September—This weeklong festival is the Big Kahuna of Santa Fe's food festivals. The program, which starts on a Wednesday, features food and wine seminars from local and guest chefs. Varying from demonstrations followed by luncheon to wine auctions and tastings, the classes fill very rapidly. Restaurant winery dinners run Wednesday through Friday, and at each, winery principals introduce their wines to guests with a special wine-pairing menu.

On Saturday, all stops are pulled out at the Grand Food and Wine Tasting, held at the Santa Fe Opera grounds. White tents like sails spring up in a giant U-shape, and food from 60 of Santa Fe's finest restaurants and vintages from 90 world-class wineries are served to a teeming, appreciative crowd.

Santa Fe Wine and Chile Fiesta, 551 West Cordova Road, Santa Fe, 87505; (505) 438-8060; www.santafewineandchile.org.

Recipes

Squash Blossom Beignets with Goat Cheese Fondue

Courtesy of Louis Moskow
315

4 servings

Tomato fondue (see recipe below)
Goat cheese fondue (see recipe below)
4 or 5 fresh squash blossoms with stamens and pistils removed
1 C. flour
1 C. soda water
1 egg
2 qts. oil
Pinch salt
Scallions, julienned

Mix flour, soda water, and egg. Heat oil to 350° F. Dip blossoms into batter and fry to a golden brown. Season with salt. To serve, place 2 oz. of goat cheese fondue on plate and spread to form base. Stack beignets on goat cheese and top with 2 oz. of the tomato fondue. Garnish with julienned scallion.

Tomato Fondue

2 oz. olive oil
1 onion, diced
Clove of garlic, minced
1 Tbsp. tomato paste
4 oz. white wine
16-oz. can plum tomatoes
5 basil leaves
1 bay leaf
Salt and pepper

Sweat onion and garlic in olive oil. Add tomato paste and cook 2 minutes over medium flame. Add wine, cook 5 minutes. Add tomatoes, basil, bay leaf, and salt and pepper to taste. Simmer 45 minutes and puree.

Goat Cheese Fondue

1 T. butter
1 shallot, minced
2 C. cream
6 oz. goat cheese
1 Tbsp. chopped herbs
Pinch cumin
Salt and pepper

Sweat shallot in butter in a small pot over medium flame. Add cream, cheese, herbs, cumin, and salt and pepper to taste. Do not boil.

Dungeness Crabmeat Tart with Creamy Avocado, Cucumber, and Tomato

Courtesy of Martin Rios
The Old House

4 servings

8 oz. clean Dungeness crabmeat
2 Tbsp. mayonnaise
2 Tbsp. Dijon mustard
Juice of a lime
Pinch of fresh thyme
Pinch of Thai basil
Pinch of cilantro
1 Tbsp. minced shallots (lightly cooked)
Salt and pepper

2 ripe avocados (pureed with a little lime juice and extra-virgin olive oil)
2 ripe roma tomatoes (concasse or coarsely chopped)
1 English cucumber (diced)
Micro greens
Vinaigrette (see recipe below)

In a small bowl, combine the crab, mayonnaise, mustard, lime juice, herbs, and shallots. Season with salt and pepper.

To Plate:
1. Place a 2-inch ring mold in the center of a dinner plate.
2. Spoon the crabmeat mixture into the ring mold about 2/3 of the way up.
3. Spread the avocado onto the crabmeat and level the puree with a offset spatula to make a clean, smooth top.
4. Remove the ring and garnish the top with micro greens.
5. Spoon the vinaigrette around the tart and serve.

Vinaigrette
1 C. cucumber juice
1 Tbsp. ponzu (ponzu is a balanced blend of soy sauce, citrus juices, and sweetener. Available at Asian food markets, it is lighter and has a fuller flavor than soy sauce.)
3 Tbsp. argan oil (argan oil is pressed from the nut of a tree grown in Morocco. It is expensive and rare. Author suggests a good nut oil as substitute.)
1 tomato (minced or confit)
1 Tbsp. calamata olives (minced)
Sugar to taste
Salt and pepper

Using a small size bowl, combine the ingredients together and whisk. Season with sugar, salt, and pepper.

A Summer Menu

Courtesy of Mark Kiffin
The Compound

Made-to-Order Summer Sweet Corn Soup
4 servings

1 ½ qts. light vegetable stock (not dark or heavily flavored)
3 ears sweet corn, shucked and cut off of the cob
2 scallions, white part only, sliced
Kosher salt and freshly ground pepper to taste

Bring vegetable stock to a simmer, add corn and scallion, and season. Bring to a boil, reduce heat, and simmer for 5 minutes. The corn should be tender but still sweet and not starchy. Puree in blender at high speed until completely smooth and slightly foamy. For a thinner soup or sauce, strain through a fine sieve. Adjust seasoning and serve hot.

Lobster Salad with Creamy Orange Vinaigrette, Sweet Corn, Red Pepper, Butter Lettuce, and Basil
4 servings

2 Maine lobsters, approximately 1 ¼ pounds each, cooked in boiling
    salted water for 6 minutes, then shocked in ice water
3 ears sweet corn, cut off of the cob
1 medium red bell pepper, cut into small dice
1 medium red onion, cut into small dice
1 small bunch basil, minced
Kosher salt and freshly ground pepper to taste
1 head butter lettuce, cored, cleaned, and spun dry, leaves should
    remain whole
Creamy orange vinaigrette (see recipe below)
1 lemon cut into wedges

Bring a small pot of water to a boil, add the corn, blanch 30 seconds, and shock in cold water. Drain completely.

Remove the lobster from the shells and cut into large pieces. Toss with the peppers, onion, basil, corn, and season to taste. Take a portion of the dressing and toss the leaves of lettuce, coated but not "wet" with dressing. Take another portion (remember you can always add more) and toss the lobster mixture with the dressing. Arrange the lettuce leaves in cold bowls, and place a portion of the lobster salad on top. Garnish with lemon wedges.

Can be served with crunchy French bread or sliced avocados.

Creamy Orange Vinaigrette
1 egg yolk
1 Tbsp. apple cider vinegar or champagne vinegar
2 C. fresh orange juice, simmered and reduced to $^1/_4$ cup, cooled
$^3/_4$ cup grapeseed or light vegetable oil
Kosher salt

In a blender place the egg yolk, vinegar, and orange juice. On high speed run to mix and slowly add oil drop by drop. As it emulsifies, add the rest in a steady steam until fully incorporated. Season with salt and chill. Will keep in the refrigerator for 1 week.

Mark Kiffin's Wildflower Honey Glazed Peaches
4 servings

4 large or 6 medium ripe peaches cut in half, pits removed
Honey glaze (see recipe below)
1 pint good-quality vanilla-bean ice cream
$^1/_2$ cup pecan pieces, slightly toasted

Heat a large Teflon or cast-iron pan to very hot, and sear the peaches, cut side down, approximately 2 to 3 minutes. Toss peaches with half of the honey glaze. Remove from heat to cool, or if you prefer, serve warm.

Cut half peaches in half again, place in chilled bowls, place scoops of vanilla ice cream on top, drizzle with the remaining glaze, and top with the pecans.

Honey Glaze
1 Tbsp. fresh lemon juice
$^1/_4$ cup wildflower honey, or any good-quality honey
1 C. water
1 vanilla bean, split

Place all ingredients in saucepan and slowly reduce to syrup to approximately $^1/_4$ cup.

Taos Pueblo

Author at Downtown Bistro

Cid Backer of Cid's Market

Taos Cookery

What draws artists and dabblers, hikers and couch potatoes, mystics and realists to Taos? And what is it that brings them back summer and winter, spring and fall? Some will say it's the beauty of the natural setting, the way a crimson sunset on the mountain is always waiting in the wings. Skiers, hikers, cyclists, and white-water rafters will tell you of the bounteous outdoor opportunities for recreation. Mystics will say it's that mysterious hum, only heard by those tuned into the cosmos. Realists will say it's a place to lay back, recreate, and enjoy the great food and shopping.

The truth lies in the perception. Taos is all things to all people depending on their need. They say the mountain either takes you in as one of its own or rejects you immediately. You'll know when you go.

Bakeries and Cafés

Dragonfly Café and Bakery

If you have ever had visions of sugarplums dancing in you head, you will be right at home at Dragonfly Bakery and Café. Home to some of the most tempting sweet bread, cakes, and pies in Taos, the café has won a regional magazine's kudos for the best baked goods in town.

The business is set back from the road, and you must look twice or you'll pass it by. Ensconced in the former Tarlton home, Dragonfly's bakery is located in the rear, off a small children's playground and parking area. Or you can enter through the front door, which brings you into the sunny café area with its butter yellow walls, 1950s collectibles, and stacks of local and regional newspapers.

Owner Karen Todd opened Dragonfly in 1999. She received her culinary training at the Cooking and Hospitality Institute of Chicago, then apprenticed with the Whole Foods chain and worked at restaurants and catering services in the Windy City.

All recipes are Karen's, and her pastry chefs are well trained. The selection they produce is a feast for eyes and taste buds. The chocolate éclairs are the most popular sweet, with the almond croissants filled with frangipani crème a close second. You'll also find items such as a flourless chocolate cake topped with Cabernet-spiked cherries; pear, walnut, and red grape galette; espresso cheesecake; and all kinds of pies and cookies. Specialty items are the chocolate truffles and the best granola in Taos. In addition to the sweet breads, the bakery daily produces nine-grain sourdough and white loaves from unbleached and unbromated flours.

The café serves breakfast and lunch with a special brunch on weekends. Specials change daily and may feature wonderful combinations such as a three-egg omelet filled with house-smoked gravlaks, cream cheese, tomato, and red onion. Other possibilities include huevos rancheros; fennel pancakes with house-made orange syrup and two eggs with choice of sausage, ham, bacon, or house-made chorizo; or the unusual *bibimbop*, two eggs over easy on rice with vegetables, kimchee, and garlic-chile sauce— a Korean treat!

Lunch means homemade soups, salads, and sandwiches such as a Duck Wrap; Roasted Vegetables; Rib Eye with roasted red peppers, portobello mushrooms, onions, Jack cheese, and sage aioli; or a Lamb Gyro with tzatziki sauce. Hot entrées include an Udon Noodle Bowl with miso broth and egg, vegetables, green onions, fresh mint, and basil. Add tofu, chicken, portobellos, shrimp, or duck, if you desire. Shepherd's Pie is always on the menu as is a quiche du jour and Campanelli Pasta in Gorgonzola cream sauce with roasted winter squash, frizzled leeks, and pistachios.

Don't pass up this great little café.

Dragonfly Café and Bakery, 402 Paseo del Pueblo Norte, Taos, 87571; (505) 737-5859; www.dragonflytaos.com.

Mainstreet Bakery & Café

Mainstreet Bakery & Café boasts "all organic—all natural—almost." Every day they craft a variety of loaves from flour suppliers in New Mexico and Arizona, and although "almost" all components are organic, some of the more difficult to obtain ingredients are nonorganic.

At this family operation, you're likely to find Anthony and Virginia Medina or daughter Andrea behind the counter. Every morning at 2:00 A.M. their bakers arrive to heat the ovens and make the dough for cinnamon-raisin, seven-grain, carrot–poppy seed, sourdough-white, orange–date and nut, white, whole-wheat, light rye, and corn breads.

Around 7:30, everything is in readiness for the first café customer stopping for breakfast or to pick up a loaf of bread to take home. A morning special of eggs, home fries, and bakery toast is a bargain. Your traditional breakfast items like buckwheat pancakes, French toast, and omelets are on the menu. If you're searching for southwestern hearty offerings, they have breakfast burritos; huevos rancheros; several egg and chile combos; and *migas*, two eggs scrambled with garlic, onions, cheese, tortilla chips, and green chile served with black beans and corn-bread. That's enough body fuel for several days!

The lunch menu lists sandwiches on your choice of breads, meatless Gardenburgers, or grilled chicken breast with choice of toppings. Salads range from grilled tofu on greens to Salade de Maison Verte, wild organic mixed greens and fresh seasonal veggies.

The bright café with its colorful red tablecloths and order counter is open daily. Lunch is served Monday through Friday only.

Mainstreet Bakery & Café, 112 Dona Luz Plaza, Taos, 87571; (505) 758-9610.

Taos Bakery

Hidden away from the main travel routes, Taos Bakery produces some of New Mexico's highest quality artisanal breads. Locally milled organic flour, local fruits and vegetables, and the finest cheeses are used in all products. Flours are whole grain, unenriched, and unbromated, and only natural leaven is used.

Seth Klein and his wife, Carla, own and operate the business. Seth's background includes 24 years as a baker. He trained at Johnson and Wales in Providence, Rhode Island, where he earned degrees in culinary arts, pastry arts, and business management.

In Woodstock, New York, he met Daniel Leader, owner of Bread Alone, who imparted to his disciple the philosophy of using local organic products and maintaining extremely high standards. On Leader's advice Seth went to Paris where he learned Old World methods and standards. Back in the States, he ran a seasonal bakery in Massachusetts and came to Taos in 1994 to work at the Ski Valley, where he met his future wife. Together they opened the Taos Bakery in July 2001.

Seth bakes approximately 700 loaves a day and distributes his wares at his two locations and at stores and restaurants throughout Taos. A sampling of his full line includes Old World rye, whole-wheat sour-dough, honey cinnamon-raisin, crusty Italian, Russian pumpernickel, 100 percent cracked wheat, French baguettes, eight-grain breads, and fruit tarts, Danish pastry, croissants, turnovers, pies, bear claws, sticky buns, and cinnamon buns. Specialty items appear seasonally.

The café serves breakfast all day, and you can order up honey-raisin French toast; a fresh fruit yogurt plate; their special breakfast burrito; *huevos compuestos*, a filling dish of eggs and red bliss potatoes baked with spinach, feta, tomatoes, and green chile; or the Parisian breakfast, two eggs baked with calamata olives, roasted red peppers, and chèvre served with potato pancakes, poultry sausage, and a fresh croissant.

Lunch, or *almuerzo*, is served after 11:00 A.M. and consists of your choice of three homemade soups, salads, calzones, pizza, lasagna, seven-ounce burgers on sourdough rolls, or sandwiches made with your choice of bakery breads. "White board" hot entrées might include a terrine, a galantine, or Chicken Française.

Due to popular demand, the Kleins have opened a satellite bakery and café north of town on Paseo del Pueblo Norte. They carry Seth's baked goods plus a limited lunch menu of soups, sandwiches, and some easily transported entrées.

Taos Bakery, 1223 Gusdorf Road, Taos, 87571; (505) 751-3734; 1299 Paseo del Pueblo Norte, El Prado, 87529; (505) 758-0434.

Brewery and Brewpub

Eske's Brew Pub & Eatery

When in Taos, where should you head for the best artisanal brewed beer? Beat feet to Eske's Brew Pub & Eatery in the historic district one-half block southeast of the Plaza. Here, in the 80-year-old, flat-roofed adobe home, beer master Steve Eskevack creates 30 different brews, all of which are made and sold on the premises.

Eske beers are fresh, unfiltered, and unpasteurized. They brew ales as opposed to lagers. Ales contain yeasts that are top fermenting, and lagers have bottom-fermenting yeasts. Six brews are almost always on tap: Millennium Pale Ale; Wanda's Wicked Wheat, a 25 percent wheat malt that is crisp and light in flavor; Taos Mountain Gold, a medium-light Munich fest ale with Mount Hood hops for spice; Scottish Ale, malty, hoppy, and assertive with Carmel, Munich, and Carapils malts blended with Chinook and Cascade hops; Seco Stout, a dry Irish-style stout; and Taos Green-Chile Beer, using New Mexico's famous green chile during fermentation. Selection varies seasonally and includes fruited ales, barley wine, and their own homemade root beer. For folks who can't make up their minds, there's a taster tray available at $1 per four-ounce sample.

Food is pub fare with burritos, vegetarian green-chile stew, Gardenburgers, regular burgers, bratwurst sandwiches, beer-battered club sandwiches, soups, salads, and snacks. Sunday night blue-plate specials run from roasted turkey to southern fried chicken with mash. Every Tuesday is sushi night with a wide selection of vegetarian, cooked, and raw sushi dishes. Each Thursday night in addition to the regular fare, Eske highlights foods from different parts of the world such as India or Greece. Weekends feature live music.

Eske's Brew Pub & Eatery, 106 Des Georges Lane, Taos, 87571; (505) 758-1517; www.eskesbrewpub.com.

Chocolatier

Xocoatl Handmade Chocolate

Xocoatl means "bitter water" in Nahuatl, the language of the ancient Aztecs. It is the name Scott Van Rixel gave to his Taos chocolate shop on Juan Largo Lane. The bitter liquid of the ancients has come a long way. Scott is a Certified Master Chocolatier, having studied with some of the finest European master chefs, pastry chefs, and chocolatiers. He and brother Tim opened the shop at its former Plaza location in April 2002, and since then Xocoatl chocolate has received wide acclaim for its devotion to quality chocolate, handcrafting, and all-natural ingredients.

All chocolates are handmade using the Venezuelan *criollo cacao* bean, which makes up less than 10 percent of beans used worldwide. The yield is small, and beans are expensive; however, the dark-roasted cherry flavor makes this chocolate stand above the rest. Xocoatl uses "El Rey" Venezuelan chocolate exclusively for its superior quality and its commitment to fair trade. Scott uses no artificial flavors, food grade wax, palm oil, or vegetable oil fillers. He uses his own blend of spices including a hint of red chile powder, which was the favorite spice of the Aztecs to flavor their cocoa.

In all, Scott creates 30 different types of confections, including his famous egg-shaped truffles. His flourless chocolate cake is made with only three ingredients, one of which is a full pound of spiced dark chocolate. Scott says, "Life without chocolate is life lacking something important." All you chocoholics beat a path to Xocoatl!

Xocoatl Handmade Chocolate, 107B Juan Largo Lane, Taos, 87571; (505) 751-7549; www.chocolatecartel.com.

Cooking Classes

Italian Cooking al Bacio

Villa Fontana and Chef Carlo Gislimberti offer a culinary adventure vacation that allows you to experience the genuine flavors of Italy without the hassles of overseas travel. These classes are fun and informative and take place in a peaceful garden setting with unrestricted views of Taos Mountain. Carlo stresses the influence of geography on the dishes of Italy as well as adapting ingredients to American markets.

From April through September, Carlo opens up his enclosed patio for three- and five-day classes in modern Italian cuisine, structured to allow for the creation of appetizers, soups, sauces, and pasta, as well as the preparation of fish, chicken, beef, and other meats.

Strictly for food lovers, not student chefs, the classes of 8 to 10 sip a little wine and watch the master prepare three recipes and learn a little lingua such as *pomodoro*, *ragu*, *saltimbocca*, *pappardelle*, *finocchio*, and *fragole*. Lunches follow each class, giving students an opportunity to sample their creations.

For more information on the restaurant and chef, look under the "Dining" section.

Italian Cooking al Bacio, Villa Fontana Restaurant, 71 NM Highway 522, Taos, 87571; (505) 758-5800; www.villafontanataos.com.

Taos School of Cooking

Want to go to night school? The Taos School of Cooking has evening programs, which although originally designed for local foodies, have grown to include many guests in the town's bed-and-breakfast community. The school, founded in 2001, is a not-for-profit organization benefiting the Yaxche Learning Center, an independent school for children from kindergarten through eighth grade.

The hands-on classes are staffed with a group of regional chefs who share their culinary backgrounds and experiences before launching into the evening's themed menu by reviewing each recipe, talking about ingredients, and sharing cooking tips. Food preparation takes place in the school's modern, well-equipped kitchen, where students are divided into work groups supervised by the guest chef. Previous menus have featured Winter Braises and Stews, Hot Wok, Luscious Lobster Cookery, and One-Dish Wonders.

Guest chefs have included Emily Swantner and John Vollertsen of Santa Fe's Las Cosas Cooking School as well as award-winning celebrity chefs Joseph Wrede of Joseph's Table, and Eric DiStefano of Santa Fe's Geronimo.

Taos School of Cooking, Yaxche Learning Center, 123 Manzanares Street, Taos, 87571; (505) 751-4419, ext. 206; www.taoscooking.com.

Cookware

Monet's Kitchen

Have you ever shopped in a store dedicated to Monet? In the historic Long John Dunn House shops between the Plaza and Bent Street, Monet's Kitchen is a leaf out of a book of Impressionist prints. This marriage of art, cuisine, and commerce is the result of high school teacher Howard Sherman's love affair with what he saw and experienced after visiting Monet's house and gardens in Giverny. The painter, a gourmet chef who cooked only for his friends and family, inspired Sherman, a Ph.D. in philosophy. Returning to Taos, Sherman opened his store and dedicated it to the Impressionist. Although Sherman passed away in 2003, the shop continues under the responsible management of long-term employee Lindsay Dinkins-Eden.

Monet's Kitchen specializes in functional cookware rather than tabletop accessories. This is the place to go for pots, pans, cooking gadgets, regional food products, and a selection of cookbooks.

Monet's Kitchen, 124 Bent Street, Ste. M, Taos, 87571; (505) 758-8003.

Taos Cookery

Taos Cookery on Bent Street is a great place to pick up specialty items such as tableware, gifts, and crafts. Owned by Cobey Senescu since 1989, the cozy shop is packed to the rafters with local products, regional pottery, pots, pans, knives, cookie cutters, and everything kitchen and dining related. When she's not in the shop during the winter, you'll probably find Cobey instructing novices at Ski Valley, and in the summer she's a true river rat, rafting white water whether on the Colorado or the Rio Grande's infamous Box.

Taos Cookery, 113 Bent Street, Taos, 87571; (505) 758-5435.

Dining

Taos

The Bavarian Lodge and Restaurant

One of the greatest dining experiences you can have in Taos is at the Bavarian Restaurant, a true chalet tucked away at the top of the ski mountain at the trailhead to William's Lake. Not easy to find but worth the trials of a narrow, rutted, and partially paved road, the Bavarian is the Schulze family's fantasy built in the Wheeler Peak Wilderness Area of Carson National Forest.

Fashioning her creation after an alpine guesthouse, Julika Schulze designed the lodge and carefully furnished it with European antiques. Today son Thomas A. Schulze and his wife, Jamie, own and operate the inn, which is a popular retreat for affluent skiers. In addition to its elegant accommodations, it has back door access to the Ski Valley's No. 4 Kachina Peak chairlift.

The Bavarian Restaurant with its huge tile oven has original antique wall paneling and ceilings from Bavaria. Its massive log walls and brick floors create a true Old World atmosphere. The kitchen is presided over by Chef Keith Harlan, who serves only traditional high mountain–shelter gourmet fare. For an appetizer, you might choose the smoked salmon or sautéed snails in herb-garlic butter. The goulash is a hearty bowl of broth, beef, pork, and potato seasoned with paprika. House specialties include Sauerbraten served with spaetzle and red cabbage; Wiener Schnitzel with parsley potatoes; Cheese Spaetzle, a homemade Bavarian pasta; or Nurnberger Brats, a pork sausage with sauerkraut, mashed potatoes, and onion sauce. For dessert, you have your choice of cheesecake, Death by Chocolate Cake, or (what else?) warm apple strudel with vanilla sauce.

On Tuesdays in the winter, the Bavarian holds special fondue nights with ski legend Godie Schuetz, who regales the guests with tales from the slopes. They prepare a three-course meal of alpine salad, cheese or beef fondue, and a surprise dessert.

Genuine beers from the 600-year-old Spaten-Franziskaner Brewery are drawn from taps, and both fine European and American wines are offered.

Summer hours are Thursday through Sunday, Memorial Day weekend through the first weekend in October, lunch, 11:30 A.M. to 4:00 P.M., dinner, 5:30 P.M. to closing. Winter hours are lunch, 11:00 A.M. to 3:30 P.M., and dinner, 5:00 P.M. to closing. Free dinner shuttles are available in winter from anywhere in the Ski Valley. Reservations requested. Closed in spring when Ski Valley ends its season until Memorial Day weekend. In fall, closed the first weekend in October until Thanksgiving weekend or the opening of the Ski Valley.

The Bavarian Lodge and Restaurant, Taos Ski Valley, 87525;
(505) 776-8020 or (505) 776-5301; www.thebavarian.net.

Downtown Bistro

Looking for an intimate spot for an engagement dinner or just a cozy meal for two? You couldn't go wrong by planning to pop the question in the decidedly romantic Downtown Bistro. Don't be put off by its location in the Pueblo Alegre Mall. The minute you open the door, a warm, intimate atmosphere surrounds you. Twinkle lights outline the bar, and the nourishing rose adobe walls are punctuated with fanciful oil paintings. A kiva fireplace is a welcoming touch on a blustery evening.

The jewel in the crown is the food. Chef Mauro Barbitta has created a menu that is the epitome of bistro cooking. Mauro, who was one of the original partners at the Trading Post in Ranchos de Taos, is an extraordinary restaurateur who believes in bringing in a young generation of cooks, especially those who do not have the financial wherewithal to attend the pricey schools of culinary arts. To this end, he has taken two local men and trained them in his methods, using his recipes. If you rave over one of the bistro entrées, Mauro refuses to take credit and says, "Be sure to tell Executive Chef Jacob Arellano and Executive Sous Chef Jesse James."

And if you're dining at Downtown Bistro, you'll be brimming with compliments. They take dishes that are found on most restaurant menus and transform them into something divine. A simple house salad is a turned into a musical composition, an intricate symphony of flavors. The slow-roasted chicken sings out in perfect harmony of crisp skin and moist, succulent meat.

The menu follows the normal bistro formula. Appetizers include dishes such as Grilled Portobella Mushroom with asparagus, tomatoes, mozzarella, yellow pepper vinaigrette, and puff pastry; Hot House Tomato Salad with buffalo mozzarella and infused shallot and basil oil; or Belgian Endive Salad with Gorgonzola cheese, red grapes, apples, walnuts, and champagne vinaigrette. For an entrée, you might choose Mushroom Ravioli served in a roasted corn essence broth with spinach, sweet peppers, and Parmesan; Soy Marinated Pork Chops with rice noodles, sautéed vegetables, and spicy cabbage relish; or Grilled Duck with mashed potatoes, dried fruit compote, natural au jus, and vegetables. Of course, there are daily specials, which might include a creamy tomato and roasted corn soup; a warm arugula salad tossed with a bacon vinaigrette and Gruyère cheese; or Mediterranean yellow fin tuna seared with tomato, capers, olives, a steamed rice medley, and julienned vegetables.

The wine list provides for glass or bottle purchase and is reasonable. Vintages vary seasonally. Desserts are classics such as tíramisu, a three-layer crème caramel, a dense rustic chocolate cake with cocoa frosting, or caramel apple pie.

Downtown Bistro is open for dinner Wednesday through Monday. Closed Tuesday.

Downtown Bistro, Pueblo Alegre Mall, 223 Paseo del Pueblo Sur, Taos, 87571; (505) 737-5060.

Joseph's Table

Joseph Wrede is a culinary legend in Taos, and the cheers reverberated off the mountains when he announced that he was reviving his much-loved restaurant, Joseph's Table, at the historic La Fonda Hotel on the Plaza. Named one of *Food & Wine*'s 10 "Best New Chefs in America" in 2000, Joseph was absent from the culinary scene after he closed the first Joseph's Table in Ranchos de Taos. Now in a new and convenient location, he is enticing locals and visitors to the beautiful revamped space.

The hotel, originally built in 1880, most recently has hosted the somewhat strange pairing of a Chinese restaurant in the old southwestern structure. The Hunan, for those who like to keep abreast of the scene, is now at 1015 Paseo del Pueblo Sur in the old Denny's building. At Joseph's Table, there's no trace of the previous décor. The space has been taken down to its elements and reconstructed in a fanciful and ethereal way. Joseph's wife, artist Kristin Bortles, and her mother, decorator Cookie Venn, have covered the warm yellow walls with frescos of tulip blossoms, some as large as tabletops. The bar area has *nichos*, for sitting with your drinks, and a kiva fireplace. Tiny iridescent butterflies cover the surfaces of walls and *nichos*, leaving you to wonder if they are flying to the light or waiting to rest delicately on your libation. Joseph says the concept is "to produce a unique culinary experience, blending food and atmosphere in a truly artistic experience unlike any other."

Although the ambience is beautiful, the food is the big draw. Joseph's innovative fare is made with the finest local organic and seasonal food. "I'm interested in indigenous foods, whether they're from the Southwest, France, Italy, or some other place," he says.

Joseph's introduction to kitchen life began at age 12, washing dishes at the Blind Lemon in Cincinnati, Ohio. His family moved around a great deal, and after high school and college, he attended the Institute of Culinary Education, formerly Peter Kump's New York Cooking School. Kump's philosophy was, "I don't want students to leave here with a sheaf of spectacular recipes to repeat step-by-step ad infinitum. No. I want them to learn to develop taste. I want them to become free to improvise, to work without recipes." Working as a line chef first at Highlands Garden Café and then at Aubergine Café, both in Denver, Joseph learned to apply this philosophy, and in 1995, after coming to Taos, he opened the original Joseph's Table.

At the time of publication, the menu was in the process of development. The restaurant will be open for lunch serving traditional New Mexican cuisine such as Duck Tamale with a tomatillo and Hatch chile *crema*. A three-course prix fixe lunch is also contemplated.

Dinners will see the revival of some past favorites such as Risotto Cake with Parma proscuitto and Parmigiano-Reggiano in portobella mushroom syrup; Hawaiian Sashimi with snapper, yellow fin, and marlin; American Steak au Poivre, a tenderloin with Madeira mushroom sauce; Risotto with fresh enoki mushrooms; and Halibut with tarragon butter and fresh strawberries. A tribute to his food and service, DiRoNA (Distinguished Restaurants of North America) has given Joseph their Award of Excellence.

Joseph's Table, La Fonda Hotel, 108 South Plaza, Taos, 87571; (505) 751-4512.

Lambert's of Taos Restaurant

Lambert's is a fixture in the Taos dining scene for good reason—consistently high-quality food founded on the basic principles of buying the best ingredients and cooking everything from scratch. It's been that way since 1989, when Chef Zeke Lambert and wife Tina gave up the gypsy life, bought the old Randall home, and opened their own place.

Prior gigs had Zeke working at ski resorts in Utah, honing his skills and developing a feel for American melting-pot cuisine. After Utah, Zeke moved to the Bay Area where he met and wed professional server Tina, and in 1985 the newlyweds landed in Taos, where Zeke chefed at Doc Martin's for several years. Four years and two children later, they founded Lambert's of Taos.

In his menu, Zeke calls upon all the techniques and ingredients he used in his culinary journey. His mix of New American, Pacific Rim, and French cuisines provide something for every palate. Signature dishes include Roasted Pepper and Tomato Soup with chive sour cream; Grilled Scallops with salsa verde and stuffed squash; Grilled Lobster Tail and hearts of palm with mango salsa and lime vinaigrette salad; Grilled Pork Tenderloin with chipotle cream sauce, garlic mashed potatoes, and sweet and sour cabbage; Medallion of Beef Tenderloin with mushroom démi-glace; Colorado Lamb lightly crusted and grilled and served with a red wine démi-glace and garlic pasta; and Pistachio-Crusted Chicken Breast filled with goat cheese and spinach in a roasted shallot–sherry cream sauce.

Desserts run from Bread Pudding with rum sauce to Warm Apple and Almond Crisp with white chocolate ice cream. Unusual post-dinner treats include a root beer float or an ice cream soda, flavors varying from chocolate to orange. Service is prompt but not intrusive, and Zeke's wine list is one of the most comprehensive in Taos.

Lambert's has a gracious ambiance. The home-turned-restaurant was built from railroad ties salvaged from the defunct Chile Line, the name of the old Denver and Rio Grande Western Railroad that ran in the area from 1887 until abandonment in 1941. In the 1940s and 1950s, Taos high school held dances in the former living room. Currently, the space is comfortable, elegant, and subdued. Tiffany-style lamps cast warm glows on the white napery, flowers adorn every table, and, hallelujah, the chairs are comfortable. It's hard to go astray when dining at Lambert's.

Lambert's of Taos Restaurant, 309 Paseo del Pueblo Sur, Taos, 87571; (505) 758-1009; www.999dine.com/nm/lamberts/info.html.

Michael's Kitchen: A Coffee Shop and Bakery

Would any visit to Taos be complete without a visit to Michael's Kitchen for breakfast, lunch, or dinner? In business since 1974, Michael Ninneman's restaurant and bakery on Paseo del Pueblo Norte has been the place for Taoseños to meet and greet for the past 40 years. A true family enterprise where sons and sons-in-law, daughters and daughters-in-law work together, Michael's is a successful and extremely busy operation that may flip (restaurant talk for changing customers) as many as 11 times a day.

Kitchen workers are old timers. Dolores has worked for the Ninnemans the full 40 years, and her brother has been with them 20 years. "It's the kind of place where when you've come here as a kid, you can bring your own kid and be waited on by the same staff," says Derek, one of the sons-in-law. "We serve healthy portions, and our consistency is legend. Our prices are geared to locals not tourists, and we keep it simple."

Describing the menu would take a very long time, but suffice it to say it concentrates on the basics with emphasis on New Mexican food. If you've overdosed on chile, there are plenty of basic American dishes from which to choose such as steak, pork chops, and fried chicken. The children's menu is more generous than most. Their bakery specializes in cakes, doughnuts, muffins, cookies, cream puffs, apple fritters, cinnamon buns, and a variety of breads including chile cheese.

The atmosphere is strictly Old West with knotty pine booths and tables, barn board walls, a big old cast-iron stove, and prints of Indian and western scenes.

Open daily except for five to six weeks from the first Monday of November until ski season.

Michael's Kitchen: A Coffee Shop and Bakery, 304 Paseo del Pueblo Norte, Taos, 87571; (505) 758-4178; www.michaelskitchen.com.

El Monte Sagrado

El Monte Sagrado is New Mexico's newest eco-resort. Using his resort to incorporate many of the earth-friendly technologies from his Dharma Corporation umbrella, entrepreneur Tom Worrell has created an incredibly beautiful karmic retreat. Using a system he calls the "living machine," they treat and recycle water for irrigation, heating, and cooling. Solar panels provide part of the resort's power.

But we're here to talk about the food, and you'll be happy to hear it stands up to its surroundings. Worrell has imported Executive Chef Kevin Kapalka from New Hampshire's renowned Village Inn. Kevin feels it is important to work with regional farmers to help sustain the local economy and provide a local flavor. He uses farm-fresh ingredients indigenous to the area, and whenever possible he incorporates produce from the resort's eco-friendly gardens. In keeping with his earth-friendly philosophy, he refuses to use endangered items such as swordfish and Chilean sea bass.

Chef Kapalka is a graduate of the Culinary Institute of America, starting his career in Florida before moving on to sous chef positions at Rockresort properties in Hawaii and the Virgin Islands. His first executive chef appointment was at the Reefs in Bermuda, after which he returned to Rockresorts where he headed the kitchens of two resorts in Jumby Bay in Antigua, West Indies. Abandoning southern climes, he chefed at the White Elephant in Nantucket before moving on to New Hampshire and then Taos.

The menu changes seasonally and, at review time, Kevin was fine-tuning the offerings. On the agenda are appetizers such as Lobster Ravioli with saffron tomato reduction, lemon-scented olive oil, and petit herbs and a Black and Blue Seared Salmon Enchilada with sweet onions, lime vinaigrette, and smoked tomato. A sample of entrées includes Grilled Petit Filet Mignon and citrus marinated beef short ribs with black bean ginger sauce, scallion sesame pancake, and sautéed cress and Colorado T-Bone Chops with roasted garlic Yukon potatoes, zucchini, carrots, white truffle oil, and sofrit.

A word about the décor: the De la Tierra Restaurant occupies a central position in the heart of the resort's "biogrande," which also houses the reception, concierge, Gardens Restaurant and Anaconda Bar, the Cellar, the fitness room, and on the second level, the library, boardroom, and a meeting salon. The restaurant's atmosphere is one of extended space broken only by the flow of entries, exits, and the exquisitely set tables with their rich black upholstered chairs embossed with Medieval French crewel designs. The rounded sandstone water wall, which reaches to the second level, is hung with moisture-loving plants.

Another wall holds James Rosenquist's *Mute Transformations I*, a colorful abstract 120-by-120-inch oil on canvas, part of Worrell's extensive art collection (N.B.: try to visit the resort boardroom where you'll see the Picasso *Reclining Nude*, another of Worrell's acquisitions). The finest settings grace the tables: premium stemware by Bormioli Rocco of Italy, silver by Guy Degrenne of France, and porcelain by Eschenbach Porzellan of Germany.

The informal dining room and overflow main room is the Garden, and it is filled with tropical trees and plants, transplanted from Worrell's Florida collection of rare specimens. Take time between bites of breakfast or lunch to examine some of the unusual specimens such as the Yaxche, or tree of life, with its thorny bark. The breakfast menu lists standards such as "Big Bowl o' Oatmeal" with golden raisins, brown sugar, and cream; Blue Corn Pancakes with piñon butter and prickly pear syrup; and Poached Eggs with duck confit hash, wilted spinach, and grilled tomato salsa.

For lunch there are both light and substantial dishes: Baby Greens and roasted golden beets with fresh herbs; Coonridge Farms goat cheese, fig balsamic vinaigrette, and pickled red onion relish; Homegrown Organic Yak (yes, yak, from Worrell's ranch) chili with Hatch green chiles, roasted pepper, and black beans; and the Duck Burger, a ground breast of duck stuffed with leg of duck confit, foie gras, caramelized onion relish, red pepper ketchup, sherry mayo, and truffled French fries. If all this is daunting, there's always a fresh garden soup.

The Anaconda Bar lives up to its name, with the body of a huge snake with glittering tile scales slithering across the ceiling on its way from the Garden to the entrance of De la Tierra. Just for fun, see if you can find its head. It's not at all scary—just another of Worrell's unique ideas.

El Monte Sagrado Restaurant and Lounge, 317 Kit Carson Road, Taos, 87571; (800) 828-TAOS or (505) 758-3502; www.elmontesagrado.com.

Orlando's New Mexican Café

No town would be complete without its prized northern New Mexican eatery. Orlando's fills the bill in Taos. The small restaurant in El Prado seats but a few inside, on the covered porch, or in fair weather, on the patio, but its reputation for authentic Mexican food dwarfs its modest size.

Owned by Orlando and Yvette Ortega, the colorful café originally housed a small store, but the Ortegas transformed it into a slice of Old Mexico. A kaleidoscope of bright green, magenta, and pumpkin lends lively notes to the walls, which are paneled with tin wainscoting. *Ristras* hang from arches, and paintings of calla lilies adorn doorways.

The Orlandos started their restaurant careers with a roadside hot cart, selling burritos and tacos to hungry Taoseños. In addition,

Orlando did cooking stints in Lambert's and Sagebrush kitchens. In 1996 they opened their place north of town, and they've played to capacity crowds ever since.

What makes Orlando's stand out from other Mexican restaurants? Consistency is one factor, and the other is their adherence to traditional recipes garnered from mothers and grandmothers. The red chile is from Grandma Tina, the *chile caribe* from Grandma Ita. When Orlando decided to make his chile sauces without meat to please the many vegetarians who frequent his restaurant, his mother exploded. "*Dios mio!*" she cried, aghast that he should deviate from the hallowed recipe. Orlando said, "Try it, you'll like it," and eventually she gave the sauce her blessing.

You don't go to Orlando's seeking some New Age fusion food. The menu is straightforward: tacos, burritos, chimichangas, tostadas, chile rellenos, carne adovada, enchiladas, nachos, taco salad, even Frito pie. If you've never eaten a Baja taco, try theirs. The two flour tortillas are filled with deep-fried cod, topped with cheese, and served with Orlando's special cucumber pico de gallo for a fresh crunch. Desserts are also traditional: flan, apple pie, ice cream sundaes, and *bizcochitos*. An exception is Kika's frozen avocado pie.

Open Monday through Saturday, lunch 10:30 A.M. to 3:00 P.M.; dinner 5:00 to 9:00 P.M.; Sunday, 5:00 to 9:00 P.M.

Orlando's New Mexican Café, 1114 Don Juan Valdez Lane, El Prado (Taos), 87571; (505) 751-1450.

The Stakeout Grill & Bar

There's no argument that the Stakeout Grill & Bar has the most dazzling location in all Taos. Located four miles south of Ranchos de Taos, the restaurant crowns a rise at the end of a dirt trail winding up Outlaw Hill, named for the desperados who used it for a lookout. From their beautiful patio you can pick out the Mesa Pedernal 80 miles south, Tres Orejas, and Cerro Vista. To the east, you'll see Picuris Mountain and beyond, the Carson National Forest and Taos Pueblo land. San Antonio and Taos Mountain are also visible as well as the twinkling lights of the town. Evenings in moderate weather, the patio is lighted for alfresco dining.

The restaurant has been a popular dining spot since it opened in 1975. Its interior is mellow with dark paneling and expansive windows looking out over the mountains and valley. Starched white napery decks the tables, and stained glass windows throw colored prisms of radiance.

Under owner Mauro Bettini's watchful eye, Chef du Cuisine Jeff Doyen prepares an appetizing range of dishes. You seldom find oysters Rockefeller on a Taos menu, but they are here along with carpaccio, escargot, baked Brie, wild mushroom risotto, and an antipasto platter. A soup du jour and both Caesar and spinach salads are available. Entrées from the grill include a selection of steaks from filet to the rib eye, chateaubriand, and venison loin. Seafood is represented by a cold-water lobster tail with drawn butter, Alaskan king crab legs, and Sunset Cioppino with shrimp, scallops, mussels, clams, and calamari in a white wine, saffron, and tomato broth. In addition, you'll find Roast Duck with Apples and Prunes served with an orange currant sauce; Chicken Oscar, a sautéed chicken breast with king crab, poached asparagus, and béarnaise; Cheese-Filled Ravioli in wild mushroom and cream sauce; and for the vegetarians, a special plate of winter or summer vegetables sautéed with fresh herbs, white wine, and cannelloni beans. Save room for dessert because you don't want to pass up the Chocolate Grand Marnier Mousse, the Blueberry Almond Bread Pudding à la mode with caramel sauce, or one of their house-made seasonal gelatos or sorbets.

The long wine list includes vintages from the States, Italy, Spain, France, and Germany—some available by the half bottle. There's a child's menu for kids 10 and under.

The Stakeout Grill & Bar, State Highway 68 (four miles south of Ranchos de Taos), Ranchos de Taos, 87557; (505) 758-2042; www.stakeoutrestaurant.com.

Tiwa Kitchen Restaurant

Long before there was a village of Taos, Tiwa Indians built their beautiful multistoried homes overlooking their sacred mountain. Every year tourists visit their pueblo, attend religious dances, and marvel at their enduring legacy. Unless you've arrived at one of their feast days when you may be invited into homes to partake of a simple meal, you haven't had the opportunity to taste their food. Remedy this by stopping at Tiwa Kitchen Restaurant owned by Ben White Buffalo and his wife, Debbie Moonlight Flowers.

The small eatery serves only traditional Native meals such as bowls of red or green chile, stuffed fry bread, a Tiwa taco (ground beef, beans, and chile on fry bread), a Pueblo-style chile steak, blue corn tacos, mountain trout, beef stew with horno bread, or *twah-chull*, grilled buffalo meat and onions over wild rice and a homemade blue corn tortilla. Fountain drinks are complemented by Indian tea and *atole*, a corn beverage. Closed Tuesday.

Tiwa Kitchen Restaurant, Taos Pueblo, 87571; (505) 751-1020.

Trading Post Café

You'd be hard-pressed to find any Taos regular who, when asked to name a favorite restaurant, doesn't mention the Trading Post Café in Ranchos de Taos. Whether it's the informal, cozy atmosphere or the Northern Italian food, it all works beautifully.

The building has a long history. Once a real trading post run by the Salad family before the Great Depression, it was a true community center and the largest general store in the Taos area. It had a soda fountain, a clothing and drug store, a canned and fresh foods area, a butcher shop, building supplies, and a liquor store. During the depression, World War I army trucks delivered goods to the elderly in the community. Today, owners Chef René Mettler and food and beverage manager Kimberly Armstrong transformed a portion of the huge, old building into a comfortable bistro that encourages that same kind of community spirit and welcome.

René has an immaculate pedigree. A native of Switzerland, where he received his initial training, he moved on to become chef du grill on Holland America's SS *Rotterdam* before landing in London, where he worked at the Hotel Piccadilly and the Hotel Saint George. His vocation then took him to the Caravelle Hotel in the U.S. Virgin Islands and to Pennsylvania's Buck Hill Falls. Next came his appointment as executive chef for the Boca Raton West Resort and Country Club in Florida.

Joining the Hyatt Corporation as executive chef at the Hyatt Regency, Dallas, he eventually transferred to the Hyatt Regency, Grand Cyprus. His last corporate position was as regional executive chef of the Hawaiian Islands, headquartered at the Hyatt Regency Waikoloa.

Opening the Trading Post in 1994 with Kimberly, he abandoned the corporate race and settled in Taos, where he daily applies his considerable skills. "We cook everything from scratch," René says, "and our portions are generous—good value for your dollar. People like our bar seating area, where they can perch and watch Kimberly and me cook in the open kitchen. They'll lean over the counter and say, 'René, leave out the onion' or 'René, I want more peppers.' We have a regular menu, but it definitely can be customized. Talk with us. If we have it, you'll get it."

Although the restaurant menu's top note is Northern Italian, many non-Italian flavors from René's past intrude—Hawaiian, Asian, French, and German. If you go for lunch, you might find a Torta Cubana Sandwich with pork or chicken, avocado, black beans, onion, and provolone cheese; Salad Niçoise; Pasta Bolognese; or good old-fashioned chicken noodle soup. The dinner menu reflects the restaurant's bistro style with a Crispy Garlic Pork Chop, Rosemary Chicken, Creole Pepper Shrimp, Oven-Roasted Half Duck, Escargot with angel hair pasta, or Piccata Milanese, a chicken breast scaloppini. Daily specials could be sautéed Colorado Coho Salmon or Indonesian Curry Chicken with wild rice, banana, raisins, and almonds on a bed of sunflower and pea sprouts. The offerings change with the seasons, what's available from local growers, and the chef's mood. On Sunday, when they're open only for dinner, a constant is the Prime Rib Roast Beef special. They have an extensive list of both international and U.S. vintages at modest prices.

Trading Post Café, 4179 State Highway 68 at Highway 518, Ranchos de Taos, 87557; (505) 758-5089; http://999dine.com/NM/Tradingpost/Trading-Post-Cafe.html.

Villa Fontana

If you conjure up an image of the Olive Garden when you think of Italian food, you definitely need to visit Villa Fontana Restaurant, five miles north of Taos on Highway 522. In fact, if you clump all Italian food into one category, you are misinformed. As Chef Carlo Gislimberti will be the first to tell you, what we've come to accept as Italian food is but a small part of the story. Like American food, Italian food is based on regional recipes and on the agricultural products of a region. You wouldn't compare a Smithfield Ham from Virginia with a cob-smoked ham from Vermont. Likewise, the food from Emilia Romana differs from the dishes of Sicily.

Carlo is an interesting man. Knighted by the president of Italy in 1999 in recognition of his contribution in promoting Italian products and for serving on the boards of the Gruppo Ristoratori Italiani and Ciao Italia, he is also a talented painter with multiple shows to his credit. Born in the Dolomites, he worked in a variety of restaurants in Italy, Belgium, Switzerland, Germany, and England, where he met his wife and business partner, Siobhan. He came to the States in 1977 and worked in Fort Worth for several years before moving to Red River, where he managed an Italian restaurant. He later moved to Taos, where he managed Casa Cordova, the predecessor of Vida.

The Gislimbertis loved Taos and dreamed of having their own restaurant there. In May of 1991, the vision solidified, and they opened the Villa Fontana. Just a year later, while preparing to cater a large wedding, Carlo had a massive heart attack. Told by the doctors that he should avoid the stress of the kitchen, he decided to take advantage of the many opportunities of a community so rich in the history of art. He took a few classes and started to paint. He says, "Cooking continues to be my profession, but painting is my passion." You can recognize the artist's eye in every dish that comes out of his kitchen.

Villa Fontana features Northern Italian cooking in its pure form. Carlo fumes at chefs who produce bastardized dishes, "If you're going to do Italian dishes, do them right. We have too many would-be chefs and not enough cooks!" At the Villa, dishes are prepared to order and might include an appetizer or Antipasti of Parma Ham with melon, celeriac, and artichoke hearts; Cured Salmon garnished with celeriac, lemon, and capers; or Beef Carpaccio alla Finice with lemon and olive oil. The *primo*, or first course, could be Risotto with Porcini Mushrooms and Salame, Cream of Wild Mushroom Soup with croutons, or a salad of wild greens with vinaigrette. You could select your entrée, or *piatti grandi*, from a list containing Veal Scaloppini sautéed in white wine, démi-glace, sage, and ham; Beef Tenderloin sautéed with mustard, brandy, and rosemary; or Grilled Filet of Salmon with fresh herb marinade.

Desserts favor Italian classics such as crème caramel, tíramisu, profiteroles, or zabaglione al vino Marsala con frutta for two. The Villa has an excellent wine list that features Italian red and white vintages as well as a good representation of American wines. For six years, the American Automobile Association (AAA) awarded the restaurant their Four Diamond Award, and it has been named to the DiRoNA (Distinguished Restaurants of North America). One of Italy's most widely read guidebooks, the *Veronelli Guide*, has named the Villa one of the top-10 Italian restaurants in the United States.

For information on the Villa Fontana Cooking School, check the "Cooking Schools" listing. Closed Sunday and annual closing from mid-November to mid-December.

Villa Fontana, 71 State Highway 522, Taos, 87571; (505) 758-5800; www.villafontanataos.com.

WesternSky Café

For a little neighborhood café, the WesternSky does very well serving patients' families, relatives, and the staff of Holy Cross Hospital. As if that weren't enough, it also produces breakfast, lunch, and dinner with a flair you won't find in many places.

Ginny Greeno, who with her husband, Arthur, owned the Apple Tree Restaurant during its glory days from 1987 to 1999, opened WesternSky in 2001. She has transferred her facility with simple ingredients to her new place, and you'll appreciate her consideration of your pocketbook.

"We're not trying for anything fancy. Our food is straight up, affordable, and especially tailored to the needs of our customers, who often come straight from the hospital. You don't want to charge someone who's just come from visiting a sick child $12 for a burger," she says.

Another convenience she's instituted is breakfast from opening to 3:00 P.M. You can get simple or hearty fare: granola with fruit and yogurt, Hemp Nut Pancakes with berry butter, a lox and bagel plate, omelets, or the traditional southwestern dishes such as huevos rancheros or a breakfast burrito.

Lunches consist of salads; burgers; hot sandwiches, such as a corned beef Rueben; and deli sandwiches, including roasted turkey and provolone. Ginny makes two soups fresh daily, one vegetarian and one with meat. Hot plates might be shrimp curry, fish-and-chips, enchiladas, or burritos.

A sample nightly entrée is Pasta with Basil Pesto and Calamata Olives, tossed with sautéed garlic, tomatoes, fresh herbs, sun-dried tomatoes, and white wine. Perhaps you'd fancy her Grilled Salmon Filet with wild rice, spicy orange sauce, and strawberry-mint salsa.

There's a child's menu, a nice little wine list, and live music most evenings. Ginny believes in supporting local musicians.

WesternSky Café, 1398 Weimer Road (across from Holy Cross Hospital), Taos, 87571; (505) 751-7771.

Arroyo Seco

Arroyo Seco is just a few miles northwest of Taos proper, but the small village is home to two restaurants you'll want to check out: Gypsy 360° Café and Espresso Bar, a small bistro, and Momentitos de la Vida, a fine dining establishment. They couldn't be more dissimilar.

Gypsy 360° Café and Espresso Bar

As chef and co-owner Sheila Guzman says, "we're an oasis for the culinary nomad." Sheila has traveled the world and has chefed at many Taos restaurants including the Apple Tree, the Taos Inn, and Lambert's. In 2002, along with her sister, Mary Ostlund, she opened the tiny café with its commodious deck. The original concept was to concentrate wholly on international street food, but that has morphed into a more sophisticated menu.

Although Gypsy's Saturday brunch is hugely popular, any time is a good time to try the café's United Nations of food. The soups are made fresh daily, and you can get a light meal of soup du jour (bowl or cup) with bread or a miso soup with brown rice. Salads range from Jamaican Jerk Chicken to Thai Grilled Beef. They make great black bean chipotle hummus and Japanese futomaki nori rolls. Their original sandwiches include the Saigon Sub, a French roll filled with pâté de campagne, aromatic lemongrass chicken patties, and slices of barbecued pork; Roasted Lamb Sandwich with sautéed radicchio and bitter greens; or Kona Club, seared ahi tuna with grilled tomato, bacon, and sauced with roasted pineapple mayo. The menu lists entrées such as Thai Green Pork Curry, Argentinean Flank Steak sparked with chimichurri sauce, and a bounteous Japanese Miso Ramen Bowl with large shrimp, tofu, and udon noodles. There's a fine selection of microbrewed and international beers, and wine is available by the glass or bottle.

Breakfast is simple: bagels with varied toppings, house pastries, and house-made granola. The coffee is organic, fair trade, and shade-grown.

If you have an adventurous palate, Gypsy 360° will please. You can even bring along your meat-and-potatoes friends. Sheila sometimes whips up her Mexican meatloaf and mashies, and there's always their "superior burger," eight ounces of all-natural Black Angus ground beef, grilled onion, crisp bacon, and choice of blue or Jack cheese with chipotle mayo.

Sunday brunch 9:00 A.M. to 3:00 P.M. Closed Monday.

Gypsy 360° Café and Espresso Bar, 480 New Mexico Highway 150, Arroyo Seco, 87557; (505) 776-3166.

Momentitos de la Vida

Momentitos de la Vida bills itself as a uniquely elegant dining experience, and we would not argue with that description. Just 4.8 miles northeast of the intersection of State Road 64 and 150, a stone's throw from the village of Arroyo Seco, Vida caters to both romantics and knowledgeable gourmands. Chef and co-owner Chris Maher and his business partner, pastry chef and co-owner Kelly Maher, have worked hard to assure this perception. Chris says, "We take pride not just in the food, service, and atmosphere, but in the details like our fine English bone china and our Corby Hall silver. Our top shelf bar is the best in Taos, perhaps the state."

Located out in the country, the former hacienda twinkles with fairy lights as you cross its broad patio. Entering, you turn to your left and step into the Bar at Vida, a large, cozy room with fantastic murals of rural life in an earlier time. Painted by Molly Spain, the art director of the Des Moines Opera Company, the images set a mellow scene. Custom-designed sofas, chairs, and coffee tables are clustered throughout, and copper pendant lights and sconces cast a soft glow. The room is so attractive you're bound to linger, and you may. There's regularly scheduled live music, and you can order either from the regular or bar menu, which might include Grilled Barbecue Baby Back Ribs, Oven Roasted Rosemary Half Chicken, Asian Noodle Greek Salad, or the Vida burger.

Each of the candlelit fine dining rooms has its own theme. The Cordova Room, named after the family that built the structure more than 100 years ago, is centered on a raised fireplace that is both ornate and functional. The Olive Room has Molly Spain frescos reminiscent of the Italian countryside and a kiva fireplace. Both rooms boast massive original vigas and tables set with immaculate napery and gleaming stemware.

Chef Chris Maher was born in Egypt and raised in Toronto and New York City. Like other chefs, he is multitalented and works as an actor when he's not at the helm of Vida. His approach to preparation was formed by his multinational upbringing, and he's not shy about his approach. "This restaurant is my concept and my baby. I design my menu to please my palate," he says, "You must truly follow the palate because all outstanding work has that derivation." As the restaurant's many aficionados attest, Maher' approach presents no problems.

The menu and its nightly creations are built around the season's availability of food. Organic produce is used whenever obtainable. Their beef is corn-fed, three-day dry-aged, from Nebraska. The lamb is from Colorado and New Mexico, and Vida prides itself on its fresh fish and oysters on the half shell.

Needless to say, the menu changes on a regular basis, but some often-requested items remain. For an appetizer, you might choose the Hudson Valley Foie Gras with rosemary shortbread, grilled habañero prawns, and an ounce of Sevruga caviar or a Grilled Vegetable and Goat Cheese Tart. Two soups are featured daily, including the flavorful house corn chowder with green chile. The classic Vida Caesar and the Grilled

Portobello Mushroom on baby greens are two frequent salad offerings. A palate-cleansing intermezzo of sweet or savory sorbet is available.

Entrées could comprise a pistachio-encrusted Colorado Rack of Lamb with potato gratin and wilted greens and a lime-chipotle démiglace; Diver Scallop Beggar's Purses in house-made savory herb crêpes with sweet pea broth; Oven Roasted Plum Glazed Ducking accompanied by roasted garlic and Parmesan bread pudding; True Red Snapper in parchment paper with white wine and sweet peppers on green rice; a Dry-Aged Export Ribeye Steak; or the "chef creations" of the day—fresh Atlantic salmon, wild game, or the featured risotto. There are no bad choices. Closed Monday.

Momentitos de la Vida, 474 State Highway 150 (Ski Valley Road), Arroyo Seco, 87514; (505) 776-3333; www.vidarest.com.

Peñasco (Taos High Road)

Sugar Nymphs Bistro

The High Road from Española to Taos winds through the foothills of the Picuris and Sangre de Cristo Mountains. The scenery is gorgeous, but watering holes are scarce. An exception to the rule is the Sugar Nymphs Bistro in the tiny town of Peñasco. Chef and owner Kai Harper Lee and pastry chef and owner Ki Holste have a culinary oasis in the hinterlands. Their cozy, country-style restaurant has a menu in the bistro tradition, using the freshest seasonal produce available from local growers. The chefs use as many organic fruits and vegetables as possible.

Kai's credentials are impressive. She trained in California under luminaries such as Alice Waters and worked for a time at the Tassajara Bakery in Cole Valley, California. In New Mexico, she headed the kitchen at the Inn of the Anasazi in Santa Fe. At Sugar Nymphs she characterizes her cuisine as "American Contemporary."

Specials change daily. There are always a homemade soup, a couple fresh salads, and poultry, beef, and vegetarian entrées. Lunch might be a Roast Chicken with Guacamole Sandwich or one of her special gourmet pizzas or calzones. The dinner menu could feature Kai's Thai Red Curry Noodle Bowl with shrimp and fresh salmon in a coconut curry broth with mushrooms, sweet potatoes, red bell peppers, and green onions, or perhaps Chicken Sautéed in White Wine, Sweet Onion, and Garlic, smothered in mushrooms and served with béchamel sauce and garlic mashed potatoes. Desserts are made fresh daily and vary except for their signature Chocolate Maple Pecan Pie, which is always available.

Open for lunch and dinner Wednesday through Saturday. Open Sunday for brunch and dinner.

Sugar Nymphs Bistro, Highway 75, Peñasco, 87553; (505) 587-0311.

Farmers' Market

The Taos County Farmers' Market, Town Hall parking lot, one block northwest of the Plaza, Taos. Saturdays, 8:00 A.M. to 1:00 P.M., May through October, (505) 776-1400.

Specialty Food Store

Cid's Food Market

You don't have to be in Taos long before you hear someone speak of Cid's as if it were a local attraction, because in a way it is. Located at the north end of town, the 13,000-square-foot market is somewhat of a coup for the town and for Cid and Betty Backer, the owners.

An eastern boy who grew up in New Rochelle, New York, Cid moved to New Mexico in 1973, attracted by the beneficial climate he remembered from his student days at the University of New Mexico. His first job was with a local co-op, but when he became disenchanted with the lack of good management, he decided to open his own place. The original 4,000-square-foot market was such a success that in 1998 he and Betty built the current super supermarket.

Cid says, "I've always believed in taking care of the customer, and I make sure our employees have the same motivation. We started out with three full-time workers and now we have 65 trained, qualified people. We provide good, wholesome food to the community."

Cid's is spacious, bright, and well arranged with a bounteous display of mostly organic produce, locally grown when available. Meats are hormone and antibiotic free. Some are certified organic. He stocks free-range chicken, organic beef from Roy, New Mexico, pork from Beeler's, local organic turkeys, and local organic lamb from Shepherd's Lamb in Tierra Amarillo, New Mexico.

Of course, there are aisles for bulk foods and a big selection of natural health and beauty products. Bakery goods come from local and

Santa Fe operations. There's a saying in Taos, "When you shop at Cid's, eventually you'll meet everyone you know."

Cid's Food Market, 623 Paseo del Pueblo Norte, Taos, 87571; (505) 758-1148.

Wine Shop

Bravo! Fine Wine, Food & Spirits

Bravo! Fine Wine, Food & Spirits is a wine and liquor shop set in a restaurant atmosphere, unusual in that you can make a choice of wine from their plentiful stock and have it with your meal. They boast of having New Mexico's largest wine selection both for retail sale and as an accompaniment to the restaurant menu. And if it's beer you're after, they stock the largest selection of microbrews in the northern part of the state.

The store and restaurant are the creation of Jo Ann Carolla, who dreamed up the intriguing floor plan. The front is divided in two with one side the bar and a small seating area and the other side filled with units displaying a selection of cheeses, pâtés, chocolates, bread, and desserts.

As you enter farther, you encounter the salad bar with its scrumptious and varied choices. This is no regular offering. Chef and business partner Lionel Garnier creates about a dozen cold items daily, varying vegetable and meat dishes. You'll find everything from an olive medley to Chicken Penne and blue cheese salad or Beef Tips with bell pepper and onions. The food is designed for consumption on the premises or as a takeout for harried home cooks. It's also the place to stop if you're planning a picnic in the countryside.

The rear of the store is a combination of wine racks and dining area, including a large common table for encouraging patron interaction.

The menu changes every six months to keep it fresh and exciting. Lunch is served from 11:00 A.M. until 4:00 P.M. and includes selections such as Pork Egg Rolls, breaded and fried Calamari with Fries and Coleslaw, Oriental Salad, and a roster of sandwiches including Reuben on rye and Philly Cheese. In addition, there's a pasta of the day and an excellent half roasted free-range chicken (author's choice).

Dinner appetizers might be sushi du jour; a cheese plate of Maytag blue, Brie, and Gruyère; or adaptations of lunch entrées. Some of the current entrées are Wild Mushroom Pasta, Half Roasted Duck au jus, Bravo! Crab Cake, Porterhouse Steak, or a selection of pizzas. Blue-plate specials change daily and include down-home specials such as Tuesday's Spaghetti and Meatballs or Friday's more exotic Seafood Bouillabaisse. Their Saturday Oven-Roasted Lamb Shank is a real winner.

Bravo! is not the place you want to take your prospective fiancée for a proposal dinner, but the variety and consistent good quality of its food and its encyclopedic wine list recommend it for casual dining. Closed Sunday.

Bravo! Fine Wine, Food & Spirits, 1353A Paseo del Pueblo Sur, Taos, 87571; (505) 758-8100.

Events

The Taos Winter Wine Festival

Last two weeks January Since 1985 oenophiles from all over the country have come to Taos Ski Valley to sample, compare, and discuss more than 300 vintages from more than two dozen wineries from the United States and Europe. Either the winemaker or owner represents each winery.

During the two-week period at different venues, master sommeliers and wine experts hold seminars on tasting wine and identifying the region of origin, varietals, and age. An extremely popular feature are the winemaker dinners, where more than two dozen local restaurants host multicourse meals paired with specific wines.

Two grand tastings and silent auctions are held the first and last Friday of the festival. Local restaurants prepare their specialties, and the winemakers provide samples of their vintages.

Taos Ski Valley, 87525; (505) 776-2291, ext. 1427; http://skitaos.org.

Son of Beer Festival

March—This spring event echoes the larger December festival with the exception of a smaller number of breweries participating and the inclusion of larger breweries showcasing their special, limited-edition beers.

Taos Ski Valley, 87525; (505) 776-2291; http://skitaos.org.

Brewmaster's Festival

December—Between 20 and 40 microbreweries from Colorado, New Mexico, Arizona, and Utah bring their best grogs to Tenderfoot Katie's in the Ski Valley base lodge for one great party with a bluegrass band providing live entertainment. Usually 60 to 70 types of beer are available for tasting, and Rhoda's Restaurant provides a good selection of pub grub.

Taos Ski Valley, 87525; (505) 776-2291; http://skitaos.org.

Recipes

CULINARY
NEW MEXICO

Carlo Gislimberti's Wild Mushroom Soup

Courtesy of Villa Fontana, Taos

6 servings

$^1/_2$ onion, finely diced
2 cloves garlic, finely chopped
Dried or fresh sage, rosemary, and bay leaf*
Lemon pepper to taste
2 Tbs. olive oil
3 Tbs. dried porcini mushrooms
2 Tbs. flour
3 qts. stock, either beef, chicken, or vegetable, hot
1 egg yolk
$^1/_4$ C. heavy cream
Freshly chopped parsley
Croutons

Sauté onion, garlic, dried herbs, and lemon pepper in olive oil. Add crumbled dried porcini mushrooms and sauté together for about 2 minutes. Add flour and make a roux, then add the hot stock. Bring to boil and boil slowly for at least 10 minutes.

Mix egg yolk with cream in a bowl and add to boiling soup. Adjust for seasonings.

Garnish with freshly chopped parsley and croutons.

*If using fresh herbs, do not sauté with onions, but add to the soup at the end of the procedure.

Stakeout Chèvre Cheesecake

Courtesy of Stakeout Grill & Bar, Ranchos de Taos

Crust
1 C. pistachios
$^1/_3$ C. breadcrumbs
$^1/_3$ C. butter
$^1/_3$ C. sugar

Place all ingredients in mixer and mix until smooth. Press into bottom of springform pan.

Cake
20 oz. cream cheese
8 oz. chèvre
7 eggs
14 Tbs. sugar
7 Tbs. heavy cream
1 Tbs. vanilla extract

Blend the cheeses in mixer adding one egg at a time. Add the rest of the ingredients and mix on low for 4 to 5 minutes. Pour into crust. Place in a covered water bath and bake at 350° F for 1 $^1/_2$ hours. Let cool slowly, *not* in refrigerator. Top it with your favorite caramel sauce and enjoy.

Stakeout Risotto

Courtesy of Steakout Grill & Bar, Ranchos de Taos

5 servings

2 oz. extra-virgin olive oil
$^1/_2$ yellow onion (diced)
1 lb. arborio rice
1 oz. garlic (chopped)
2 oz. dried porcini mushrooms
1 C. white wine
1 $^1/_2$ qt. chicken stock, hot
1 C. rock shrimp
4 oz. grated Parmesan cheese
$^1/_2$ C. heavy cream
Salt and pepper
Parsley to garnish (diced)

1. Heat oil in large sauté pan, add onion, and cook until soft.
2. Add rice and cook in oil until all the grains are covered in oil and very hot to the touch.
3. Add garlic, mushrooms, and wine and cook until dry.
4. Add stock (4-oz. ladles at a time).
5. When the rice has absorbed the first ladle of stock, add the next one and repeat until stock is gone.
6. Add rock shrimp, half of cheese, and heavy cream and cook until smooth. Adjust with salt and pepper to taste.
7. Place in a bowl, top with rest of cheese, and garnish with parsley.

Grilled Shrimp with Serrano-Braised White Beans and Sofrito

Courtesy of Chef Kevin Kapalka
El Monte Sagrado, Taos

4 servings

Serrano-Braised White Beans
1 C. dry white beans, soaked overnight in 4 C. water.
$^{1}/_{2}$ C. onion, diced small
1 Tbsp. extra-virgin olive oil
1 clove garlic, crushed
3 oz. Serranno ham, diced (the heel works well)
1 sprig fresh thyme
2 bay leaves, fresh if possible
2 C. chicken stock
Salt and pepper

Cook beans in water to cover until tender. Set aside. Sweat onions in extra-virgin olive oil. Do not brown. Add garlic and cook one more minute. Add all other ingredients, including beans, and reduce heat to low simmer. Continue to cook until most of the liquid is absorbed. Season to taste with salt and pepper. Hold in warm place until service.

Sofrito
$^{1}/_{2}$ C. salt pork, small diced and soaked overnight in 2 C. water. Drain and dry on a towel.
$^{1}/_{2}$ tsp. annatto seed
$^{1}/_{2}$ C. onion, diced small
1 clove garlic, crushed
$^{1}/_{2}$ C. bell pepper, diced small
1 C. tomato, seeds removed and diced small

Pinch of chile flakes to taste
Salt and pepper

Heat saucepan and add salt pork. Slowly cook to render out fat. Remove pieces of salt pork when golden brown and save for garnish. Add annatto seed to fat and cook lightly. Add onion and continue to sweat. Add garlic, cook another minute, and then add pepper. When pepper is soft, add tomato and chile flakes. Reduce heat and simmer until it starts to thicken lightly. Season with salt and pepper to taste.

Shrimp
12 raw, peeled, and deveined shrimp, with tails left on
Salt and pepper
1 Tbsp. canola oil
Leek, mache, or micro greens for garnish

Season shrimp with salt and pepper. Heat sauté pan to the smoke point. Add canola oil. Add shrimp to hot oil, being sure not to crowd the pan and lose the heat. Briefly cook, approximately 2 ½ minutes per side or until just cooked. They may still be a bit translucent in the center.

To Plate:
Place beans in the bottom of a shallow bowl and place a small mound of sofrito in the center. Place all three shrimp around the mound of sofrito with the tails up and to the center. Wrap a blanched strip of leek or garnish with mache or micro greens. Sprinkle remaining crisped salt pork around dish.

Ranch Kitchen
Gallup

Coffee Works
Farmington

Displays
Coffee Works

Navajo Weaver
Gallup

New Mexico's vast northwest is lonesome country. Only a few towns hug the highways, and you can drive for hours without seeing another soul. The primary towns are Aztec/Bloomfield, Farmington, Gallup, and Grants.

The northwest is also Indian Country, home to a large portion of the Navajo Nation as well as containing both the Zuni and Jicarilla Apache reservations. Landmarks such as Mount Taylor, Ship Rock, El Malpais, and Cabezón Peak as well as the Bisti Wilderness Area and the Chuska Mountains have profound associations with Native American lore.

The Ancestral Puebloan people also claimed this land as attested to by the ruins in Chaco Culture National Historical Park, Aztec Ruins National Monument, Salmon Ruins, and a number of small sites throughout the region. Terrain is a combination of mesas, volcanic cones, oil fields, and desert. Water is scarce except in the Farmington area. The damming of the San Juan River, which joins the La Plata and Animas Rivers in Farmington, created Navajo Lake. The waters of the San Juan below the dam are considered among the state's best fishing areas.

Aztec

Aztec is one of New Mexico's atypical small towns. Streets are lined with trees and the homes are mainly wood and brick, not adobe. A short distance out of town, Aztec Ruins National Monument is one of the most important ruins in the Southwest, and its Grand Kiva is the only one existing rebuilt to an approximation of its original appearance. Mistakenly named for the Aztecs thought to have been the builders, the pueblo was constructed in the 11th or 12th century by the Ancestral Puebloans. The name of both town and ruins reflects that error.

Dining

The Main Street Bistro

The Main Street Bistro on the corner of Main and Blanco has undergone a transformation from filling station in the 1950s to oil equipment storehouse in the 1980s and finally to a funky little café. The sunny, bright interior walls are painted with vivid shades of chartreuse and red. The ceiling is horizon blue and scattered with puffy white clouds. There's an outdoor patio for alfresco dining.

Owners Tony and Susan French serve espresso, "not quite espresso" (brewed coffee drinks), breakfast all day, and from-scratch desserts and pastries. Two or three times a week they do hot entrées such as a Beef Vegetable Stir Fry or Shrimp Scampi, and daily specials may include Spinach, Artichoke, and Feta Quiche; Green-Chile Stew; or their "Ultimate Sandwich," a freshly baked croissant piled with thinly sliced turkey breast, thickly sliced bacon, provolone cheese, and fresh avocado, then topped with a creamy dressing. Check the chalkboard for daily specials.

The Main Street Bistro, 122 North Main Street, Aztec, 87410; (505) 334-0109; www.aztecmainstreetbistro.com.

Farmington

As its name denotes, Farmington was founded in 1901 as a farming community after William Hendrickson led a small party of pioneers to this well-situated spot at the confluence of three rivers. Known mainly for its fruit crops and extensive cattle and sheep raising, the city underwent a huge transformation when large-scale oil and gas field development began in the 1950s. Farmington is still the center of the Four Corners oil, gas, coal, and power generating industries today.

Bakery and Tea Room

Something Special Bakery and Tea Room

Something Special Bakery and Tea Room was founded as a restaurant in 1980 by Charliene Barns, and the bakery was added in the late 1980s by her son Dean, who has taken over the burgeoning business from his mother. Housed in a tidy cottage with outdoor dining on a shaded patio, the popular bakery and lunch spot is bright and cheery with local art on the walls and white arches painted in the Bavarian style.

The bakery specializes in Old World breads, cookies, and muffins. The desserts (to go or eat in) are a dieter's downfall. The most outrageous number is the Strawberry Napoleon, berries slathered with real whipped cream and sandwiched between layers of crisp puff pastry dough. And the cream pies are so rich, you'll swear they're illegal.

The restaurant serves two specials every day, one meat and one vegetarian. A month's menus are printed on cards so patrons will be sure not to miss their favorite dishes, which might include Green-Chile Chicken Enchiladas or Chile Rellenos made with filo dough and cream cheese. The ingredients are scrupulously fresh, and all sauces and dressings are homemade.

Something Special Bakery and Tea Room, 116 North Auburn Avenue, Farmington, 87401; (505) 325-8183.

Brewery and Brewpub

Three Rivers Eatery and Brewhouse

The Three Rivers Eatery and Brewhouse was established in 1997 by John Silva and Bob and Cindy Beckley. It was formerly the Andrews Building, housing the Farmington Drug Store and the *Farmington Times-Hustler* (now the *The Daily Times*).

The unique décor consists mostly of items found in the building during the renovation. The restaurant was expanded in July 1999. The addition includes an outdoor private patio, a bar, and the largest beer label and beer coaster collections in New Mexico.

Head brewer Casey Gwinn brews about 20 different beer styles a year, including a selection of ales, lagers, ciders, and seasonals. They use two different gases to carbonate the beer—nitrogen or carbon dioxide or a mixture of the two depending on the beer style—and they serve their beer at two temperatures to authenticate the subtle differences in styles. In addition, they home brew a selection of sodas: root beer, cream soda, and six other seasonal sodas.

There's the usual selection of pub food including soups, salads, appetizers, burgers, sandwiches, and entrées. Daily specials for soup, lunch, and dinner are posted on a chalkboard. Beer and soda are available to go in half-, five-, and 15-gallon kegs.

Three Rivers Eatery and Brewhouse, 101 East Main Street, Farmington, 87401; (505) 324-2187; www.threeriversbrewery.com.

Cookware and Specialty Food Store

Coffee Works

Although the name would indicate a coffee bar, the Coffee Works is much more. In addition to selling specialty caffeinated drinks, owner Christie Irvin and daughter Meghan stock a fine line of gourmet food products, fine toiletries, specialty herbs, Stahmann's candies, Eagle Ranch pistachios, and cookware. You'll find All-Clad pans, Crabtree and Evelyn lotions and potions, American Spoon Food fruit butters, Stonewall rubs, and much more.

In addition to coffee and cooking supplies, Coffee Works has an extensive lunch menu of wraps, sandwiches, salads, and soups. Try the lean roast beef with tomatoes, red onions, mixed baby greens, and blue cheese in a garlic herb wrap or the fresh fruit salad with poppy seed dressing. "We use only the finest ingredients," Christie says. "We strive for quality with fresh, wholesome food." Two soups are made fresh daily and might include gazpacho in summer or beef and veggie barley in winter. Closed Sunday.

Coffee Works, 1901 East 20th Street, Farmington, 87401; (505) 326-6048.

Dining

The Bluffs

Opened in 2002 by restaurateur Kelly Ledbetter and wife Ivy, the Bluffs fills a need in Farmington for a quality steak and seafood dining experience. Located on the eastern edge of town surrounded by the strip malls that have embraced the area, the Bluffs stands alone as an independent Bronx cheer to the prevailing glut of chains.

Named for the sandy bluffs lining the San Juan River flowing through the heart of the city, the restaurant décor echoes the landscape. Walls are sponge painted in shades of sandstone and terra-cotta. Stone construction reminiscent of the masonry of Chaco Canyon fronts the fireplace and section dividers. Frosted and worked-glass partitions mirror the bluffs theme.

Lunch and dinner menus are similar, with dinner selections expanded and refined. Here you won't need to query, "Where's the beef?" They serve premium gold Angus steaks cooked at 1,200° F. You can choose the petite eight-ounce filet or the monstrous 24-ounce bone-in rib eye. Even their "small cut" prime rib is too much to finish. There's also a choice of chicken breast, double-cut pork chop, or Colorado rack of lamb.

Seafood is their second specialty, and if you're wondering why order seafood in landlocked New Mexico, may we remind you that Federal Express and other services do overnight delivery from any place in the United States.

In their "Offshore" items, the Ahi Tuna Sesame, seared rare with ginger soy, wasabi, and pickled ginger, is the best seller. Other alternatives include salmon, halibut, trout, king crab, and cold-water lobster tails. If you wish, you may mix and match meat and seafood to create your own "surf and turf."

Four pasta dishes are on the regular menu, ranging from Fettuccine Alfredo with Parmigiano-Reggiano and Pecorino-Romano to Linguine with vodka, artichoke hearts, sun-dried tomatoes, and olives.

Appetizers vary from Lump Meat Crab Cakes with roasted red pepper coulis and smoked pepper mayonnaise to Seafood-Stuffed Artichoke with garlic aioli and remoulade. The daily blue-plate special is chef's choice and includes a dinner salad. Other nightly specials round out the selections.

Desserts change daily and may include Warm Sour Cream Apple Pie with Dutch topping, Crème Brûlée, Baily's Irish Cream Chocolate Mousse, or Sticky Pecan Cheesecake.

The Bluffs, 3450 East Main Street, Farmington, 87402; (505) 325-8155.

Los Hermanitos

No town in the northwest would be complete without a good northern New Mexican restaurant, and Los Hermanitos in Middlefork Square qualifies. Sam and Cathy Gonzales opened the restaurant in 1992, and they have been going strong ever since.

The restaurant décor is the typical adobe walls, hanging *ristras*, and Mexican scenes, with one exception—a large, extremely colorful mural by Leander Begay.

The menu lists appetizers such as chili con queso, soups including posole and menudo, and *especialidades* such as Sam's Special Carne Adovada and Liz's Tamale Plate. Of course, there are burgers, tacos, burritos, and chimichangas. Of particular note are children's and seniors' menus, as well as "Food for Life," items deemed a healthier choice than the standard high-fat offerings.

Breakfast is a busy time at the restaurant. They serve the usual American-style pancakes, eggs, and bacon, ham, or sausage, but it's their breakfast burritos that really stand out. They bill them as "World Famous," and although that may be a bit of a stretch, they are mighty fine.

Los Hermanitos, 3501 East Main Street, Farmington, 87402; (505) 326-5664; www.loshermanitos.com.

Gallup

Gallup bills itself as "Gateway to Indian Country," and it is a busy trade center for Navajo and Zuni Indians, whose reservations lie nearby. Originally nothing more than a stop of the Westward Overland Stage, the coming of the railroad conferred a degree of prominence on the city.

The still-active Burlington, Northern, and Santa Fe rails dictated the town's linear layout with the railroad edging the eastern margin of Old Route 66, the main drag, and shops, motels, and restaurants on the other side. An average of 70 trains a day pass through.

Still a bit rough around the edges, today Gallup remains the center for Indian art and a stopping point for travelers passing through on nearby Interstate 40.

Dining

Chelle's

If you're looking for fine dining in Gallup, the only place to go is Chelle's, owned by Irene Ferrari and Chef Bob Witte. The building itself is unimpressive and has housed a teen club, a jewelry store, and a trading post. The interior, however, is more polished with knotty pine and barn board walls and ceiling, a pretty stained glass window announcing "Chelle's, a good place to eat," and room dividers of stained glass.

Bob has been a chef for more than 30 years, and his experience shows in the food and its presentation. *Chelle,* meaning "little chef," is the nickname his grandmother gave him because he was always in her kitchen.

Everything on the menu is homemade, and dinners have several pleasant touches such as complimentary soup and a sherbet palate cleanser between first and second courses. Entrées lean to steak and seafood, although there is a light menu for those watching their fat and salt intake. In addition, a children's menu is available.

Nightly specials might include Top Sirloin topped with pico de gallo, cheese, and ratatouille or Beef Tenderloin stuffed with ricotta and bathed in a mushroom-Cabernet sauce. The most popular desserts are Bob's sinful chocolate cake, tiramisu, or *tres leches* cake.

Chelle's is open only for dinner and closed Sunday.

Chelle's, 2201 West Highway 66, Gallup, 87301; (505) 722-7698.

Earl's Family Restaurant

Earl's Family Restaurant is a Gallup landmark that bills itself as "where the locals eat." Done in an adobe and teal color scheme and owned by the Richards family since 1947, the huge dining rooms are always bustling with tourists and Native Americans.

Tourists love Earl's because in addition to its good, basic New Mexican cooking, they are treated to the sight of a constant parade of Indian vendors winding their way among the tables with trays loaded with jewelry and art. If you prefer not to be disturbed in your dining, you can pick up a card requesting privacy to place on your table.

Breakfast is one of the most popular times at Earl's, but lunch and dinner can also draw crowds. There's a child's menu, soup and salad bar, and daily specials. The regular menu lists "Sharon and Steve's Gourmet

Sandwiches," and "Chef's Suggestions" that include favorites such as chopped sirloin, ham steak, chicken-fried steak, breaded shrimp, belly buster haddock, roast pork and scalloped apples, calves liver and onions, and steaks ranging from 7 to 16 ounces. Needless to say, Mexican dishes also have a prominent place in the menu, including the Pride of Earl's, a steak and enchilada combo.

Earl's Family Restaurant, 1400 East Highway 66, Gallup, 87301; (505) 863-4201.

The Ranch Kitchen

If the bustle at Earl's is too much to handle, head west of town to the Ranch Kitchen, a down-home eatery with well-prepared food and big portions. Opened by Earl Vance in 1954 and managed today by stepson John Marbury, the Ranch Kitchen is lodged in a rustic building with multiple dining rooms, brick floors, wagon wheel chandeliers, and Native American art on the walls.

The food is all prepared on the premises, and the menu is extensive with typical New Mexican favorites, soups, salads, sandwiches, and dinner entrées ranging from steak to chicken and dumplings. Their barbecue is smoked at the restaurant and can be ordered as pork ribs, half chicken, beef brisket, or a ribs and chicken combo. The Ranch Kitchen is also one of the few places where you can order Navajo food such as lamb stew, and they're known as the first restaurant in town to serve Navajo tacos.

Service is good and the management likes to make people feel at home by placing a small flag with their state or international home on the table. "We love to see folks come in here road-weary and leave feeling better than when they arrived," John says.

The restaurant also houses two retail shops, one where they sell New Mexico souvenirs and their Ranch Kitchen Southwestern BBQ Sauce, and the second with good-quality jewelry and art. Open Tuesday through Sunday, 5:00 to 9:00 P.M.

The Ranch Kitchen, 3001 U.S. 66 West, Gallup, 87301; (505) 722-2537; www.ranchkitchen.com.

Grants

The sleepy town of Grants has a history that belies it current quiet status. Originally founded to service the building of the railroad, it grew as a center of logging in the Zuni Mountains from the late 1880s to the early 1940s. During the 1930s and 1940s it was also known as "the carrot capitol of the world" until the process of cellophane wrapping began, bulk shipping was no longer viable, and California took over the title.

Grants' biggest boom was during the 1950s when uranium was discovered in the vicinity. It lasted until the mines were closed in the 1980s following the Three Mile Island nuclear power plant incident, which drastically reduced the demand for uranium as a raw material for nuclear power generation.

Today Grants is a stop along Interstate 40 and a jumping off point for attractions such as Mount Taylor, El Malpais and El Morro National Monuments, Acoma, Laguna, and Zuni Pueblos, and the Ice Cave and Bandera Volcano.

Dining

El Cafecito

Angie and Larry Baca have run El Cafecito since 1986, and you'll find they live up to their motto of "authentic New Mexican cuisine." Whether it's a morning order of huevos rancheros, a lunch of a sopapilla stuffed with beans and meat, or a dinner combo plate of tacos, enchiladas, and chimichangas, the emphasis is on chile in its many and varied forms. Tortillas are homemade, and their taco salad is the best you're likely to find anywhere. Desserts are their special *frittas* with cherry, peach, or apple filling.

The restaurant is bright and immaculate with white stucco walls, Saltillo tile floors, and lots of greenery. Busy all day long, El Cafecito is a favorite of locals and tourists alike.

El Cafecito, 820 East Santa Fe Avenue, Grants, 87020;
(505) 285-6229.

La Ventana

More formal in atmosphere yet warm and inviting, La Ventana is Grant's best all-round restaurant. It can be a challenge to find, hiding out off the main street behind the New Mexico Department of Labor building. La Ventana's décor is a little bit rustic, a little bit New Mexican adobe, with Indian masks, sand paintings, and weavings adorning the walls.

Open for lunch and dinner, the restaurant has some of the best beef in the state. Their signature prime rib is a local favorite, and the steaks are not far behind.

Owner Ray Renon states, "I expect our customers to eat like I like to eat, the best in meats and produce. We don't skimp on quality."

"Appeteasers" include coconut shrimp, deep-fried cauliflower, or sautéed mushrooms. Chicken is prepared Mexicali, teriyaki, or barbecue style on the mesquite grill. Seafood entrées run from Alaskan king crab legs to halibut. You can order the usual cast of New Mexican dishes or go with other entrées such as barbecued baby back ribs, rack of lamb, or their special beef kabob.

There's a good wine list, and the restaurant has periodic seven-course wine and food paired meals. Call for dates.

La Ventana, 110 ¹/₂ Geis Street, Grants, 87020; (505) 287-9393.

Farmers' Markets

Aztec Farmers' Market, Westside Plaza, 1409 West Aztec Boulevard, Wednesday, 4:00 to 7:00 P.M., mid-July to October, (505) 334-9121.

Farmington Farmers' Market, Animas Park off Browning Parkway, Saturday, 8:00 to 11:30 A.M., Tuesday, 4:30 to 6:30 P.M., mid-July through October, (505) 327-7757.

Grants Growers' Market, Grants City Hall, Santa Fe and Iron Streets, Saturdays, 8:00 A.M. to noon, early August through October, (505) 287-8070.

Ramah Area Farmers' Arts and Crafts Market, Ramah Café parking area, Highway 53, Saturdays, 10:00 A.M. to 1:00 P.M., mid-July through October, (505) 783-4704.

Events

New Mexico Spirits

May—More than 25 New Mexico wineries and breweries come to Farmington for a one-day tasting festival. Food booths complement the beer and wine.

New Mexico Spirits, McGee Park, off highway 64, Farmington; (505) 325-0279 or (888) 325-0179.

A Taste of Gallup

September—Area restaurants give samples of their cuisine, and there's a bike race and car and motorcycle show as part of the event. Jugglers, stilt walkers, and clowns entertain, with balloons and face painting for the kids. An opportunity to learn to climb is held at Mentmore rock climbing area.

A Taste of Gallup, Downtown Gallup; (505) 722-2228.

Aztec Octoberfest

October—Main Street, Aztec celebrates the season and German heritage with a complement of Teutonic food, beer, music, and contests.

Aztec Octoberfest, Main Street, Aztec; (505) 334-7605.

Recipes

Navajo Lamb Stew

Courtesy of the Ranch Kitchen, Gallup

8 to 10 main course servings

1 pound dried or frozen posole (hominy)*
3 bay leaves
$^1/_2$ tsp. garlic powder
1 $^1/_2$ tsp. salt
$^1/_2$ tsp. black pepper
5 lbs. diced lamb
1 bunch of celery, chopped in half-inch pieces
10 carrots, chopped in half-inch pieces
$^1/_2$ C. New Mexico chile powder**
$^1/_4$ cup strong beef stock

Boil posole in water to cover generously approximately one hour. Add bay leaves, garlic, salt, and black pepper. Continue boiling another hour. Check water level and add more as needed. Add diced lamb. Simmer another hour. Add celery, carrots, chile powder, and beef stock. Simmer for approximately 30 minutes.

Author's notes:

*Posole in both dried and frozen form is available in almost all New Mexico markets. The dried posole varies in quality depending on its age. The older the kernels, the longer they need to cook. Frozen posole is easier to use as its age is arrested at freezing, and it takes shorter cooking time.

**Use chile powder made from red chile pods. Do not use commercial chili powder, which includes cumin, garlic, and salt.

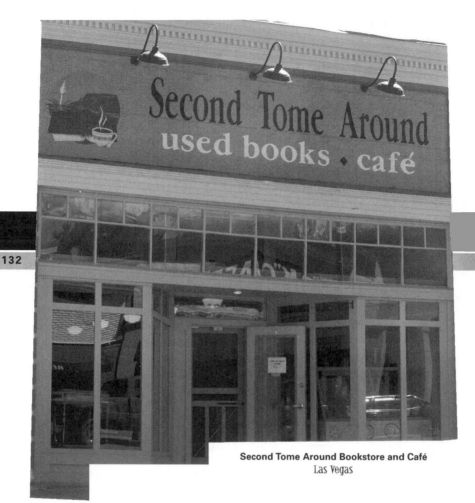

Second Tome Around Bookstore and Café
Las Vegas

Ardys Otterbacher
Second Tome Café

Charlie's Spic & Span Café
Las Vegas

Estella's Café
Las Vegas

NORTHEAST NEW MEXICO:
WHERE THE MOUNTAINS MEET THE PLAINS

If you're traveling Interstate 25, it's a long distance between towns in New Mexico's northeast quadrant. You're roaming the route where the western end of the Great Plains meets the eastern slopes of the Rocky Mountains. This is the path of the Santa Fe Trail, and communities such as Las Vegas, Cimarrón, Eagles Nest, and Raton retain the Old West flavor. Watering holes are rare, so plan your culinary adventures with this in mind.

Las Vegas

Las Vegas was not named for the gambling mecca whose birth the New Mexico town predates by more than 150 years, but for the region's "big meadows," part of the 1821 land grant to Luis Maria C. de Baca. Originally a farming and commercial center, the city became an important stop on the Santa Fe Trail and later, in 1879, on the Atchison, Topeka, and Santa Fe Railroad. The railroad builders bypassed the old town, or West Las Vegas, and routed the line east of the Rio Gallinas, creating the new Victorian area, East Las Vegas.

Once separate communities, the two sections eventually incorporated, although each retains its distinct characteristics to this day—Old Town heavily Hispanic, and East Las Vegas mainly Anglo. Parts of the city seem caught in a time warp. Few places survive that still have a drive-in theater.

The Victorian homes of West Las Vegas keep their stately charm, and the original Andrew Carnegie library is still the town's bookshelf. Other areas have not fared so well, although there are encouraging patches of renovation and new business, especially on Bridge Street.

Bakeries and Cafés

Charlie's Spic & Span Bakery & Café

Las Vegas does not strike you as a town where you'd find Starbucks coffees, but if you stop at Charlie's Spic & Span Bakery & Café near the old Serf Theatre, you'll find that and much more. Like Estella's on Bridge Street, the Spic & Span is a city institution. Opened in the early 1960s by Carmen C. DeBaca and currently owned by Charlie Sandoval and his wife, Elizabeth, the bright, cheery restaurant is "the meeting, greeting, eating place of Las Vegas." This is no small hole-in-the wall. There's seating for 200 upstairs and for 100 downstairs in the banquet area. The interior is indeed spic and span with its peach walls and sky blue cornice. Susan West's delicate artwork covers the walls with faux *nichos* and borders of prickly pear cactus. An intricate painted swag of flowers adorns the center arch.

Charlie has owned the restaurant for five years, and all the fine touches are his. He says, "We try to keep our food and baked goods traditional—things people here in town would make if they had the time." Baker Pedro Garcia has had 25 years of experience, and he and his helpers turn out a variety of breads: wheat, white, French, raisin, jalapeño, potato, and chocolate chip. Pastries include all types of doughnuts including a glazed variety that rivals Krispy Kreme. In addition, there are éclairs, napoleons, cream puffs, six kinds of pie, carrot cake, strudel—the list goes on. Of course, they specialize in *bizcochitos* and long johns. During the holidays, they bake old-time items including empanaditas and tamales.

Fresh tortillas are another draw. If you arrive for breakfast, you'll find the tortilla machine and grill in action. This contraption takes balls of dough, rolls them thin, and spits them out onto the griddle where a baker tends them. They puff up like baby balloons, and he gives them a good whack before mounding them on a cooling rack. Weekdays they bake about 100 pounds of wheat dough for tortillas a day, but on weekends, they can go through 200 to 250 pounds. Some of this is for the restaurant use. The balance is sold "to go" in lots of a dozen.

The café menu is traditional New Mexican with breakfast customers favoring the huevos rancheros and breakfast burritos. Lunch diners order from fajitas, tacos, tostadas, enchiladas, burritos, stuffed sopapillas, quesadillas, or Navajo tacos. If you want to try a bit of everything, get the combo plate of enchilada, homemade tamale, and a taco. Soups, salads, green-chile stew, sandwiches, and burgers flesh out the selections. There's even a menu *por los ninos* (kids).

If you plan on coming for dinner, you'll have to arrive early because although they open early at 6:30 A.M., they also close early—5:30 P.M. Dinner offerings include pork chops, hot roast beef, an eight-ounce rib eye, and that old standard, chicken-fried steak. Sunday hours are abbreviated from 7:00 A.M. to 2:00 P.M.

Charlie's Spic & Span Bakery & Café, 715 Douglas Avenue, Las Vegas, 87701; (505) 426-1921.

Second Tome Around Used Bookstore and Café

You'd never expect to find the former pastry chef of Santa Fe's Bishop's Lodge baking and managing a small used bookstore-*cum*-café in Las Vegas. However, Ardys Otterbacher found the slow pace and friendly atmosphere of Las Vegas to her liking, and she teamed up with Nancy Colallillo, owner of Tome on the Range bookstore, to open Second Tome Around.

Like its sister store across Bridge Street, the Second Tome is bright, attractive, and colorful. Nancy and Ardys have used a retro 1950s color scheme combining lavender, turquoise, chartreuse, yellow, and pink walls with a rotating gallery of local artists' work.

The first room is devoted to second-hand books and has comfortable seating areas and game tables. The second room is the bakery and coffee bar, and the third and fourth rooms hold the seating areas. A back patio is brought to use in the warm months.

Only coffees and pastries are served, not a full café menu. All breads and pastries are baked fresh daily by Ardys, a graduate and former professor at the New England Culinary Institute in Montpelier, Vermont. Schooled in the European tradition of bakers and pastry chefs, she makes a range of yeast breads: baguettes; batards, either plain or studded with calamata olives or sun-dried tomatoes; various whole-grain loaves; sourdoughs; and challah.

Popular pastries include her double-chocolate mousse tart, a fresh lemon curd tart, and a piñon tart, which she developed for Indian Market while working in Santa Fe. Other specialties include a flourless chocolate cake and her New York–style cheesecakes. On weekends, she bakes dynamite cinnamon rolls using brioche dough. Scones, muffins, cookies, brownies, biscotti, and cakes are part of the daily offerings.

Second Tome Around Used Bookstore and Café, 131 Bridge Street, Las Vegas, 87701; (505) 454-8511.

Dining

BlackJack's Grill at the Inn on the Santa Fe Trail

The Inn on the Santa Fe Trail is a historic property, built in the 1930s. Originally it had a couple cabins and a campground fronted by a gas station. Today it is an attractive motel-*cum*-restaurant set in the middle of expansive gardens.

That it has survived, even thrived, into the 21st century is a tribute to the vision of current owners David and Lavinia Fenzi. Professional hoteliers, they have renovated the single-story hacienda-style motel building and converted what once were three units into the BlackJack Grill, where Lavinia is head chef.

When it was first opened in 1998, the restaurant was named for the outlaw Black Jack Ketchum. The Fenzis thought tying it to Las Vegas Old West history would be a proper theme, but in the process of establishing the décor and planning the menu, something strange happened. Lavinia's Italian heritage asserted itself, and now BlackJack's resembles nothing more than a Tuscan bistro. The walls are in distressed tones of sienna, and the walnut sconces and Old World prints take the décor beyond the Southwest. Adding to this impression is the large oil painting of a peasant woman with chickens by Alejandro Morales. The woman could be any Mediterranean nationality, but she certainly looks like someone's *nonna*.

The evening mood is soft and romantic, with seating inside or on the patio in warm weather. Soft jazz plays in the background, and the mellow lighting casts glints off the copper-topped tables.

The menu is divided into distinct categories. The grill concentrates on steaks, chicken, pork chops, and trout. BlackJack's specialties feature the restaurant's Southwest dishes: Old Mexico Pork Tenderloin, pan-seared pork medallions topped with roma tomatoes, Mira Sol chile, and mushrooms; Seafood Enchilada with shrimp, scallops, crab, scallions, and feta cheese layered between blue corn tortillas and topped with a special green-chile cream sauce; and Lamb Tacos, two tortillas stuffed with shredded lamb, Jack cheese, tomatoes, and scallions.

Needless to say, there are Italian dishes. You might try the Linguine con Aglio e Gamberi, shrimp sautéed in garlic, sun-dried tomato, pesto, and basil, served over linguine or perhaps the Scaloppini de Salmone, sautéed salmon filet topped with lemon butter, garlic, and capers in a white wine sauce, served over angel hair pasta. Vegetarians will delight in the Melanzana Florentine, lightly breaded eggplant medallions topped with Parmesan cheese and marinara, served on a bed of herb ricotta and wilted spinach over angel hair pasta.

Nightly specials are listed on the white board in the entry and are recited by the waitstaff. On any night, you might find Pecan Encrusted Black Sea Bass with mandarin orange and cranberry chutney or Sautéed Red Snapper with raspberry coulis.

House-made soups change daily, and there's a selection of salads ranging from Caesar to Garlic Shrimp with mango and spinach. A light tapas menu is available and can be augmented with soup or salad and two side dishes. You'd have a choice of crab cakes, artichoke and crab casserole, escargot, and mussels, to name a few alternatives. Desserts stick with the standards: cheesecake, tiramisu, and Key lime pie.

When queried about her culinary philosophy, Lavinia says, "We've traveled all over the world and have eaten in the finest restaurants. With my recipes, I've tried to take the best and incorporate it into our cuisine. We use only the freshest ingredients and everything is cooked to order. I guess you could say it's 'contemporary Italian' with a twist on the traditional."

BlackJack's Grill at the Inn on the Santa Fe Trail, 1133 North Grand Avenue, Las Vegas, 87701; (505) 425-6791; www.innonthesantafetrail.com.

Estella's Café

When writing about hometown restaurants, it's frequently difficult to separate the food from the physical surroundings. This is especially the case for Estella's Café, a landmark restaurant in Las Vegas. The food is quintessential northern New Mexican and a classic of the genre. The building, however, is old and in dire need of renovation. "Don't panic," as Emeril Lagasse says, "and don't call 911!" Be brave, enter the old hardware store turned restaurant, and you'll be rewarded with some very good chow.

Estella's is named for Estella Gonzales, who opened the restaurant in the 1950s, and her son Alfredo and his daughter Adelita Lujan currently manage it. On any day, it is the most popular lunch spot in town, often with locals waiting for tables. You will hear as much Spanish as English spoken, and service is snappy.

The menu lists all the traditional dishes: flautas, tostadas, burritos (both undressed and smothered), enchiladas (add one or two eggs, if you wish), and tacos. If you're undecided, try the combination plate with posole, an enchilada, relleno, taco, rice, and beans. The pinto beans are perfectly prepared, and Estella's has not switched to the black variety currently so popular in metro areas. Their rellenos are luscious with a crispy deep-fried crust and melting cheese stuffed into a New Mexico roasted green chile. The portions are reasonably sized. *Calditos* (soups or stews) come as bowls of red or green chile, posole, menudo, or green-chile stew. A few Anglo sandwiches and burgers are also available.

Open for lunch every day except Sunday, the restaurant serves dinners only on Friday and Saturday. From 4:00 to 8:00 you can order specials such as their Huachinanago a la Veracruzana (red snapper), Camarones al Caribe (shrimp), Carne de Res Asada (an eight-ounce rib eye), or an empanada filled with cheese, green chile, onion, tomato, parsley, mushrooms, olives, and avocado with choice of meat.

Estella's Café, 148 Bridge Street, Las Vegas, 87701; (505) 454-0048.

Pastime Café

Bridge Street's Pastime Café is a neat little bistro tucked into two storefronts next to the old Kiva Theatre. If Estella's is the place to find Las Vegas's Hispanic population, the Pastime draws businesspeople and Anglos.

Classically schooled in painting and sculpture at the University of Southern California, owner and chef Larry Callahan left the art world for the life of a small-town restaurateur. There's been a felicitous carry-over. The artist's eye has been at work in the café décor. The front room, with its tapas bar, its Italian ceramic plates and plaques, and its colorful fabrics and geometric Pakistani rug, is a meld of Old World and New. The dining room is a contrast. The large front windows with their white café curtains light up the room with its cream and dark green walls. One side is broken by a gallery of the work of local artists, giving the space just enough definition without being spare.

Open since 1998, the café serves lunch weekdays and Saturday and dinners Wednesday through Saturday. The lunch menu has homemade soups, salads, sandwiches, quiches, and hot dishes such as Oriental Vegetables with Tofu, crisp-steamed and served with ginger sesame sauce on soba noodles; Green-Chile Meatloaf with mushroom gravy; and Salmon Croquettes with scalloped potatoes. All dishes are made from scratch using fresh ingredients.

The spinach and feta and the mushroom quiches are lunch favorites as are the specialty sandwiches. You might try the Gallinas, smoked turkey breast, Swiss cheese, guacamole, and tomato with chipotle mayonnaise, or the Salmon Big Boy, a cumin-spiced patty of salmon, potato, and apple on a kaiser roll. A Mediterranean influence sneaks in with the Pan Bagna Niçoise, albacore tuna, anchovies, olives, red onion, and tomato packed into a French roll and panini-grilled for maximum flavor.

The dinner menu starters are Mushroom Caps stuffed with spinach, feta, and apples, bathed with cream or Salmon Mousse, fresh poached salmon, green peppercorns, and cucumber. For an entrée, you might order the rib eye, which is marinated and grilled to order, or the Pasta

Capricorn, linguine tossed with aged goat cheese, smoked salmon, tomato, roasted peppers, and garlic. Your server recites weekly specials, and Lemon Soufflé Pudding and Coffee Flan are always on the dessert list.

Pastime Café, 113 Bridge Street, Las Vegas, 87701; (505) 454-1755.

Farmers' Markets

Clayton Five State Producer Growers' Market, Ranch Market parking lot on 1st Street, Clayton. Wednesday and Saturdays, 10:00 A.M. to sell-out, July to October, (505) 374-9582.

Las Vegas Tri-County Farmers' Market, old Safeway Parking lot at Douglas and 7th Streets, LaLoma, Saturdays, 7:00 A.M. to noon, Wednesdays, 2:00 P.M. to sellout, July through October, (505) 427-4115 or (505) 427-7016.

Tucumcari Farmers' Market, Whales Park, corner of Lake Street and Tucumcari Boulevard, Tucumcari. Tuesdays, 5:00 P.M. to dusk, Saturdays, 8:00 A.M. to sellout, July to October, (505) 461-1161.

Specialty Food Product

Tucumcari Mountain Cheese Factory and Mediterranean Café

The Tucumcari Mountain Cheese Factory is located in the old downtown district. It does not have retail sales, but if you visit the Mediterranean Café operated by factory owner Charles Krause's wife, Sylvia, you may purchase any one of their many specialty cheeses. Best known for their Asiago and feta, they also make small amounts of other varieties for local consumption: cheddar, Jack, provolone, Parmesan, mozzarella, and longhorn. While you're at the café, you might want to try one of Sylvia's excellent gyros, dolmas, or spanokopitas. Closed Sunday.

Tucumcari Mountain Cheese Factory and Mediterranean Café, 1804 East Route 66, Tucumcari, 88401; (505) 461-3755.

Winery

Madison Vineyards and Winery

Madison Vineyards and Winery is a small family operation owned by Bill and Elise Madison and producing less than 5,000 gallons per year. Bordering the Pecos River, the vineyards produce both dry and semi-sweet wines, much of it from French hybrid grapes.

The tasting room is open Monday through Saturday, 10:00 A.M. to 5:00 P.M., Sunday, noon to 5:00 P.M. Open March 1 through January 31, February by appointment.

Madison Vineyards and Winery, HC 72, Box 490, Ribera, 87560; (505) 421-8028.

Events

Chuck Wagon Cookoff

April—Every year the Logan Chamber of Commerce organizes a Chuck Wagon Cookoff at Ute Lake State Park. Wagon cooks from the Southwest prepare a meal of meat (usually chicken-fried steak), potatoes, bread, and dessert. Judging is at 12:30, after which dinner is served to guests with tickets. There's live entertainment and an evening dance.

Chuck Wagon Cookoff, Logan; (505) 487-2284.

Red Cross Chili Cookoff

August—The annual American Red Cross Cookoff and Fundraiser Challenge is held at Victory Ranch in the Mora Valley, one mile north of Mora on Highway 434. Surrounding counties, towns, fire departments, as well as individuals compete for the title of Champion Chili Cooker and Best Presentation.

Red Cross Chili Cookoff, Mora; (505) 387-2020.

Bean Day

Labor Day Saturday—Bean Day has been a tradition in Wagon Mound since 1914. The town once known for its bean farms now celebrates its heritage with a rodeo, free beef and bean barbecue, parade, dance, and horseshoe-pitching contest.

Bean Day, Locations throughout town, Wagon Mound; (505) 666-2262 or (505) 666-2408.

Recipes

Ardys Otterbacher's Piñon Tart

Courtesy of Second Tome Around Used Bookstore and Café, Las Vegas

8 to 12 servings

1 C. honey
1 C. sugar
3 eggs
1 lemon, juice and zest
3 Tbs. melted butter
1 Tbs. flour
2 C. piñons, lightly toasted
1 unbaked 9 or 10" tart shell

1. Mix honey, sugar, eggs, lemon juice and zest, butter, and flour. Strain if necessary to avoid any lumps.

2. Place piñons in tart shell.

3. Pour over just enough filling to bind the nuts together; there will be enough for two tarts, but extra may be kept in the refrigerator and used later.

4. Bake (use sheet pan to catch any spills) at 400° F for 10–15 minutes; lower temperature, bake at 325° F for an additional 15 minutes until pie is set in the center.

Attention: baking temperatures are for high altitudes.

Roast Beef Enchilada Plate

Courtesy Charlie's Spic & Span Bakery & Café, Las Vegas

1 serving

2 stone-ground corn tortillas
6 oz. cooked and shredded roast beef
8 oz. red or green chile
4 oz. shredded cheddar and Monterey Jack cheese
Chopped lettuce and tomatoes
4 oz. refried beans
4 oz. posole (hominy stew) or Spanish rice

Fry two corn tortillas to soft texture (12–18 seconds). Place flat on plate. Place 3 oz. of beef on each tortilla. Roll up, center each one on end of plate, and cover enchiladas with 8 oz. of red or green chile (or both for "Christmas"). Sprinkle cheese on top. Garnish with fresh lettuce and tomatoes. Serve piping hot with beans and posole or rice on the side. Traditionally served with a fresh sopapilla.

Hillsboro Apple Festival

A.I.R. Coffee Company
Silver City

Chile fields
Hatch

Hatch Chile Express

South of Albuquerque, the Rio Grande takes a lazy sweep through the heart of New Mexico's fertile valley. To the west lies the state's largest body of water, Elephant Butte Lake, and nearby Caballo Reservoir, both fed by the great river. On the river south of Socorro, the Bosque del Apache National Wildlife Refuge fills with all species of waterfowl as they begin their spring and fall migrations.

Numerous mining towns such as Hillsboro and Silver City dot the western mountains, giving way to expanses of creosote bush desert as the border with Mexico looms to the south. Las Cruces, the state's second largest city, and historic Mesilla round out *rio abajo*, or lower river's, mix of desert, mountains, and towns.

Las Cruces and Mesilla

With a population of nearly 180,000 and the campus of New Mexico State University, Las Cruces is a bustling town. Situated in the Mesilla Valley with the rugged Organ Mountains to the east, the city's long history begins with Paleo-Indian habitation circa 200 B.C. It extends through the rise and fall of the Puebloan people around A.D. 300 and includes the Spanish *entrada* by Alvar Nunez Cabeza de Vaca in 1535 as he made his way from a shipwreck in the Gulf of Mexico. Five years later Coronado captained the first organized expedition through the Mesilla Valley in pursuit of his search for the Seven Cities of Gold, and in 1598 Don Juan de Oñate passed through this area. For the next 245 years it was the stopping place on El Camino Real between Mexico City and Santa Fe. Indian raids were constant. In fact the city's name means "the crosses" in Spanish because the whole area was a "garden of crosses" due to Apache massacres of travelers passing through.

With the ratification of the Gadsden Purchase in 1854, Las Cruces became a major supply center for Organ Mountain miners and soldiers stationed at Fort Selden. Nearby Mesilla was a major stopover on the Butterfield Overland Stage route. Today Las Cruces is both a cultural and agricultural center. Fields of cotton, groves of pecans, and acres of vineyards dot the outskirts.

Neighboring Mesilla dates back to the 1500s. The Gadsden Purchase was signed on the plaza in 1854, annexing Mesilla to the United States and fixing the international boundaries of New Mexico and Arizona. In 1861 the village was the western headquarters of the Confederacy. Today the shady plaza is highlighted by San Albino Church, one of the oldest in the valley, and ringed by restaurants and upscale shops selling everything from jewelry to fine art.

Bakery and Café

Old Mesilla Pastry Café

A few blocks off the plaza on Old Route 28, the Old Mesilla Pastry Café is the felicitous combination of bakeshop and restaurant. Owner Gabriel Mendoza says, "The restaurant does a brisk business, but our bakery and breads are the real hook that brings customers back time after time."

Serving the folks from the Mesilla Valley since 1996, they specialize in a wide variety of breads and pastries created by Paula Freeman, a self-taught baker with 17 years' experience. Her repertoire contains more than 25 varieties, several of which appear in each day's selection. You might find cranberry pecan, Absolutely Apricot, rye, 12-grain, black olive–Parmesan, fresh tomato with Swiss and basil, French baguette, or, on the Day of the Dead holiday, *pan de muerto*. Add to this list fruit-filled Danish, pecan rolls, fruit croissants, brownies, and cookies. No preservatives are used.

Of course, the café uses Paula's output in their breakfast and lunch offerings. Chef Robert Smith prepares daily specials using as many local products as possible. You might find *calabacitas* enchiladas with squash and corn fresh from the farmers' stand down the road, or maybe you'd like to dig into one of their soups or sandwiches such as their Smoked Trout on a Bun served with Jack cheese, tomatoes, onions, and fresh sprouts.

In addition to the full-service Mesilla location, Gabriel has opened an outlier named OMPC in Las Cruces with the same menu but with self-service features. Bakery and café open Wednesday through Sunday.

Old Mesilla Pastry Café, 2790 South Highway 28, Mesilla, 88046; (505) 525-2636; OMPC, 810 South Valley, Las Cruces.

Brewery and Brewpub

High Desert Brewing Company

You know those high-visibility brewpubs with faux gaslights and view rooms with gleaming copper kettles? Well, High Desert Brewing Company is not like that. Located on a small side street off Valley in Las Cruces, the modest one-story adobe brick building more resembles a roadhouse than high-end brewpub.

Owned by Mark Cunningham and brewmaster Bob G. Gosselin, High Desert makes up in quality what it lacks in ambiance. Their lagers consist of Amber Lager, Dark Bock, Bohemian Pilsner, Octoberfest, Steam Beer, and Pale Bock. Ales include amber, brown, India pale, peach wheat, wheat, porter, and stout. All are handcrafted using the finest grains and hops, and they brew in small batches of about 100 gallons, ensuring that all beers are at peak freshness. High Desert beers have been consistent winners at state fair competitions. Some beers are seasonal, such as the Holiday Ale, Hefeweizen, and Imperial Stout. Although they strive to keep all beers on tap at all times, sometimes one or two may not be available for a few days. Beer to go is available in half-gallon growlers (jugs), five- and 15 ½-gallon kegs.

The food is simple pub grub with appetizers such as jalapeño poppers and nachos. There's an assortment of quesadillas and chicken sandwiches, and their burgers are big and juicy, served, if you wish, with their original potato salad. Open daily with live music on Tuesday, Thursday, and Saturday.

High Desert Brewing Company, 1201 West Hadley Avenue, Las Cruces, 88005; (505) 525-6752; www.highdesertbrewing.20megsfree.com.

Chocolatier

J. Eric Chocolatier, Inc.

Deprived chocoholics need only to stroll Old Mesilla Plaza to discover J. Eric Chocolatier. The sweet-smelling little bandbox is owned by Linda Ramiriz, who purchased it in 1998 from original founder Eric Rathgeber. Eric is still involved, helping out in the back of the shop preparing his specialty, truffles.

On any day you'll find turtles of rich caramel and pecans and milk or semisweet chocolate; English toffee coated in milk chocolate and pecans; homemade caramels dipped in milk or semisweet chocolate; maraschino cherries in milk, white, or semisweet chocolate; milk or semisweet meltaways in pecan or plain; premier truffles of pure chocolate or flavored with liquor; and almond or pecan bark in milk, white, or semisweet chocolate. Almost all chocolates are made on the premises, except for some specialty items such as creams and chocolate boxes. Hard candies are from outside purveyors.

Linda prepares holiday specials on Christmas and Valentine's Day, and during Mesilla's hot summers, she uses cold packs to prevent her fine chocolates from melting. Her confections contain no waxes or preservatives. A second store is located in Vista Village, Las Cruces.

J. Eric Chocolatier, Inc., 304 Calle Guadalupe, Old Mesilla, 88046; (505) 526-2744; Vista Village, 3850 Foothills Road, Las Cruces, 88011; (505) 522-3456; www.j-eric.com.

Dining

Conti's Restaurant and Wine Bar

Those who have complained of the lack of fine dining in Las Cruces have obviously not discovered Conti's Restaurant and Wine Bar in Commerce Center. Opened in December of 2002 in the same space that had housed the well-known Millennium Restaurant, Conti's offers the highest level of dining, service, and culinary presentation.

Beth Conti, a California transplant and a graduate of a California school of culinary arts and hospitality, is the force behind the restaurant. Her chef, Alex Sanchez, studied under Martin Rios at the Old House in Santa Fe. Everything is made in house: soups, stocks, sauces, breads, and dessert—even the ice cream and sorbets. Beth calls their approach "new American cuisine," which she defines as fusion of southwestern and Asian with some Italian and French thrown in for good measure.

The menu changes seasonally. In summer, you might start with Mediterranean Crab Cakes of stone and snow crab with field greens and aioli or perhaps a bruschetta with shrimp, garlic, Limoncello, and chives on toasted bread. Maybe you'd like to try their Wild Mushroom Soup en Croute, an unctuous combination of porcini, white, portobello, and crimini mushrooms in a vegetable stock enriched with cream.

Conti's prides itself in its fish presentation, and one of their best-selling entrées is pan-seared halibut with blood orange vinaigrette and a spinach and pancetta salad. The chef uses organic and local products whenever possible.

Except for the penne and linguine, which they purchase fresh, all pastas are made in house. The Wild Mushroom Cannelloni is a marvel—white, field, porcini, and portobello mushrooms moistened with Marsala wine, wrapped in a delicate crêpe, and bathed in a silky white Romano sauce.

Desserts are stunning presentations as appealing to the eye as the taste. The summer menu lists Crème Brûlée, Lemon Tart with fresh berries, Strawberry Shortcake with lemon verbena cream, Liquid Chocolate Cake (think a chocolate volcano), and house-made ice cream and sorbet.

Conti's is open for lunch and dinner. Monthly wine dinners are scheduled with an occasional national figure such as Walter Schug presiding. In addition, Chef Alex conducts monthly four-course demonstration cooking classes in the restaurant's Gathering Room. Closed Sunday.

Conti's Restaurant and Wine Bar, 1120 Commerce Drive, Las Cruces, 88011; (505) 522-7777; www.contisrestaurant.com.

Double Eagle/Peppers Restaurant

Prepare yourself to be stupefied if you've reserved a dinner table at the Double Eagle on Old Mesilla Plaza. Upon passing through the post–Civil War, 1,000-pound cast-iron and gilded gates, you will be dazzled by the glittering gilded Baccarat crystal chandelier, the jewel tones of tens of stained glass panels, the proliferation of priceless antiques, and the collection of monumental oil paintings, some quite naughty.

There are two restaurants sharing the same building. The first is the Double Eagle with its sumptuous, turn-of-the century rooms, and the second is Peppers, an informal restaurant with southwestern cuisine. Peppers's menu is available on the Billy the Kid Patio with its fountain and plant-filled atrium and in the Juarez Room with its Mexican theme.

The Double Eagle specializes in classic continental cuisine served up with an elegant backdrop. The building has been recognized by the U.S. Department of the Interior as the oldest structure on the historic plaza and has been placed on the National Register of Historic Places as significant for both historical and architectural reasons. First constructed in the late 1840s by original owners Señor and Señora Maes, the building remained a private resident for decades. Through the years, it served many purposes, and in the 1950s, it was abandoned for a time.

In 1972, Robert O. Anderson restored it, narrowly preserving it from the wrecking ball. Finally in 1984 a major restoration was undertaken by the present owner, C. W. "Buddy" Ritter, a fifth-generation Mesilla descendent. The exposed patio was covered, the building fitted with modern heating and air-conditioning, and the "back porch" enclosed to produce the sumptuous Isabela Ballroom. The massive antiques and heroic paintings were collected by the well-known designer John Meigs, who also designed the décor for the Tinney Restaurant in Tinney, the Lodge in Cloudcroft, and the Maria Theresa in Albuquerque's Old Town.

The Maximilian Room is truly the max with its tin ceiling covered in 18-carat gold. Meigs's original plans called for 24-carat, but when Anderson discovered his decorator's extravagance it is not known whether he first grabbed his heart, his wallet, or Meigs's throat. The single 24-carat square Meigs applied may still be seen, outshining its less valuable brethren. Huge Baccarat crystal chandeliers light the room that also incorporates a music balcony with a gold-leafed brass-railing cast in the lyre pattern. Tiffany-style stained glass panels over the double doors are further embellishments.

If you can put the décor at the back of your mind for a minute, you'll remember the Double Eagle is a restaurant, not merely a museum. How's the food? Have no fear. It lives up to its surroundings.

First courses might include their southwestern Tortilla Bisque soup, a salad, or an order of their crispy Green-Chile Cheese Wontons with their refreshing salsa of pineapple, red and green pepper, and jalapeños. Perhaps you'd favor their Smoked Salmon on sourdough points, topped with minced purple onion and capers and garnished with sour cream.

Double Eagle's specialty is beef, and their signature dish is the Chateaubriand Bouquetiere for two, center-cut tenderloin broiled to your order, caressed in a béarnaise and special mushroom Marsala sauce, and presented and carved tableside. If you wish to order solo, try the New York Strip steak, the Filet Mignon in six, 10, and 18 ounces, or the Top Sirloin. There are 14 individual sauces to enhance the flavor of your steak, from a simple béarnaise to a bourbon peppercorn bordelaise.

Other popular entrées include Friday and Saturday nights' Prime Rib, Chipotle Shrimp in red-chile butter sauce, Pork Tenderloin with a raspberry-jalapeño glaze, and Veal Tenderloin braised and served over baby spinach sautéed with garlic and prosciutto and topped with Chianti red wine–mushroom sauce. As a gesture to the Southwest, the Plato Rio Grande has a petite filet mignon with red-chile sauce, a three-cheese chile relleno, a green-chile chicken enchilada, and their special black beans Santa Fe.

Chef Laruo Campos prepares a pasta of the day, and there's a full complement of seafood and poultry dishes from Scallops Saint Jacques to Chicken Jerusalem, a breast sautéed in butter with fresh garlic, shallots, and Fumé Blanc wine, capped with artichoke hearts and whole mushrooms.

The signature dessert is their Bananas Enchiladas, crêpes filled with fresh bananas, bathed in a confection of maple syrup and pecans, and graced with a scoop of vanilla bean ice cream.

The Peppers menu, which is available for lunch and dinner, is strictly southwestern (N.B.: in spite of their proximity, you cannot divide a table's orders between Peppers's and Double Eagle's menus). You'll find a couple of the same dishes on both menus, but that's the exception. Peppers serves tapas including their Ceviche Mesilla, shrimp and whitefish cold-cooked in lime juice and served with cucumbers, cilantro, jalapeños, and tomatoes. Other appetizers include a Tularosa Taco Salad and Tortilla Soup, and entrées embrace favorites such as their special Rellenos in Tomatillo Green-Chile Sauce and spicy Shrimp Enchiladas. Specialty sandwiches and burgers also are available. Save room for dessert, especially their out-of-the-ordinary Capirotada, a Mexican bread pudding with apples, coconut, raisins, and a brandy cream sauce. Everything is made in the Double Eagle kitchens except for their Death by Chocolate dessert. As general manager Jerry Harrell says, "Our supplier is so good we decided not to fool with perfection."

Double Eagle/Peppers Restaurant, 2355 Calle de Guadalupe, Mesilla, 88046; (505) 523-6700; www.doubleeagledining.com.

International Delights Café

International Delights Café is that happy combination of a restaurant serving Mediterranean food and a grocery where ingredients for home cooks may be found. Owner Abdelahfatah Hafassa opened it in September 1998 "to arouse [customers'] taste buds while enjoying a pleasant dining atmosphere."

Located in the corner of a mall next to Albertsons supermarket, the café's exterior is welcoming with its fountain, arches, and outdoor seating area. The interior is divided into two dining rooms and the grocery. Customers order at the counter, and their choices are delivered to their tables. Above the pastry counter clocks keep track of the time in Algiers, Las Cruces, France, Colombia, Turkey, Kenya, Greece, Italy, and Morocco. Balalaikas, Turkish hookahs, and copper pots compete for attention.

When you place your order, you will be tempted with the large selection of baklava made with your choice of walnuts, pecans, or pistachios. Every day there is a special soup and hot entrée. Lentil soup is always on tap plus Greek salad, Machoula salad (marinated roasted bell peppers, tomatoes, and onions), and hummus (a puree of chickpeas and tahini), baba ghanouj (roasted eggplant, tahini, and lemon), tabbouleh (parsley and cracked wheat mixed with tomatoes and green onions), and dolma (grape leaves stuffed with rice and marinated in olive oil and lemon). There are several specialty plates: falafel, gyro, *kebsa* (lamb shank, rice, and Greek salad), lamb couscous (lamb shank with vegetables on a bed of steamed couscous), or *mezza*, a sampler. Chicken, shrimp, or lamb kabobs are available from the grill.

International Delights Café, 1245 El Paseo Road (on the corner of Brazito Plaza), Las Cruces, 88001; (505) 647-5956; www.internationaldelightscafe.com.

Lemongrass Thai Cuisine

It may be a typical hot Las Cruces summer day, but when you walk into Lemongrass Thai Cuisine, you enter a cool, more peaceful world. Kimberly Ming's spacious and elegant restaurant in Hadley Center is an oasis of muted earth tones of beige, taupe, and black. Asian accents are refined and sophisticated.

Kimberly is a native of Bangkok, and when she arrived in the States, she opened the Ming Palace, a Thai and Chinese restaurant, which flourished from 1982 until 1993. After a five-year hiatus, she launched Lemongrass using her accumulated expertise and cooks from her native Thailand.

The menu calls upon the classics: Gai Gaprow (basil chicken), Pananag (rich red curry), Goong Pad Pak (jade shrimp), and of course, Pad Thai, thin rice noodles pan fried with eggs, crushed chile, bean sprouts, fried tofu, and chives and topped with ground peanuts, crispy shallots, and your choice of shrimp or chicken. Many dishes are vegetarian, and many can be made using vegetarian substitutes such as tofu, soy gluten, or shitake mushrooms.

Appetizers run from Mieng Kum, leaf wrapped savories, to the Ha Sa Hai, a five-of-a-kind combo with coconut shrimp, spring rolls, green-chile egg roll, crab Rangoon, and golden chicken wings. Their signature soup is Tom Uum Goong, a hot and sour shrimp soup with straw mushrooms in a lemongrass, galangal, and Kaffir lime leaf broth, accented with cilantro, green onion, and roasted chile paste.

All the traditional beverages including Emerald Cream Soda, Sparkling

Ruby, and Thai iced coffee and tea are available, and desserts can be seasonal, for example sticky rice with mango or Thai pumpkin custard.

If you are in Las Cruces on a Saturday evening, be sure to stop in for their Mongolian barbecue, where you select the ingredients and the chef prepares them for you over the specially constructed unit at the rear of the dining area.

Lemongrass Thai Cuisine, 2540 El Paseo Road, Las Cruces, 88001; (505) 523-8778.

Lorenzo's de Mesilla Ristorante Italiano

Perhaps you harbor certain reservations when considering an Italian restaurant. You may have been the victim of soggy pasta, red sauce with enough oregano to blister your tonsils, and bread slathered with margarine and garlic salt. Lorenzo's de Mesilla puts all your fears to rest.

Owner Lorenzo Liberto doesn't try any fancy culinary tricks. Using many of his grandmother's recipes from Sicily, he is very good at what he does. The restaurant buys the best quality imported dried pasta and cooks it perfectly al dente. The flatbread is baked fresh several times a day. The romaine salad greens are crisp and clad in a light herbal dressing. The carbonara sauce is not cloying but light and creamy. The red sauce sings of acid-balanced fresh tomatoes and just a hint of spice.

You have your choice of appetizers including fried calamari; salads such as a combo of artichoke hearts, dry meats, mozzarella, mushrooms, and green onions; and all varieties of pizzas from *formaggio* to the Mesilla Valley Special with green chile, pepperoni, mushrooms, olives, green onions, and jalapeños. Pastas run from six types of ravioli, including lobster, to Italian *paste* in many varieties. Cannelloni, eggplant Parmigiano and green chile, and meat lasagna are always on the menu, as is a seafood selection ranging from fresh sautéed sea scallops to Fettuccini al Salmone with thin sliced smoked salmon in a crème sauce. Daily specials are recited by your waitperson. If you're fortunate, you might reserve a table the evening they're serving linguine with fresh mushrooms and pepper flakes. Divine!

Lorenzo's is located in the new Mesilla Mercado, on NM 28 a short distance off the old plaza. The interior décor is a tasteful salute to Italy with a large mural of the early Roman countryside backing the service bar and window treatments of city-themed painted valences. Open lunch and dinner daily.

Lorenzo's de Mesilla Ristorante Italiano, 1750 Calle de Mercado, Suite #4, Las Cruces, 88005; (505) 525-3170; www.lorenzosdemesilla.com.

Mix Pacific Rim Cuisine

Tatsu Miyazaki has been a prominent figure in the Las Cruces restaurant scene with his namesake restaurant, Tatsu, and his work with the Purple Sage at the New Mexico Farm and Ranch Heritage Museum, Saffron, and Way Out West. Sadly, Tatsu and Saffron have closed their doors, but there's a new star on the horizon, and it's Mix Pacific Rim Cuisine, owned by Tatsu's brother, Haruya Miyazaki, and his wife, Chiaki. Both trained under Tatsu, he worked with them in developing the concept of Mix.

Not a large space, Mix is exquisitely decorated starting with the bronze door handles in the shape of carps. Upon entering, you face a curved rust-enhanced iron screen with slender reed outcroppings. Walls are painted in gilded shades of stone and taupe, and the sushi bar is slashed with banners inscribed with Japanese calligraphy. Black lacquer tables are deep laminated with an amalgamation of chopsticks, coins, good luck charms, rice dishes, old photos, and more. Tiny high-intensity lights hang from the rafters on thin wires.

Voted the "Best Asian Restaurant" by *Las Cruces Sun-News* in 2001 and 2002, Mix represents all countries of the Pacific Rim. You'll find dishes from Thailand, Japan, China, Korea, Vietnam, and Australia, as well as the Hawaiian Islands. Of course, there's a complete selection of sashimi and *negri* sushi from the sushi bar.

Appetizers include fresh Vietnamese Spring Rolls, Ribs Chinois in a Polynesian barbecue sauce, Baked New Zealand Mussels, and Malaysian Chicken Satay, to name a few. Salads range from a Sesame-Seared Tuna with mixed greens to Char-Grilled Salmon and Skin with mixed greens and a jalapeño dressing. Bento boxes with various combinations of *maki, nigiri,* and *inari* sushi are listed, as are both Thai and Tokyo curries. Seafood specials range from Kaki Fry (breaded oysters with an apple and Worcestershire sauce served with wasabi mashed potatoes and stir-fried vegetables) to Fresh Swordfish fried in tempura batter with a spicy ginger sauce. No Mix menu would be complete without the noodle dishes, Pad Thai (rice noodles with grilled shrimp and chicken and lemon-lime vinaigrette), Fusion Noodle (rice noodles with tempura shrimp and tamarind sauce), or Mix Noodle (stir-fried soba noodles with your choice of vegetables, chicken, beef, or shrimp topped with crispy wontons and Japanese *nori*).

Dinner entrées run the gamut of countries of origin. Korean Bulugogi is marinated beef, seafood, or shrimp sautéed with an Asian barbecue sauce; Japanese Ebi Fry is pecan-breaded shrimp with chile tartar sauce; and Australian Steak Wrap is fresh asparagus wrapped with grilled New York steak.

If you still have room for dessert, try their tíramisu, Banana Spring Rolls (bananas wrapped, fried, and sprinkled with cinnamon and sugar, topped with ice cream), or their Frio Grande, tempura-fried green tea ice cream. Open lunch and dinner. Closed Sunday.

Mix Pacific Rim Cuisine, 1001 East University Avenue, Las Cruces, 88001; (505) 532-2042; www.nm-mix.com.

La Posta de Mesilla

Like its neighbor the Double Eagle and most of the early buildings on the plaza, La Posta de Mesilla was constructed in the 1840s of adobe brick in the Territorial style, with the north and west sides of the building retaining the Greek Revival pediments. It is listed on the National Register of Historic Buildings. Sam Bean and his more famous brother, Judge Roy, operated a freight and passenger service line from the property to the mining community of Pinos Altos in the 1850s, and after the Civil War, the La Posta Compound was an important stop of the Butterfield Stagecoach Line.

The building had other owners and served various purposes until Katy Griggs Camunez bought the property in 1939 and transformed it into a restaurant. After Katy's death, a great niece, Jerean Camunez Hutchinson, and her husband, Tom, aka "Hutch," acquired La Posta. They continue to maintain the cuisine and ambiance Katy made famous.

The 10,000-square-foot building is a warren of rooms. The entry, or *zaguán*, houses a New Mexico chile shop, a small dress shop, and a jeweler. The atrium contains an aviary, a large cage filled with parrots, macaws, and a cockatoo. Several very large red piranhas swim in aquariums, and the Oriental goldfish are separate but equal in their own tank. One of the most popular rooms has a huge wall embedded with lava stone and webbed with green plants. Fountains tinkle from one nook or another.

Check out the bar with its stained glass window portraying a run of the Butterfield Stage with the Organ Mountains in the background. More than 100 varieties of tequila are stocked, and you have to try their Chile Rita, a margarita made with tequila, lime juice, Cointreau, and just a dash of Besito Caliente, a locally made syrup of blackberries and habañero peppers. Maybe you'd prefer their spicy Bloody Maria, vodka and tomato juice with a generous zing of La Posta's red salsa.

The menu has many recipes handed down through the years from the Fountain, Chavez, and Griggs families, and customers firmly reject any attempts at turning good New Mexican food into nouvelle or fusion anything. Kitchen help has seniority. In fact, cook Conchita Flores has been with La Posta for 40 years.

House specialties include the Tostada Compuesta, which first came on the menu in 1939. The dish consists of a toasted corn tortilla cup filled with frijoles, red chile con carne, and topped with chopped lettuce, diced tomatoes, and grated cheddar cheese. Another favorite is the Sour Cream Enchilada, corn tortillas smothered with green-chile sauce, topped with grated Monterey Jack cheese and sour cream.

Of course there is all order of tacos, burritos, chimichangas, enchiladas, rellenos, and combination plates. Burgers and charbroiled steaks complete the entrées, and desserts run from flan to fruit empanadas. **La Posta de Mesilla, 2410 Calle de San Albino, Mesilla, 88046; (505) 524-3524; www.laposta-de-mesilla.com.**

Specialty Food Stores

CULINARY NEW MEXICO

International Delights

(See "Dining.")

Stahmann's Country Store

In 1932 Deane Stahmann planted 4,000 acres with pecan trees in the fertile Mesilla Valley. Through the years, the Stahmanns became the largest pecan producing family in the United States, and when Deane's son planted 2,000 acres in Australia, the family became the largest pecan producing family in the world. Today two varieties are harvested, the Western Schley and the Bradley, both known for a high-quality yield and a soft shell. The farm produces between 8 and 10 million pounds of nuts a year and uses no chemical insecticides, relying on green and black aphids to control natural predators.

Stahmanns' products range from roasted and unroasted pecans to candies, fudge, pecan logs, and gift baskets. During non-harvest season, tours of the shelling and candy plants take guests through the process of preparing the candy and nuts for market.

Driving through the shady groves and stopping at their Country Store on NM 28 south of Old Mesilla makes a pleasant excursion. Or you can visit their store on Old Mesilla Plaza, their outlet at the New Mexico Farm and Ranch Heritage Museum, or order online. **Stahmann's Country Store, 22505 South Highway 28, La Mesa, 88044; (800) 654-6887 or (505) 526-8974; www.stahmanns.com.**

Zen Oriental Market

Zen Oriental Market is owned by Haruya and Chiaki Miyazaki (see Mix Pacific Rim Cuisine under "Dining"). It is located next to the restaurant and stocks Asian spices, fresh sushi, sushi-grade seafood, groceries, and housewares. **Zen Oriental Market, 1001 East University Ave, D-3, Las Cruces, 88001; (505) 532-5553.**

Silver City

Looking east from the hills of Silver City, you catch a glimpse of the rock formation called the Kneeling Nun keeping watch over the huge terraced hole in the ground, which is the Chino copper mine. Minerals, especially copper and high-grade chloride silver, were the lure that originally brought miners and later settlers to this remote region tucked in between the Mogollon Mountains, the Black Range, and the Gila Wilderness.

Later came the railroads, telephone service, and a college, now Western New Mexico University. The town grew during the early Victorian Age, and that period's brick and mortar are still evident in the many early Territorial-style homes.

Today Silver City still retains an air of its Victorian past, from the city museum to University Hill. Bullard, the main street, is lined with restaurants, stores, and gift shops. It replaced what was then the prime commercial thoroughfare after the Flood of 1825 swept through the city's heart, turning Main Street into a giant ditch 35 feet below street level. The Civilian Conservation Corps built dams on the stream in the 1930s, and now, green and lush, it is Big Ditch Park.

Today the city's well-deserved reputation for excellent climate and a vibrant arts community has lured both travelers and retirees. In addition, it is the jumping off place for attractions such as the Gila Cliff Dwellings National Monument, the old mining community of Pinos Altos, City of Rocks State Park, Lake Roberts, the Cat Walk, and Mogollon Ghost Town.

Coffee Roaster and Café

A.I.R. Coffee Company

A.I.R. Coffee and the coffeehouse have been fixtures in Silver since Halloween of '93. The gaily painted old storefront houses a coffee bar amid the sprawl of mismatched tables, chairs, and varying degrees of caffeine-stoked residents. The sidewalk tables facing Yankie Street provide a place to consume your java, dig into one of their homemade pastries, and watch the parade of visitors filter in and out of the street's art galleries.

The actual coffee roasting is done at the plant in Bayard where they prepare their blends: the Jaguar, the Lioness, the Kodiak, and the Llama. Jaguar is their most popular and is the foundation for all espresso beverages. It consists of organic coffee from Colombia, organic Gayoland Sumatra, organic estate coffee from El Cerro in Costa Rica, and Monsoon Malabar from the east coast of India.

Lioness is a blend of African selections; the Kodiak Organic has Guatemalan, Sumatran, and Colombian beans; and the Llama is a decaf using organic Peruvian beans and the Swiss water process. Owner Jacqueline Shaw is extremely proud to be one of only four New Mexico roasters to be certified organic. Coffee is available through their Web site or by the pound at the coffeehouse.

A.I.R. Coffee Company, 112 West Yankie Street, Silver City, 88061; (866) 892-3009 or (505) 388-5952; www.aircoffee.biz.

CULINARY
NEW MEXICO

Dining

Café Un Mundo

It's a gas station, it's a transmission shop, no, it's Café Un Mundo, a neat little eatery in a morphed garage. When Julie Good and partner Manuel Martinez bought the building, it was in sad need of repair. Fortunately, Julie's dad is in construction, and with his help, they transformed the wreck into a surprisingly chic little café.

The former auto bay is the main dining room, with steel and wood tables and chairs. Carpeting and walls are soft lavender. There's a handsome oak juice bar for smoothies and health drinks.

Julie's specialty is her soups, which she artfully crafts from available ingredients and her own fertile imagination. "All our foods are flavor driven," she says. "We don't do bland." The lunch menu also includes fresh salads and sandwiches on homemade rolls with sides of hummus or salsa. Breakfast is a choice of omelets, eggs, or an egg or tofu burrito. Closed Sunday.

Café Un Mundo, 700 North Bullard, Silver City, 88061; (505) 534-4406.

Diane's

If you were to ask anyone in Silver City where to go for fine dining, they undoubtedly would say "Diane's" without reservation. Opened as a bakery in 1997 by Diane Holloway, the business has grown into a very popular eatery patronized by both locals and travelers.

Diane's credentials are impressive. From the humble beginnings as a graduate of Albuquerque's Technical Vocational Institute, she rose to the position of pastry chef for the prestigious Ritz Carlton in Hawaii. Currently, Diane's son Bohdi Werber is co-managing and acting as chef. Bohdi did his apprenticeship in the northern California wine country and on the island of Maui.

When discussing the business, Bohdi says, "We're always looking to progress, both in the menu and in the ambiance of our dining rooms. If you were to describe our food, I'd have to say we're a blend of many, a fusion of European, Pacific Rim, and, of course, a touch of New Mexican."

Popular dinner entrées are their Crab Cakes served crispy with jicama salad and chipotle dipping sauce; Thai Coconut Curry with assorted seafood and Asian vegetables in a spicy coconut and green curry sauce; or the Lemon Chicken, a large, juicy breast served with fettuccine Alfredo and smothered in rich citrus caper gravy.

Breakfast specials include all types of omelets and eggs. Especially toothsome is their Hatch Benedict, chile cheddar toast with a thin slice of ham and cheddar and two poached eggs topped with hollandaise sauce and fresh salsa. Chiles show up again in a lunch favorite, Green-Chile Alfredo, Hatch green chile in a Parmesan cream sauce with fettuccine.

With Diane's expertise, you can expect spectacular desserts; her Mildred Pierce chocolate cake brings gasps with its size and super chocolate flavor. Actual measurement of the uncut pastry is 12 inches in diameter and more than six inches in height. Her white cakes are equally impressive.

Restaurant décor is simple: two dining rooms with seating for 93. A garden theme is carried throughout, and in winter, a gas-fired stove adds to the ambiance. Closed Monday.

Diane's, 510 North Bullard Street, Silver City, 88061; (505) 538-8722.

Jalisco Café

If you're searching for good home-style Mexican food in Silver, you can't go wrong at the Jalisco Café, owned and operated by the Mesa family from Guadalajara since 1984. The restaurant has moved once from its original location at the corner of Texas and Spring Streets, but it has been at its current location since 1989.

The block-long building, built in 1923, has housed a variety of establishments, including a CCC infirmary during the 1940s. It is easy to see how the multiple dining areas once housed storefronts that are now joined to create the 108-seat restaurant. Jalisco's is clean and cheerful with its buff-colored walls delineated by a chair rail embossed with hand-painted stencils.

The chef is Michael Mesa, a Culinary Institute graduate. His father, George, is manager. Their menu is typical Mexican, reflecting the family's

Jalisco roots. Their "bowl of green" is one of the best, filled with hunks of beef and chile and bathed in a rich, savory sauce. It's served with or without beans—your call.

Chile is more than featured. It is elevated to a work of culinary art. In fact, the menu warns, "The Jalisco Café specializes in red and green chile. Our chile is spicy so we recommend that if you're not familiar with your choices that you ask for a taste tester before placing your order." A bit of preprandial salsa and chips illustrates their point. It's not incendiary, but close.

Every green chile is fire roasted on the premises, and in 1999, they processed 28,000 pounds. This assures a consistent product, and consistency is a byword at Jalisco's. Their red-chile sauce is made from sun-dried pods, not powder, giving it more richness and depth.

Menu changes are planned to include more steaks and seafood, but you can always count on these to be seasoned with a touch of Mexico. Closed Sunday.

Jalisco Café, 100 South Bullard, Silver City, 88061; (505) 388-2060.

Shevek and Mi

When you enter Shevek and Mi (formerly Pinon Café & Bakery) you know imaginative minds have been at work. Big blue patio umbrellas hang from the ceiling like psychedelic morning glories, and the minimal art decorating the white walls is a pole festooned with ceramic representations of men's ties of every color and design. A second room contains floor-to-ceiling bookcases and has the intimate atmosphere of a library. The effect is both funky and sophisticated.

Chef Shevek Barnhart and front-of-the-house manager Mike Barnhart are the individuals responsible for bringing this welcome bistro to Silver. Shevek has had 32 years in the restaurant business, having worked at a variety of prestigious establishments such as the Moosewood Restaurant in Ithaca, New York, the Quilted Giraffe in New York City's SoHo, the Ivy Inn in Charlottesville, Virginia, and early in his career, at New York's Russian Tea Room.

The menu changes periodically, and at review time was especially strong in Italian cuisine as attested to by entrées such as Porcini Mushroom Ravioli in light basil cream sauce, Chicken Marsala, and Tuscan Pork Loin. Shevek's Chicken Ashke has been copyrighted. It's a lightly curried, grilled chicken breast wrapped in smoked Atlantic salmon and topped with béarnaise sauce and fresh scallions.

Future menu additions will lean more to pan-Mediterranean cuisine melding Portuguese, Spanish, French, Italian, and Greek dishes. Shevek will also experiment with some Middle Eastern items.

Shevek and Mi is the first Silver City restaurant to be chosen for the AAA Guide. It has a comprehensive wine and beer list with specials featured every three months. Open breakfast, lunch, and dinner.

Shevek and Mi (formerly Pinon Café & Bakery), 602 North Bullard, Silver City, 88061; (505) 534-9168; www.silver-eats.com.

Vicki's Eatery

Vicki's Eatery is a little hole in the wall café-*cum*-patio on Yankie Street. During the restaurant's six years in business, both locals and visitors have learned that it lives up to its credo: "We are dedicated to preparing your meal using the freshest, most minimally processed ingredients from the most local sources we are able to locate."

Breakfast might feature French toast made from La Brea Bakery's nutty organic whole-grain bread with maple syrup or apple–black currant chutney or Vicki's special Gold Dust, two eggs on a biscuit smothered in sausage gravy.

The lunch menu has soups, salads, sandwiches, and hot entrées. Favorites include the Mediterranean salad of greens dressed with sun-dried tomato vinaigrette and topped with feta, calamata olives, mushrooms, and artichokes and served with hummus and dolmas, or Stormy's Sandwich, turkey, provolone, guacamole, cucumber, and sprouts on a kaiser roll.

On the dinner menu you might discover a portobello mushroom stuffed with caramelized onions, spinach, feta, provolone, ricotta, and red bell pepper served over pasta with marinara sauce and garnished with toasted pine nuts. Brats grilled and served with seasoned sauerkraut and German potato salad is another choice and reflects the years owner Vicki Sontheim spent in Europe.

All desserts are homemade, and the list runs from Pineapple Upside Down Cake to Bee Sting, filo pastry layered with whipped cream and topped with brown sugar, almonds, and honey. Open for breakfast and lunch. Dinners served Friday and Saturday from Memorial Day to Labor Day. Closed Sunday in winter.

Vicki's Eatery, 107 West Yankie Street, Silver City, 88061; (505) 388-5430.

CULINARY
NEW MEXICO

Ice Cream

Alotta Gelato

Silver City may have the only gelato store in New Mexico. Alotta Gelato on North Bullard stocks a variety of flavors including the delicious Romeo and Juliet, vanilla crème with dark chocolate chunks; Dulce de Leche; and Chocolate Hazelnut, among others. Their lactose-free fruit flavors come in a rainbow of colors and tastes.

Planned expansion includes serving desserts and the sale of bulk candy.

Alotta Gelato, 619 North Bullard, Silver City, 88061; (505) 534-4995; www.alottagelato.com.

Specialty Food store

Silver City Food Co-op

Residents of Silver City are indeed fortunate to have the co-op in their community. The 2,000-square-foot store specializes in high-quality organic produce, rBGH-free dairy products, healthful groceries, bulk foods, and herbs, supplements, and natural body care products.

Unlike some co-ops, this operation serves the entire community, not merely its members. Founded in 1974, its longevity attests to its importance in the area. It is the first independent grocery in New Mexico to be certified organic. Customers can be assured that all staff is trained in preserving the integrity of the store's organic products. Closed Sunday.

Silver City Food Co-op, 520 North Bullard, Silver City, 88061; (505) 388-2343; www.silvercityfoodcoop.com.

Wine Shop

The Twisted Vine

A wine bar in Silver City is a most unusual endeavor, but on the corner of Broadway and Bullard, the Twisted Vine occupies a mellow space. Owned by Jim Kolb, the former art gallery has been transformed into a chic blend of gourmet grocery and purveyor of New Mexico wines.

The front room contains shelves filled with gourmet goodies while the side room houses the wine bar and comfortable seating arrangements. There's a lovely deck overlooking the Big Ditch for alfresco sipping.

Tastings are free, and wines are available by the glass or bottle. Open noon to 10:00 P.M. daily.

The Twisted Vine, 108 East Broadway, Silver City, 88061; (505) 388-2828.

Socorro

If you're approaching the southwest from Interstate 25, you'll pass the exits to Socorro, a staging ground for a visit to the Bosque del Apache National Wildlife Refuge and its yearly Festival of the Cranes. Socorro once was a stopping grounds for the Juan de Oñate expedition on its way to establishing a colony in Santa Fe. The Piro Indian villagers gave the wanderers food and shelter, and the Spanish left behind two Franciscan priests who established the mission of San Miguel and named the place Nuertra Señora de Perpetus Socorro. Later it was simplified to Socorro, which means "help" or "aid" in Spanish.

Brewery and Brewpub

Socorro Springs Brewing Company

Mic and Molley Heynekamp dreamed of opening a restaurant and brew house even as Molley was finishing her thesis at New Mexico Tech in Socorro. The subject of the work was, of course, a restaurant business plan. In October 1999, they found the old Juan Jose Baca House a block off the plaza and went to work with the tedious job of restoring the old mercantile, which had sustained heavy fire damage. In 2003, listening to their customers' "want lists," they built a new restaurant on Socorro's main drag. The southwestern-style adobe building has the same wood-fired pizza oven and grill as the original restaurant, but its larger kitchen space allows for an expanded menu, adding more pasta and grilled dishes. The bar and dining area are separate and are divided by an interior courtyard. The bar has a viewing window so customers can watch the brewing process, and the dining room has an open kitchen with a family atmosphere.

The menu is typical pub food with daily specials, soup, salad, sandwiches, and wood-oven fired pizzas, lasagna, and calzones. Their beers and ales are sold only at the restaurant, but you can purchase a half-gallon jug called a growler to take home and refill. The selection runs from their most popular Pick Axe Indian Pale Ale, with lots of maltiness, strong hop aroma, and a balanced bitterness, to Prohibition Stout, the first beer commercially brewed in Socorro since Prohibition and the brewery's version of classic dry Irish Stout.

Socorro Springs Brewing Company, 1012 California Street, Socorro, 87801; (505) 838-0650; www.socorrosprings.com.

CULINARY
NEW MEXICO

Dining

Martha's Black Dog Café

Just off Kittrel Plaza, Martha's Black Dog Coffeehouse is a sun-drenched café where you're likely to find an assortment of town regulars and savvy travelers ordering up what owner Martha Rimmel calls her "yuppie chow." The décor is basic, with mismatched tables and chairs and an abundance of plants. Walls are decked with work by local artists.

Defining her menu selections as "more raw than fried," Martha maintains she cooks what she likes, and that means "no turnips or peanut butter and jelly." What you will find is good, fresh, homemade food. Specialties include Steamed Blue Mussels in a garlic, wine, and tomato sauce; House-Smoked Turkey Breast with whole-cranberry chipotle chile mayonnaise, avocado, and cream cheese; and her notorious chocolate cake, "Dog Overboard." There are daily specials.

Martha describes her place as a coffeehouse morphing into a café. "A coffeehouse," she maintains, "is a quiet place with a limited menu where people can gather, read a book, or just relax. A café has a more extensive menu and a faster pace."

Martha's Black Dog Café, 110 Manzanares Avenue East, Socorro, 87801; (505) 838-0311.

Farmers' Markets

Las Cruces Farmers' Market, (mostly crafts), downtown mall, Wednesday and Saturday, 8:00 A.M. to 12:30 P.M., year-round, (505) 541-2556.

Mesilla Mercado on the Plaza, 2205 Avenida de Mesilla, Sunday, noon to 4:00 P.M., Thursday, 10:00 A.M. to 2:00 P.M., year-round, (505) 524-3262.

Silver City Farmers' Market, Downtown, 7th and Bullard, Saturdays, 8:30 A.M. to noon, Tuesdays at Gough Park, 5:00 P.M. to dusk, mid-May through late October, (505) 536-9681.

Socorro Farmers' Market, Socorro Plaza, Saturdays, 8:00 A.M. to sellout, Tuesdays, 5:00 to 7:00 P.M., July through October, (505) 838-0555.

Sunland Park Farmers' Market, Ardovino's Desert Crossing, Ardovino Drive, Friday, 7:00 to 11:00 A.M., May through October, (505) 589-0653.

Truth or Consequences Farmers' Market, three locations: Ralph Edwards Park, Saturday, 8:00 A.M. to noon; Route 195 in Elephant Butte near the near Post Office, Saturday, 7:00 to 11:00 A.M.; Charles Motel on Broadway, T or C, Tuesday, 8:00 A.M. to noon. Season: mid-July through mid-October, (505) 744-4747.

Wineries

Blue Teal Vineyards

Blue Teal Vineyards was founded in 1983 by Herve Lescombes and is still owned by the Lescombes family. Its wines are made entirely of grapes grown in New Mexico. Currently produced by sixth-generation winemaker Florent Lescombes, Blue Teal wine offers 11 varieties of still wine including Cabernet Sauvignon, Merlot, Chardonnay, and Sauvignon Blanc, plus three sparkling wines including their Imperial Kir, a delicate semisweet champagne flavored with raspberry liqueur. Popular dessert wines are Muscat and Ratafia.

Blue Teal specializes in hand-painted bottles, employing local artists to paint custom designs on champagne bottles for unique gifts. The winery has two tasting rooms, featuring free samples.

Blue Teal Vineyards, 1710 Avenida de Mesilla, Las Cruces, 88005; (505) 524-0390; Wines of the Southwest, 2641 Calle Guadalupe, Mesilla, 88046; (505) 524-2408; www.Southwestwines.com or www.blueteal.com.

Mademoiselle Vineyards

New Mexico grapes play the starring role in the wines of Mademoiselle Vineyards. In Mesilla they produce a Cabernet Sauvignon, Merlot,

Chardonnay, Muscat, Sauvignon Blanc, and more. Their tasting room is located inside the Old West Brewery.

> Mademoiselle Vineyards, 1710 Avenida de Mesilla, Las Cruces, 88005; (505) 524-2408; www.nmwine.net/mademoiselle.html.

St. Clair Winery

St. Clair is New Mexico's largest winery. Located in the Mimbres Valley, their high elevation of 4,500 feet creates warm days and cool nights. Currently 70 acres are planted with Cabernet Sauvignon, Chardonnay, Zinfandel, and other varietals. By 2005, they hope to have 100 acres in grapes. They have a 5,000-gallon production capacity.

Winery tours are available Saturdays and Sundays, and the tasting room for free samples is open daily. St. Clair also sells wine in bulk.

> St. Clair Winery, 1325 De Baca Road SE, Deming, 88030; (505) 546-1179; www.stclairvineyards.com or www.nmwine.net/stclair.html.

La Viña Winery

New Mexico's oldest winery has a new home in La Union, a section of Anthony just 30 minutes northwest of Las Cruces. La Viña covers 42 acres with 25 devoted to grapes for the production of varietals available only in New Mexico. Established in 1977, current owners Ken and Denise Stark have 10,000 feet dedicated to production facilities, tours, and tastings as well as a two-acre yard with room for festival celebrations.

Their output includes estate-bottled wines from plantings of Italian and Rhone grapes for Cabernet, Zinfandel, and Chardonnay.

> La Viña Winery, 4201 Highway 28, Anthony, 88021; (505) 882-7632; www.nmwine.net/lavina.html.

Events

Cuchillo Pecan Festival

February—The one-day event celebrates the New Mexico pecan with approximately 30 craft and four food vendors. A blacksmith, spinner, and weaver of rugs conduct demonstrations, and about 400 pecan pies are for sale. Attendance runs around 2,000. The proceeds go to the New Mexico Boys and Girls Ranches.

The Cuchillo Pecan Festival, 101 West Highway 52, Cuchillo; (505) 743-3201.

Southern New Mexico Wine Festival

Memorial Day Weekend—One of five special three-day festivals sponsored by the New Mexico Wine Growers Association brings together more than 20 wineries from across New Mexico. Tastings, live entertainment, gourmet food, and fun are the order of the day, with an arts show and a contingent of craftspeople and vendors of agricultural products to add to the festivities.

Here's your chance to sample a variety of vintages and speak with the vintners themselves. Wine is available for purchase by the glass, bottle, or case. The expected attendance is 10,000.

Southern New Mexico Wine Festival, Southern New Mexico Fairgrounds, Las Cruces; (505) 834-0101; www.nmwine.net.

Hatch Chile Festival

August—If you're a chile head, you need to go to Hatch on Labor Day weekend for their annual Chile Festival. A real celebratory atmosphere holds sway in this tiny town 30 miles northwest of Las Cruces. The Mesilla Valley abounds in agricultural products from pecans to cotton, but the crop for which it's best known is its famous green and red chile. More than 30,000 acres are under cultivation.

Arriving at the Hatch Airport you'll find food booths featuring pungent chile dishes: burritos, enchiladas, *gorditas, caldillo, chile verde con carne,* tacos, chile rellenos, and chile burgers. You can buy chile *ristras* and bulk chile in 40-pound bags ready for roasting. The delicious smell pervades the festival grounds.

The lively festival draws thousands of tourists from around the world and features a chile cookoff, arts and crafts, music, and a parade led by the newly crowned Ms. Chile. Carnival and pony rides keep the children amused, and an old-time fiddlers' contest is scheduled for the afternoon. Evening events feature a big barn dance at the airport.

Hatch Chile Festival, Hatch Airport, Highway 26, Hatch; (505) 541-2444.

Harvest Wine Festival

Labor Day Weekend—One of five special festivals sponsored by the New Mexico Wine Growers Association. See listing for Memorial Day.

Harvest Wine Festival, Southern New Mexico Fairgrounds, Las Cruces; (505) 834-0101; www.nmwine.com.

Hillsboro Apple Festival

Labor Day Weekend—Each Labor Day weekend the small ex–mining town of Hillsboro plays host to the Apple Festival. On display are a range of apple-related products from apple pies to apple jams to apple bread. The festival also draws a diverse assortment of visitors from area locals and out-of-town tourists to local and visiting bikers.

Hillsboro Apple Festival, NM Highway 152, Hillsboro; (505) 895-5686.

The Pie Festival

September—Little Pie Town comes alive every September with their annual Pie Festival. People from all over Catron County as well as a generous helping of visitors from all over come for the country breakfast at the firehouse, cowboy beef barbecue dinner, Old Time Fiddle Contest, pie eating contest, horny toad race, hot air balloon ascension, and of course, pie sampling. You might find a selection including blueberry, cherry, peach, apple crumb, peach crumb, apple, oatmeal walnut raisin, oatmeal pecan, pecan, and coconut, plus five or six cream pies.

Craft vendors line the town park, and there are children's games. A festival king and queen are crowned, and the results of the town pie-baking contest are announced.

Pie Festival, Lester Jackson Park, Pie Town; (505) 772-2525; www.pietown.org.

The Whole Enchilada Fiesta

September—Las Cruces is a happening place every year during the annual Whole Enchilada Fiesta. Continuous weekend-long entertainment is scheduled including a variety of music for street dancing, a

Harley Davidson fashion show, a rods and rides show (cars and bikes), and children's activities. A parade features more than 73 floats, 15 high school marching bands, 10 horse units, and nine walking units.

The preparation of the world's largest enchilada is the festival's high point. Local volunteers do the honors using 750 pounds of stone-ground corn for masa, 75 gallons of red-chile sauce, 175 pounds of grated cheese, 50 pounds of chopped onions, and 175 gallons of oil to cook the tortilla.

Whole Enchilada Fiesta, Downtown Mall, Las Cruces; (505) 524-7824; www.twefie.com or www.las-cruces.org.

St. Clair Wine Festival

October—This annual event features the wines of southwest New Mexico with food and craft vendors, live music, and a corkscrew competition. The entry fee covers free samples and a souvenir glass. St. Clair, St. Rita, Blue Teal, and Mademoiselle are several of the vineyards participating.

St. Claire Winery, 1325 De Baca Road SE, Deming; (505) 546-1179; www.stclairvineyards.com.

La Viña Wine Festival and Grape Stomp

October—La Viña's annual harvest festival features food, entertainment, and wine tasting. Ride the LaViña Wine Train around the orchard and try out the fine art of grape stomping. The admission charge includes a complimentary glass with six tastes of wine or a glass of wine of your choice.

La Viña Winery, 4201 Highway 28, Anthony; (505) 882-7632; www.nmwine.net/lavina.htm.

Recipes

Chile 'Rita

Courtesy of Las Posta de Mesilla, Mesilla

1 $^1/_2$ oz. Sauza Hornitos 100 percent blue agave tequila
$^1/_2$ oz. Cointreau
2 oz. Tavern Sweet and Sour Mix
$^1/_2$ oz. fresh-squeezed lime juice
$^1/_2$ oz Besito Caliente (blackberry habañero sauce. See note)

Combine Hornitos, Cointreau, sweet and sour, lime juice, and Besito Caliente with ice in a shaker. Shake lightly and pour into salted or unsalted margarita glass. Salud! Hot stuff for cool people!

Note: Besito Caliente is a product of the Truck Farm, Las Cruces, (800) A1-HONEY.

CULINARY
NEW MEXICO

Wild Mushroom Pâté

Courtesy of Chef Shevek Barnhart
Shevek and Mi, Silver City

2 porcini mushrooms
2 morels
2 chanterelles
2 oz. any other gourmet fresh dried mushroom available
$^1/_4$ lb. of butter
2 dried shitake mushrooms, ground in a food processor or coffee mill
1 oz. any dried mushroom available
$^1/_2$ cup sherry
$^1/_2$ Tbsp. fresh basil
$^1/_2$ Tbsp. minced garlic
1 tsp. brown sugar
1 tsp. salt
1 Tbsp. Hungarian paprika
1 sun-dried tomato

Roughly chop the porcinis, morels, chanterelles, and gourmet fresh dried mushrooms and sauté in butter for five minutes. Add the rest of the ingredients to the sautéed mushrooms. Poach until all the sherry is absorbed. Put into a food processor and blend until the consistency of caviar. Add $1/2$ tsp. black pepper and chill.

Serve with a fine crackers or crostini.

Diane's Green-Chile Fettuccine Alfredo

Courtesy of Chef Bohdi Werber
Diane's, Silver City

8 servings

8 C. heavy cream
$1/4$ C. fire roasted hot green chile
Splash of Worcestershire sauce
Salt and pepper
Fettuccine noodles for eight, boiled until al dente
1 $1/2$ C. freshly grated Parmesan cheese
Fresh chopped parsley

Place large saucepan on burner and put cream, green chile, and Worcestershire in the pan. Reduce liquid to about half (bubbles will start to thicken as liquid reduces). When reduction is complete, season to taste and add fettuccine noodles.

Toss mixture with pasta fork until pasta is warmed and sauce is thick. Finally, add Parmesan cheese. Toss. Top with additional Parmesan and chopped parsley. Serve right away!

Banana Enchiladas

Courtesy of Double Eagle Restaurant, Old Mesilla

2 servings

1 Tbsp. butter
1 C. pecans, large pieces or rough chopped
$1/8$ tsp. salt
1 C. maple syrup
1 C. Karo light corn syrup
4 crêpes
2 bananas, peeled and sliced into $1/2$-inch rounds
Vanilla bean ice cream
Whipped cream

Melt butter in a small sauté pan at medium heat, add pecans, and stir occasionally until toasted. Sprinkle with salt and set aside to cool. Heat maple syrup and Karo syrup in saucepan over low heat just until warm. Add pecans and stir well. Set aside.

On a dessert plate, line middle of crêpe with banana rounds and fold. Use two crêpes per plate. Top banana stuffed crêpes with a scoop of vanilla bean ice cream and spoon pecan sauce over top. Crown with whipped cream and serve.

Roswell's Aliens

Farm Stand
Ruidoso

Crash Down Diner
Roswell

Viva New Mexico
Ruidoso

SOUTHEAST NEW MEXICO:
OUTLAWS AND EXTRATERRESTRIALS

Home to legends such as Billy the Kid and little green men from the fabled UFO crash, New Mexico's southeast is a jumble of desert, plains, and high mountains. Ruidoso is a favorite destination in both summer and winter. The warm months find refugees from the heat of Texas, New Mexico, and Arizona fleeing to its cool summits and clear, bubbling creeks. In winter, the same cast favors the area for its skiing at Ski Apache, owned by the Mescalero Apache tribe and located on Sierra Blanca, the area's highest peak. The village itself is filled with galleries, boutiques, and a few restaurants worthy of merit.

Capitan, just a short drive from Ruidoso, is home to Smokey Bear, the Forest Service's durable symbol of fire safety, and the small state historical park named in his honor. It was in the nearby mountains on May 9, 1950, that a crew fighting the Los Tablos forest fire found a badly singed black bear cub clinging to the side of a burnt pine tree.

Roswell is best known for the 1947 UFO incident in which the U.S. Air Force issued a press release that stated a "flying saucer" had crashed in the area and debris had been found. The military later retracted its initial report, stating that the object actually was a weather balloon. No matter. There are still many believers in the extraterrestrials, and that lure brings visitors to Roswell, a desert town struggling with a depressed economy. Roswell's other claim to fame is the New Mexico Military Academy.

Ruidoso

Bakery

Cornerstone Bakery & Café

If your sweet tooth needs feeding, go on over to the Cornerstone Bakery & Café in the Gateway section of Ruidoso. Owner Delphine Salai is a classically trained pastry chef who has graced the kitchens of the Radisson Hotel in Austin and more recently the Inn of the Mountain Gods near Ruidoso. Her daily offerings include Italian cream cake, Key lime pies, strawberry chiffon cakes, tarts, éclairs, brownies, and other assorted goodies. She even has two Dr. Atkins–approved desserts: New York–style cheesecake and chocolate–peanut butter cookies.

Her breads number favorites such as French baguette, German dark rye, honey wheat, sourdough, and green chile–cheddar, not to mention her bagels and focaccia. To ensure depth of flavor, all yeast dough is begun with a starter (mother or biga).

The café serves breakfast and lunch featuring the bakery's fine breads, pastries, and their selection of European cheeses. The lunch menu always has a weekly special, a homemade soup, salads, quiches, and sandwiches. Special Atkins dishes are available. To keep customers apprised of specials, Delphine publishes a weekly newsletter, which she will fax to anyone requesting it.

Cornerstone Bakery & Café, 359 Sudderth Drive, Ruidoso, 88345; (505) 257-1842.

Coffee Roaster

Ruidoso Roastery and Espresso Bar

A block off Sudderth behind Mountain Arts Gallery, the Ruidoso Roastery and Espresso Bar perfumes the air with the rich aroma emanating from its big red roaster. The only trademarked "high altitude" roaster in the United States is housed in a 75-year-old log cabin among the ponderosas.

Linda and Clyde Stinnett have been lovingly toasting beans since purchasing the business from the previous owner in November 2001. Every other day they fire up the roaster to resupply their stock of 12 different blends. In addition, Linda bakes brownies, cranberry muffins, carrot-raisin muffins, and Scotties for her customers. Plans are to include takeout ceviche, tabbouleh, and pickled shrimp specialties.

Ruidoso Roastery and Espresso Bar, 113 Rio, Ruidoso, 88345; (505)257-3676; www.zianet.com/roastery/espress.htm.

CULINARY
NEW MEXICO

Dining

Le Bistro

At Le Bistro Richard Girot brings his years in the restaurant business to bear at his snug octagonal restaurant specializing in French country cuisine. A smaller and less ambitious undertaking than La Lorraine (see page 178), Le Bistro's menu concentrates on fresh meats and produce prepared simply.

"We try for honest cuisine and an honest price," Girot explains. "Everything is fresh here, all our soups and sauces are house made, and we buy quality meat. Even our wines are reasonable, none more than $25 a bottle." This must appeal to a great many customers if the profusion of bottles hanging from the rafters or the cork-filled front case is any indication.

The lunch menu features a variety of crêpes, a daily quiche, sandwiches such as French dip and *croque monsieur*, a luncheon steak, and of course, great desserts. An extensive dinner menu starts with Soupe à l'Oignon Gratinée, Saumon Fumé, Pâté de Campagne, Cuisses de Grenouilles, and Escargot à la Bourguignon. Entrées include such favorites as Coquille St. Jacques, Moules Marinières, or Filet de Canard au Poivre Vert. Mille-feuille, profiteroles, and chocolate, strawberry, or banana crêpes show up on the dessert menu.

On Friday and Saturday nights local musical groups perform downstairs in "La Cave." Closed Sunday.

Le Bistro, 2800 Sudderth Drive, Ruidoso, 88345; (505) 257-0132.

La Lorraine

Ruidoso's classic French restaurant is an AAA four-diamond property. La Lorraine prides itself in "elegant dining" with white tablecloth service, romantic lighting, a draped ceiling, and stained glass panels separating the eating areas. The color scheme is a rich wine and pearl gray, and huge urns of silk flowers embellish the dividers. Oil paintings in heavy gilt frames adorn the walls, and a heavy antiqued chandelier with crystal drops sprinkles rainbow prisms on the diners.

Tom and Kathy Gerber run the restaurant, having purchased it in 1995 from a previous owner who, in turn, took it over from Richard Girot, who founded the landmark in 1985. The chef is David Keaton.

The menu is classic French with appetizers such as Shrimp La Lorraine, spicy sautéed crustaceans in a Chardonnay cream sauce; Escargot sautéed in garlic butter and served on puff pastry with roasted red and yellow pepper vinaigrette; or Scallops sautéed with white wine and orange chipotle butter. Soups are lobster bisque or onion. Entrées cover the spectrum of beef, veal, lamb, pork, chicken, duck, pasta, and vegetarian and change seasonally.

On any night, you might find a thick and juicy Pan-Seared Veal Chop served with polenta primavera, Grilled Rack of Lamb with fresh mint apricot marmalade, Roasted Long Island Duckling with a choice of orange or cherry sauce, or Black Angus Rib Eye with horseradish cream, fresh vegetables, and whipped potatoes. All desserts are made at the restaurant, and a selection might include crème brûlée, napoleons, chocolate torte, and lemon tart.

An extensive wine list features 27 whites, 36 reds, champagnes, and a "rare and exceptional" collection of premiums. Lunch is served Wednesday through Saturday and dinner Monday through Saturday. Closed Sunday.

La Lorraine, 2523 Sudderth Drive, Ruidoso; (505) 257-2954.

Restaurant Jezebel

Restaurant Jezebel is the shining star in Ruidoso's restaurant scene. Chef Parind Vora and partner Débora Santos provide a dining experience that can compare with top restaurants in any major city. Their small establishment located in the Gazebo Shopping Center has it all—gracious ambiance, fantastic food created from impeccable ingredients, a massive wine list, and a caring, thoughtful staff. "We aim for a three-star dining experience without the cost and stuffiness," Parind says.

Although of East Indian descent, Parind grew up in the States and got his culinary training in Germany, Austria, and Switzerland. In addition, this 34-year-old wunderkind has completed three years of medical school.

Attention to detail is his watchword. All cold-water fish are ordered via Federal Express from Brown's Trading Company in Portland, Maine. His beef is prime aged filet, which he further ages 21 days in house. Tuna is sushi grade, and wild game is brought in from Broken Arrow Ranch in Texas. All poultry is free range. Plugrá butter is used with its higher butterfat and lower moisture content. Baking chocolate is Chocolat Noel from Belgium or El Rey from Venezuela. Even the bottled water is special—Source's Tŷ Nant imported from Bethania, Wales, United Kingdom.

When a customer has wine with dinner, Parind checks the variety and matches his sauce to the wine's acidity. A bold wine of high acidity requires bolder seasoning, while a softer wine needs a gentler touch. All entrées are prepared to order, and Parind strives to incorporate the four flavors of sour, sweet, spice, and salt in each dish. Distilled water is used for all cooking to produce a pure taste without interference from the local hard water.

The menu is "new contemporary American," with starters such as Roasted Garlic and Bread Soup, Salad of Salmon Carpaccio with Pecorino-Romano cheese and white truffle oil, or Pan-Seared Fois Gras with wildflower honey glaze. Main courses could include roasted Chilean Sea Bass and Maine Lobster with a mango-fresh curry leaf sauce; Espresso Rubbed Ahi Tuna with raspberry hollandaise; Roasted Semi-Boneless South Carolina Quail with black currant-lavender sauce; Pan-Seared Porcini Crusted Filet Mignon served with roasted potato cake and citrus hollandaise sauce; or a Napoleon of Roasted Portobello Mushrooms, Gorgonzola cheese, spinach, and roasted red pepper with balsamic pan sauce. A local favorite is Peekie Toe Crab cakes made from young Atlantic blue crab.

End the meal with one of Parind's special desserts: Tahitian Vanilla Bean Crème Brûlée, the rich Belgian Chocolate Mousse with raspberry truffle sauce, or tropical fruit and lavender infused Key Lime Pie. A cheese tray with a selection of imported and domestic artisan cheeses is available as are French press coffee service, six black teas and six green teas by the pot, "sherries, ports, and such."

That's just the food. Tableware is fine German Rosenthal, and all stemware is hand blown. Steak knives are French Laguiole. Table under-skirts are saris from Parind's mother's collection. The rooms are painted in vivid colors of yellow, blue, green, and wine, shades that mirror Parind's Indian heritage and Débora's Brazilian roots. Large framed nude figure studies by Tom Darrah, a New Mexican artist, line the walls. Shawls are available for women customers on cool nights, and there are reading glasses for those who've forgotten their specs. Book lights are provided for those who find it difficult to read the menu in the low-lit romantic atmosphere.

Restaurant Jezebel is extremely popular and is open only for dinner. Make reservations as far in advance as possible, or you're liable to lose out. They are closed Wednesday.

Restaurant Jezebel, 2117 Sudderth Drive, Ruidoso, 88345; (505) 257-5883; www.restaurantjezebel.com.

The Texas Club Grill & Bar

If you're a devoted carnivore, mosey over to the Texas Club Grill & Bar, slightly off the beaten path on Metz Drive in a condo development. Owner Linda Kelso specializes in all those down-home dishes such as chicken-fried steak and the gamut of steaks ranging in size from the prudent six-ounce rib eye to the gargantuan 20-ounce Trailboss Porterhouse. Of course, there's a selection of appetizers, soups, salads, seafood, and pastas, but make no mistake, it's the beef the majority of diners request. If you order one of their steaks but are restricting your salt intake, you might be advised to tell your waitperson to leave off the rub. It is delicious but definitely salty.

Dessert selections run from bread pudding with whiskey sauce to Chocolate Stampede, a rich chocolate pecan cake with hot fudge sauce and vanilla ice cream. A child's menu is available. Open lunch and dinner. Closed Monday and Tuesday.

The Texas Club Grill & Bar, 212 Metz Drive, Ruidoso, 88345; (505) 258-3325.

The Village Buttery

Lunch in Ruidoso finds people scurrying to the Village Buttery, open only from 10:30 A.M. to 2:30 P.M. The husband-and-wife team of Becky and Frank Walston have converted a small shop into a replica of a European cottage with wide porches and umbrella-shaded tables.

Their specialties are gourmet sandwiches, salads, homemade soups, and rich dessert pies. There's a quiche of the day, perhaps a ham, green chile, and cheddar or maybe spinach, mushroom, and Swiss cheese. There's a variety of green, fruit, chicken, crab, and tuna salads, but the best sellers are the pastas: rotini with dill, feta, green and black olives, and broccoli with a raspberry walnut vinaigrette or tortellini with water chestnuts, baby corn, broccoli, red peppers, and sugar peas with a sun-dried tomato-basil vinaigrette. The most preferred sandwich is good old chicken salad prepared from roast chicken breast, celery, sweet relish, and mayonnaise. Becky's buttermilk pie sells out fast. Hot blue-plate specials are served from Labor Day until Memorial Day, and the restaurant is open daily except for a week in mid-September when the Walston's take a much-deserved vacation.

The Village Buttery, 2107 Sudderth Drive, Ruidoso, 88345; (505) 257-9251.

Specialty Food Stores

The Herb Stop

Although the Herb Stop in the Gazebo Shopping Center is best known as the local source for botanical healing, it is a great place to purchase dry culinary herbs in bulk at reasonable prices. You'll find everything from anise to sweet woodruff.

Owner Rosemary Cascio is a gentle soul with infinite patience, and she can advise you on your questions, whether they are how to flavor your stew or relieve insomnia. She is a trained herbalist, having studied with Swiss teacher Leilah Breitler and Arizona guru Michael Moore.

The Herb Stop, 2117 Sudderth Drive Suite B #2, Ruidoso, 88345; (505) 257-0333; www.herbstop.com.

Viva New Mexico

If you're searching for a New Mexico food product for a gift or special occasion, Viva New Mexico is the place to stop. Located in the old Winfield House on Sudderth, the shop carries a bonanza of gourmet foods, coffees, and teas; "Heart of the Desert" pistachios; Stahmann's pecan nuts and candies; candles; books; and bath products.

Perhaps its greatest treasure is its wine cellar, with 24 New Mexico wines available to purchase by the bottle or glass. To enable you to pick a favorite, they have a wine bar with free tastings. Owned by Scott and Jessica Willmon, proprietors of Willmon Vineyards in Deming, the store is bright and cheerful with a sun porch for lazing or sipping a sample of the grape.

Viva New Mexico, 2811 Sudderth Drive, Ruidoso, 88345; (505) 257-8482; www.winesofnewmexico.com or www.endofthevine.com.

The Wild Herb Market

You'd never confuse it with the mega natural food markets like Wild Oats or Whole Foods, but the Wild Herb Market serves its community in a more modest fashion. Owner Elizabeth Byars, who has had the store since 1997, describes her business as "a cross between the large natural retailers and a vitamin shop." Her main concern is to "educate my customers in good nutrition and the use of new products to make life better for themselves and to aid in the protection of the environment."

The cheery store, with deep purple walls, wide windows, and a bright yellow floor, stocks all-organic produce and some frozen organic meats. There's a wide selection of vitamins and supplements. A deli in the rear has a juice and smoothie bar as well as prep space for soups, salads, and sandwiches.

The Wild Herb Market, 1715 Sudderth Drive, Ruidoso, 88345; (505) 257-0138.

Wine Boutique, Gourmet Food, and Tableware Shop

End of the Vine

End of the Vine is another enterprise of Scott and Jessica Willmon. Located in Vision Shopping Center, the 2,800-square-foot store is elegant and upscale with its terra-cotta walls, grapevine display racks, fireplace seating area, and game tables.

A wide selection of tableware and gourmet items is available including Riedel glasses; Scharffen Berger chocolates; Ritzenhoff stemware; Gourmet Gardens' relishes and pickles; Stonewall Kitchen products; Cuisine Perel vinegars, pâtés, and mousses; and cheeses from all over the world. A wine bar provides free tasting, and New Mexico wine is sold by the glass or bottle. A tobacco humidor occupies in the rear.

End of the Vine, 2801 Sudderth Drive, Ruidoso, 88345; (505) 257-8482; www.endofthevine.com or www.winesofnewmexico.com.

Capitan

Dining

The Greenhouse Café

In the small community of Capitan, the Greenhouse Café resides on the corner of NM 48 and Smokey Bear Road. Formerly the Hotel Chango owned by Gerald Flores, this reincarnation bears much physical resemblance to its previous life. Gerald's eclectic décor is still in place, and decorations run from Ndebele dolls to Yoruba statues and fabric art. There are a couple dining rooms and a porch overlooking an enclosed garden. Gerald's original jewelry is displayed everywhere.

The food, however, has changed. Tom Histen's first association with the restaurant was providing Gerald with fresh hydroponic greens and herbs grown in his greenhouses. When Gerald stepped down as chef, Tom and his wife, Gail, took over and revamped the menu. Tom has had 35 years in the food business, and he classifies his cuisine as "groundbreaking and eclectic."

The lunch menu might include Pacific Rim Double Noodle soup, a variation on the Thai or Vietnamese meal in a bowl; Chicken Casserole; Blackened Tilapia Salad with a Caribbean masala served over mixed greens and snow peas; or Meatball Lasagna layered with cream cheese mousse, caramelized onions, roasted garlic, and fresh herbs.

At dinner, Tom always includes a chicken, pork, and filet dish. Appetizers could be Oriental Pot Stickers; Fresh Scallops, sautéed and served with a deglazed sauce made from white chocolate, Chardonnay, garlic, and fresh dill; or a flawless Mixed Green Salad with Très Fin endive, arugula, and Persian Garden cress. Entrées might be a Rib Eye Steak au Poivre; Orange Roughy Northern Italian, baked with roasted red bell pepper and garnished with just-picked basil; or Pacific Rim Pork Loin marinated in sesame and pecan milk, coated with panko breadcrumbs, sautéed until golden brown, and served with caramelized onions and roasted garlic chaka soba noodles.

The menu changes with ingredient availability and Tom's frame of mind. "Like a musician, a chef needs inspiration," he says. "We have a few standards like the salad and lasagna, but I like to try new groundbreaking combinations."

The Greenhouse Café is open for lunch in the summer Wednesday through Saturday and dinner year-round Wednesday through Saturday.

Sunday brunch is served 9:00 A.M. to 1:00 P.M.

The Greenhouse Café, 103 South Lincoln, Capitan, 88316;
(505) 354-0373.

Roswell

Panadería

Pan Dulce Bakery

Pan Dulce Bakery is a true old-fashioned *panadería*. Housed in a battered building that appears to have been a convenience store, the operation bakes Mexican pastries, breads, *bolillos*, long johns, doughnuts, and good *bizcochitos* fresh every day.

Take-away burritos are available for breakfast and lunch, and you may purchase *barbacoa*, tamales, chile, adovada, carnitas, and salsa by the pound. Closed Monday.

Pan Dulce Bakery, 912 East 2nd Street, Roswell, 88201;
(505) 622-5970.

Dining

The Crash Down Diner

This listing is just for kicks. When you visit Roswell, you can't help but become exposed to the UFO incident, and one café has capitalized on this association. The Crash Down Diner is basically a burger joint decorated with little green men. A trio of aliens smiles from a wall mural welcoming you to Roswell, and blown-up greenies hang from the rafters.

Frank and Marni Gamboa's menu reflects the theme with Galactic Beverages, Planetary Delights (ice cream), Hungry Alien subs and sandwiches, Space Burgers, and Little Martians (children's menu).

Is this all a little funky? Yes. Is it commercial? Yes. But it's also fun, especially for the young and young at heart.

The Crash Down Diner, 106 West 1st Street, Roswell, 88203; (505) 627-5533.

Nuthin' Fancy

If it's good enough for George W., it's good enough for us. During a stop in Roswell, the president got hungry for ribs, and with a local recommendation, he stopped at Nuthin' Fancy for a take-out order to share with his entourage.

Nuthin' Fancy is somewhat of a landmark in the town. Former owners Frank and Ellen Bramlet opened the restaurant in 1993, and current proprietor Armando Aceves has kept their recipes and their pledge to cook everything from scratch.

"Home cooking without the mess" is their motto, and they follow that up with old-time favorites such as Mama's Meatloaf, Chicken-Fried Chicken (for a change), Char-Broiled Pork Chop, and Deep-Fried Catfish. There's the usual selection of New Mexican dishes including the UFO Quesadilla, a green-chile tortilla filled with beef, pico de gallo, and cheese, and enchiladas, tacos, and carne asada. You can order salads, sandwiches, and even a "soup of yesterday," which costs more than today's soup because everyone knows soup tastes better the second day. Daily blue-plate specials run Monday through Friday.

Décor is basic country, and the service is prompt and friendly. Open daily for breakfast, lunch, and dinner. Prices are very reasonable.
Nuthin' Fancy, 2103 North Main, Roswell, 88201; (505) 623-4098.

A Taste of Europe Restaurant

A Taste of Europe is a touch of heaven in Roswell, a city populated by fast food emporiums and chain restaurants. Owner Eve Strzyzewski owns and manages an attractive, bright restaurant, discreetly tucked into one wing of a building housing a Days Inn.

Interior décor is a little bit Polish, a little bit mixed European. The brick walls are covered with scenes from the Continent, and dark green shutters frame the windows. Dolls and nutcrackers are on display at the service area.

Eve and husband Lech emigrated from Poland in 1984, and in 1998 Eve opened the business. Although she serves both European and American favorites, her Polish dishes from her great-grandmother's recipes are the star attraction. Her "entrées from the Old Country" list such specials as *golumpki*, fresh cabbage stuffed with ground beef, pork, and rice and topped with tomato sauce and baby dill; *bigos* and kielbasa, the traditional dish of pork, mushrooms, and beef stewed in sauerkraut and served with sausage and potatoes; pierogies made fresh daily and stuffed with either a mixture of ground beef, pork, and veal or a delicious blend of mashed potatoes and cheese and topped with sautéed onions and bacon bits; schnitzel, a fresh cut of pork breaded and fried and served with *bigos* and steamed red potatoes; or Hungarian goulash with gnocchi. If you can't decide, try the combination platter.

For the less adventurous, there's pasta, a New York strip, grilled pork chops, shrimp scampi, chicken Parmigiano, veal scaloppini, and more. Eve's is open for breakfast as well as lunch and dinner, and in addition to the standard pancakes, eggs, omelets, waffles, and French toast, she prepares *twarozek*, a dairy dish consisting of cottage cheese, chopped green onion, radish, and sour cream. It's served with a toasted bagel and fruit. Closed Monday.

A Taste of Europe Restaurant, 1300 North Main Street, Roswell, 88201; (505) 624-0313.

Carrizozo

Brewery

Sierra Blanca Brewing Company

Under the Sierra Blanca label, master brewer Richard Weber crafts and bottles his Alien Amber, Nut Brown Ale, German-Style Pilsner, and English Pale Ale at the Carrizozo microbrewery. In addition, he prepares Imperial Stout, India Pale Ale, American Lager, and American Wheat beer for sale in kegs. The brewery is open for retail sale, tours, and tastings Monday through Friday.

Sierra Blanca Brewing Company, 503 12th Street, Carrizozo, 88301; (505) 648-6606.

Farmers' Markets

Alamogordo Farmers' Market, County Fairgrounds, Saturday, 7:30 to 11:00 A.M., June through October, (505) 437-6092.

Carlsbad-Eddy County Growers' Market, San Jose Plaza, Wednesday and Saturday, 8:30 A.M. to noon, June through October, (505) 887-6595.

Chaparral Farmers' Market, 101 County Line, Saturdays, 9:00 A.M. to noon, May through October, (505) 824-4114 or (505) 824-3250.

Clovis Farmers' Market, North Plains Mall, parking lot west of JC Penney's, Saturdays, 8:00 A.M. to sellout, Tuesdays, 4:00 P.M. to sellout, June to October, (505) 763-6505.

Portales Farmers' Market, corner of West 1st and Avenue B, Mondays and Thursday, 4:00 P.M. to sellout, June to first freeze, (505) 760-0690.

Roswell: Pecos Valley Farmers' and Gardeners' Market, south side of courthouse between Main and Virginia, Tuesday and Saturday, 6:30 A.M. to noon, July through first freeze, (505) 624-0889.

Wineries

Arena Blanca Winery

Arena Blanca Winery is located at Pistachio Tree Ranch and McGinn's Country Store, which offers a selection of New Mexico foods and gifts as well as a full line of their vintages. Their wines include Chardonnay, Cabernet Sauvignon, White Zinfandel, and Pistachio Blush. Open daily.

> **Arena Blanca Winery, 7320 Highway 54/70 North, Alamogordo, 88310; (505) 437-0602 or (800) 368-3081; www.pistachiotreeranch.com.**

Tularosa Vineyards and Winery

Tularosa Vineyards and Winery is a small family-owned vineyard and winery operated by the Wickham family. Wines are primarily varietals produced from vinifera grapes and include most of the standard varieties as well as some unusual offerings. Visitors are welcome for tours, tastings, and sales from noon to 5:00 P.M. daily. Calling ahead is encouraged.

> **Tularosa Vineyards and Winery, No. 23 Coyote Canyon Road, Tularosa, 88352; (505) 585-2260 or (800) 687-4467; www.tularosavineyards.com.**

Events

Taste of Carlsbad

March—Carlsbad's annual sampling of area restaurants and bakeries attracts a crowd to the Pecos River Village. Each year a different theme is chosen, new decorations are prepared, and the participants tailor their food to the subject. Willmon Vineyard provides the wine.

    Pecos River Village, 711 Muscatel, Carlsbad; (505) 887-6516; www.carlsbadchamber.com.

Mescal Roast

May—The third weekend of May Carlsbad's Living Desert Zoo and Gardens State Park and the Mescalero Apache tribe hold the annual Mescal Roast. The four-day event begins Wednesday with harvesting the mescal agave plants, which are a staple in the diet of the tribe. The plants are placed in hand-dug pits Thursday and roasted in the traditional Apache manner. The pits are opened Sunday morning and guests are invited to taste the sweet, stringy pulp. Mescalero Feast Dinners are held Friday and Saturday evenings, and Mountain Spirit dancers perform.

    Living Desert Zoo and Gardens State Park, 1504 Miehls Drive, off U.S. 285 northwest of Carlsbad; (505) 887-5516; www.livingdesertzoo@zianet.com.

Carlsbad Chili Cook Off

June—The annual June event began in 1993 and features bands and parades in addition to the cookoff, which is sanctioned by the Chili Appreciation Society International (CASI). Between 10 and 20 cooks vie for prizes and points to be applied to the national CASI contest held in Terlinguas, Texas.

    Band Shell Park on the Pecos, Carlsbad; (505) 887-7563.

Cloudcroft Pie Auction and Barbecue

June—Townsfolk bake up their favorite pies, which are auctioned off to the highest bidders from the Chamber of Commerce back porch. A barbecue dinner is served. Proceeds go to Chamber projects.

Chamber of Commerce, 1001 James Canyon Highway, Cloudcroft; (505) 682-2733.

High Rolls Cherry Festival and Fiddling Contest

June—On the third full weekend in June, High Rolls hold its annual Cherry Festival and Fiddling contest. The village has always been known for its fruit orchards, and cherries are the stars of the spring event. You'll find baskets of fresh fruit, pies, and cherry cider. Entertainment and an arts and crafts sale add to the festivities.

High Rolls, off NM 82, past mile marker 8; (505) 682-1151.

Carlsbad Caverns Bat Flight Breakfast

August—The National Park celebrates it 300,000-bat colony the second Thursday of August at the annual breakfast event. Starting at 5:00 A.M., visitors gather at the opening of the famous caves to watch the resident bats return from their nightly foraging flights. A hot breakfast is served when the critters are tucked away for their daylong sleep, and for those attending, the national park offers a free day pass through the self-guided sections of the caves.

Bat Flight Breakfast, Carlsbad Caverns National Park, Carlsbad; (505) 785-2232; www.nps.gov/cave.

Toast Yer Tailfeathers Hot Wing Cookoff

September—Benefiting Big Brothers and Sisters of Otero County, Toast Yer Tailfeathers Hot Wing Cookoff brings together lovers of the fiery flappers in a culinary challenge. Scheduled to coincide with liftoff at the annual White Sands Balloon Invitational, individual teams compete for prizes, and, after judging, samples of the wings are available for purchase by hungry bystanders.

Washington Park, Washington Avenue, Alamogordo; (505) 437-7120.

Annual Lincoln County Cowboy Symposium and Chuckwagon Cookoff

October—Sid Goodloe, an area resident, founded one of southeastern New Mexico's most popular events, the Lincoln County Cowboy Symposium and Chuckwagon Cookoff, in 1989. Cowboy poets and storytellers from all over the West compete for prizes, and there's music, western art and craft displays, as well as rodeo and roping events for the kids. Friday and Saturday nights swing dances hold forth.

By far one of the most popular events is the chuckwagon cookoff in which as many as 20 chuckwagons from New Mexico, Texas, Arizona, and Colorado compete for prizes. The sponsor, the Hubbard Museum of the American West, provides the basic ingredients, and the cooks are up and about before dawn's early light on Saturday morning to prepare the chow. Categories for meat, beans, potatoes, bread, and desserts are judged as well as overall food presentation. In addition, the wagons themselves are rated for authenticity.

Tickets to the events and chuckwagon meal tickets are available from the museum's Web site or by calling direct.

The Hubbard Museum of the American West, 841 Highway 70 West, Ruidoso Downs; (505) 378-4142; www.hubbardmuseum.org.

High Rolls Apple Festival

October—As with their June Cherry Festival, the village of High Rolls again celebrates its fruitful bounty in October. Apples in a range of varieties are available as well as apple pies, apple butter, and apple cider. An arts and crafts sale is scheduled as well as an array of entertainment.

High Rolls, off NM 82, past mile marker 8; (505) 682-1151.

Ruidoso Octoberfest

October—Come lift a stein of beer, dig into those brats and sauerkraut, contribute of few "*ja, ja*'s" to the chorus of "*Du, Du Liegst Mir Im Herzen*," or take a turn on the dance floor at the Ruidoso Octoberfest. There'll be German food, beers, wine, arts and crafts, dancing, and a special Kinderhall for children.

Convention Center, 111 Sierra Blanca Drive, Ruidoso; (505) 258-5500 or (866) 211-7727.

Recipes

Buttery Tomato Basil Soup

Courtesy of the Village Buttery, Ruidoso
24 servings

1 ¹/₂ cans whole tomatoes (6 lb., 6-oz. cans or 102-oz. cans)
4 Tbsp. dried basil or 12–14 fresh basil leaves
3 Tbsp. butter
1 qt. heavy whipping cream
3 Tbsp. condensed chicken stock
Parmesan cheese

In a blender or food processor, puree tomatoes and basil a little at a time. Pour into double boiler; add butter, whipping cream, and chicken stock. Warm completely (do not boil or it will separate). Sprinkle with Parmesan cheese and serve.

Crème Brûlée

Courtesy of Chef Parind Vora
Restaurant Jezebel, Ruidoso

9 servings

Everything that I cook covers the five taste buds ... sweet, salt, sour, bitter, and pain receptors (what you taste carbonated beverages and hot peppers with). I achieve balance by equalizing salt and sour, sweet and pain, acidity and richness, flowery aromatics with an earthy component and only adding slight bitterness to add depth of flavor. —Parind Vora

1 qt. /liter full-fat cream (heavy whipping cream) (adds richness to the dish)
1 Tahitian vanilla bean or 1 ¹/₂ of other type of vanilla bean (adds sweetness and floweriness to the dish)
15 yolks from large organic eggs (adds richness to the dish)
1 C. castor sugar (extra fine granulated sugar, *not* confectionery sugar. Adds sweetness to the dish)

A small pinch salt (adds salt flavor to the dish)

A small pinch coarse ground black pepper (pain receptor stimulation and balances sweetness and richness in the dish)

A splash of good balsamic vinegar (adds needed acidity and sourness to the dish)

A small pinch ground coffee (slight bitterness and earthiness to balance the floweriness in the dish)

Sugar in the raw (turbinado sugar as needed for the topping)

Set oven to 250° F, gas mark 1, 110 C. Scald 1 cup of heavy cream and turn off the heat. Split the vanilla bean(s) lengthwise and scrape the contents into the scalded cream and add the vanilla bean shell as well and let steep until completely cool. In a large bowl, mix the cooled vanilla-infused cream, vanilla bean and all, with all the other ingredients, using a wooden fork. Do this slowly as you do not want to make the mixture too frothy. (Note: when separating eggs separate them into another bowl and after a few, add them to the main bowl and continue until all the eggs are separated. This is so if you get a bad or bloody egg, it does not ruin the whole batch). Strain the whole mixture through a fine mesh strainer into a pitcher. Fill 9 5- to 6-ounce ramekins with the custard mixture.

Line a lasagna pan with a clean cloth dishtowel (this will protect the bottom of the custard so it does not overcook), add the filled ramekins, and add water so that comes up to about one-half of the height of the ramekins.

Bake in the preheated oven until the custards jiggle like a slightly firm style of Jell-O when shaken slightly. (Cooking time is dependent on a lot of factors. Do not open the door for at least 45 min., and then check every 5–8 min. until done. If watery, they are not done … remember, Jell-O. If they have puffed up at all, they are overcooked and you have to start over.)

Once cooked, take them out of the water right away, let them come to room temperature, and then refrigerate until cold.

Take out the chilled custard, sprinkle with sugar in the raw until a single layer coats the top of the custard, and wipe off the excess.

Caramelize with a MAPP torch. (You can find these at hardware stores. Do not use propane as it leaves a residual petrol taste in the topping. Butane can also be used but it's not as hot, so it will be slower than a MAPP torch.) I like a fairly dark caramel in order to balance the rich custard beneath.

Enjoy and repeat often! This recipe can be scaled up as needed.

Farmers' Market
Taos

Linda Stinnett
Ruidoso Roasters

Farmers' Market
Santa Fe

Bill Smith and Rick Hogan
Bees Brothers Winery

Appendix A

Indian Pueblo Feast Days

January 23
Annual San Ildefonso Feast Day
San Ildefonso Pueblo

February 2
Annual Nuestra Señora de las Candelarias Feast Day
Picuris Pueblo
San Felipe Pueblo

March 19
Annual Saint Joseph Feast Day
Old Laguna Village

May 1
Annual San Felipe Feast Day
San Felipe Pueblo

May 3
Annual Santa Cruz Feast Day
Taos Pueblo

June 13
Annual San Antonio Feast Day
Picuris Pueblo

Sandia Pueblo
San Juan Pueblo
Santa Clara Pueblo
Taos Pueblo

June 24
Annual San Juan Feast Day
San Juan Pueblo
Taos Pueblo

July 14
Annual San Buenaventura Feast Day
Cochiti Pueblo

July 18–20
Fiesta de Santiago y Santa Ana (Saint James and Saint Ann)
Taos Pueblo

July 26
Annual Santa Ana Feast Day
Santa Ana Pueblo
Taos Pueblo

August 2
Annual San Persingula Feast Day
Jemez Pueblo

August 4
Annual Santo Domingo Feast Day
Santo Domingo Pueblo

August 10
Annual San Lorenzo Feast Day
Picuris Pueblo

Annual San Lorenzo Feast Day
Acomita Village (Acoma Pueblo)

August 12
Annual Santa Clara Feast Day
Santa Clara Pueblo

August 15
Annual Our Lady of Assumption Feast Day
Zia Pueblo

Assumption of Our Blessed Mother Feast Day
Laguna Pueblo (Mesita Village)

August 28
Annual Saint Augustine Feast Day
Isleta Pueblo

September 2
Annual Saint Steven Feast Day
Old Acoma Pueblo

September 4
Annual Saint Augustine Feast Day
Isleta Pueblo

September 8
Annual Nativity of the Blessed Virgin Mother Feast Day
Laguna Pueblo

September 19
Annual Saint Joseph Feast Day
Old Laguna Village

September 25
Annual Saint Elizabeth Feast Day
Laguna Pueblo

September 30
Annual San Geronimo Feast Day
Taos Pueblo

October 4
Annual Saint Francis of Assisi Feast Day
Nambe Pueblo

October 17
Annual Saint Margaret Mary Feast Day
Laguna Pueblo

Nov. 12
Annual San Diego Feast Day
Jemez Pueblo
Tesuque Pueblo

Dec. 12
Annual Nuestra Señora de Guadalupe Feast Day
Pojoaque Pueblo

The Pueblo of Zuni's annual feast day is a religious ceremony and visitors are not encouraged. Instead, they have three monthly harvest festivals. Call for more information and specific dates.

July
Zuni Summer Solstice Market Festival

August
Zuni A: Shiwi Festival

October
Zuni Indian Summer Festival

Pueblo phone contacts:
Acoma, (888) 759-2489 or (505) 552-6604
Cochiti, (505) 465-2244
Isleta, (505) 869-3111
Jemez, (505) 834-7235
Laguna, (505) 552-6654
Nambe, (505) 455-2036
Picuris, (505) 587-2519
Pojoaque, (505) 455-2278
Sandia, (505) 867-3317
San Felipe, (505) 867-3381
San Ildefonso, (505) 455-3549
San Juan, (505) 852-4400
Santa Ana, (505) 867-3301
Santa Clara, (505) 753-7330
Santo Domingo, (505) 465-2214
Taos, (505) 758-1028
Tesuque, (505) 983-2667
Zia, (505) 867-3304
Zuni, (505) 782-4481

Appendix B
Regional Contacts

New Mexico Travel Offices

For state map and state travel guide:

New Mexico Department of Tourism
495 Old Santa Fe Trail
Santa Fe, NM 87501
(800) 733-6396 or (505) 827-7400
www.newmexico.org
enchantment@newmexico.org

For information on cities and towns in *Culinary New Mexico*, contact:

Albuquerque Convention and Visitors' Bureau
20 1st Plaza, Ste. 601
P.O. Box 26866
Albuquerque, NM 87125
(800) 284-2282 or (505) 842-9918
www.itsatrip.org
info@itsatrip.org

Santa Fe Convention and Visitors' Bureau
P.O. Box 909
Santa Fe, NM 87504
(800) 777-2489 or (505) 955-6200
www.santafe.org
santafe@santafe.org

Taos County Chamber of Commerce
P.O. Drawer 1
Taos, NM 87571
(800) 732-8267 or (505) 758-3873
www.taoschamber.com
info@taoschamber.com

Northwest

Farmington Convention and Visitors' Bureau
3041 East Main Street

Farmington, NM 87402
(800) 448-1240 or (505) 326-7602
www.farmingtonnm.org
fmncvb@cyberport.com

Gallup Convention and Visitors' Bureau
P.O. Box 600
Gallup, NM 87305
(800) 242-4282 or (505) 863-3841
www.gallupnm.org
genuine@gallupnm.org

Grants/Cibola County Chamber of Commerce
P.O. Box 297
Grants, NM 87020
(800) 748-2142 or (505) 287-4802
www.grants.org
discover@grants.org

Northeast

Las Vegas/San Miguel County Chamber of Commerce
513 6th Street
Las Vegas, NM 87701
(800) 832-5947 or (505) 425-8631
www.lasvegasnm.net
lvsmcc@zialink.com

Southwest

Las Cruces Convention and Visitors' Bureau
211 North Water Street
Las Cruces, NM 88001
(800) 343-7827 or (505) 541-2444
www.lascrucescvb.org
cvb@lascruces.org

Silver City/Grant County Chamber of Commerce
201 North Hudson Street
Silver City, NM 88061
(800) 548-9378 or (505) 538-3785
www.silvercity.org
scgcchamber@cybermesa.com

Southeast

Ruidoso Valley Chamber of Commerce
720 Sudderth
P.O. Box 698
Ruidoso, NM 88355
(800) 253-2255 or (505) 257-7395
www.ruidoso.net
info@ruidoso.net

Capitan
P.O. Box 441
Capitan, NM 88316
(505) 354-2273
www.smokeybearpark.com

Roswell Chamber of Commerce
131 West 2nd Street
P.O. Box 70
Roswell, NM 88202
(877) 849-7679 or (505) 623-5695
www.roswellnm.org
roswellcc@dfn.com

CULINARY
NEW MEXICO

Appendix C

Ingredient Sources

New Mexico Products Online or by Mail Order

505 Southwestern Organics
5555 Montgomery Boulevard, #16
Albuquerque, NM 87109
(888) 505-CHILE

Hot and mild green-chile sauce, red enchilada sauce, fajita marinade, hot, medium, and mild salsa.

The Chile Lady
P.O. Box 685
Hatch, NM 87937
(866) 279-1690
www.hatchchilelady.com
customerservice@hatchchilelady.com

Fresh red and green chile in season (early August to late September), *ristras*, wreaths, green-chile salsa, green-chile sauce, red-chile sauce, frozen green chile, habañero powder, habañero sauce, and chipotle powder.

Los Chileros de Nuevo Mexico
Gourmet New Mexican Foods
P.O. Box 6215
Santa Fe, NM 87502
(505) 471-6967
www.hotchilepepper.com
info@hotchilepepper.com

Exotic chiles, New Mexico chiles, New Mexico specialties, rubs and mixes, snack foods, blue and white corn products, gift packs.

Chimayo To Go
HCR 65, Box 71
Ojo Sarco, NM 87521
(800) 683-9628
www.chimayotogo.com or www.cibolojunction.com
info@chimayotogo.com

Fresh chile and sauces, dry chile and spices, coffee, tea, and cocoa, mixes, jellies and jams, *ristras,* cookbooks.

Da Gift Basket: Chile Products of New Mexico
P.O. Box 2085
Los Lunas, NM 87031
(505) 865-3645
www.dagiftbasket.com

Fresh chile products and fresh spices for true New Mexican/southwestern cooking.

Gift Baskets Just for You!
Online and phone order distributor of Bueno Foods
P.O. Box 9443
Albuquerque, NM 87119-9443
(505) 410-8559
www.giftbaskets-justforyou.com
info@giftbaskets-justforyou.com

In addition to providing the highest quality professionally designed gourmet gifts, Gift Baskets Just for You! is a supplier of all Bueno® Products ordered via the Internet, mail order, and 800 number. Products include flame-roasted fresh frozen green chile, red chile, salsas and sauces, tortillas, dried chile pods and chile powders, tamales, enchiladas, and more. Celebrating its 52nd anniversary this year, Bueno is one of the nation's largest Hispanic-owned companies, certified minority and women-owned.

Jane Butel's Pecos Valley Spice Company
P.O. Box 964
Albuquerque, NM 87103
(800) 473-TACO
www.pecosvalley.com

Butel's library of southwestern cookbooks brings to life the spirit of a region where flavors are always clear and strong. Twelve new videos each offer a menu designed around a uniquely southwestern theme. The Chile Lovers Kit, a tortilla press, barbecue mixes and rubs, Native American teas, and southwestern spices make ideal gifts, as well as perfect products for the serious chef. (See description of cooking school in Albuquerque chapter.)

Monroe's New Mexican Food
6051 Osuna Road NE
Albuquerque, NM 87109
(505) 881-4224
www.monroeschile.com
info@monroeschile.com

Green-chile sauce, red-chile sauce, red-chile honey, salsa, combination packs. (See description of restaurants in Albuquerque chapter.)

The New Mexico Connection
6401 Cochiti SE
Albuquerque, NM 87104
(800) 933-2736
www.nmchile.com
tab@nmchile.com

Hatch brand chile, sauces and picante, kitchen and pantry items, Sadie's of New Mexico products, dried chiles, coffees, teas, and candy, frozen green and pintado chiles, chile seeds.

El Pinto Restaurant
10500 4th Street NW
Albuquerque, NM 87114
(505) 898-1771
www.elpinto.com
elpinto@elpinto.com

Salsas and green-chile sauces (see description in Albuquerque chapter).

Santa Fe School of Cooking Online Market
116 West San Francisco Street
Santa Fe, NM 87501
(505) 983-4511
www.nmchile.com
cooking@santafeschoolofcooking.com

Ceramics, clothing, coffee, tea, and cocoa, cookbooks and prints, cooking tools, fun stuff, gift baskets, herbs and spices, jams, music from New Mexico, New Mexican chiles, nuts from New Mexico, salsas, snacks, barbecue, soaps and lotions, specialty soups. (See description of cooking school in Albuquerque chapter.)

Learn All about Chiles

The Chile Pepper Institute
New Mexico State University
Box 30003, MSC 3Q
Las Cruces, NM 88003
(505) 646-3028
www.chilepepperinstitute.org

Everything you could possibly want to know about chile from the Chile Capital of the World. Order seeds—grow your own!

Native American Foods

The Cooking Post
Pueblo of Santa Ana
2 Dove Road
Bernalillo, NM 87004
(888) 867-5198 or (505) 771-8318
www.cookingpost.com
info@cookingpost.com

Red corn hominy, Tamaya blue corn, tea and coffee, salsa, chile and hot sauce, wild rice, syrup and spreads, processed meats, gift packs and samplers, Bedre chocolates.

Pueblo Harvest Foods
P.O. Box 1188
San Juan Pueblo, NM 87566
(505) 747-3146
www.puebloharvest.com

Native American and southwestern dehydrated soups and stews.

Spice Specialists

B. Riley Fresh Herbs
670-A Juan Tabo NE
Albuquerque, NM 87123
(505) 275-0902 or (800) 427-1756
www.brileyfreshherbs.com
See description in Albuquerque chapter.

Penzeys Spices
19300 West Janacek Court
Brookfield, WI 53008
(800) 741-7787
www.penzeys.com

We try to concentrate on New Mexico firms, but Penzeys offerings are so comprehensive, we've included them in this list. Their herbs and spices are immaculately fresh and are packaged in several different sizes. They stock even hard-to-find items such as *epazote*. Order online, through the 800 number or visit one of the retail stores in Wisconsin, Minnesota, Michigan, Illinois, Ohio, Indiana, Pennsylvania, Missouri, Connecticut, Kansas, Florida, and Texas.

Other New Mexico Products

Pecan Producers

Stahmann's Country Store
22505 NM Route 28,
La Mesa, NM 88044
(800) 654-6887 or (505) 526-8974
www.stahmanns.com

Established in 1932, Stahmann Farms is the largest family-owned pecan farm in the world. Drive through their orchards or visit their gift shop. (See description in Southwest chapter.)

Pistachio Producers

Eagle Ranch Pistachio Groves
7288 Highway 54/70
Alamogordo, NM 88310
(800) 432-0999 or (505) 434-0035
www.eagleranchpistachios.com
sales@eagleranchpistachios.com

Home of the award-winning Heart of the Desert Pistachios®, this family farm is owned and operated by George and Marianne Schweers. It contains New Mexico's first and largest-producing pistachio groves. The first trees were planted in 1972, and new groves were, and continue to be, added on a regular basis. Today, Eagle Ranch is home to more than 12,000 pistachio trees. The trees are cultivated, harvested, and the crop totally processed on the premises. Eagle Ranch is home to the only pistachio salting and roasting plant in New Mexico. The original recipes for red chile– and green chile–flavored pistachios were also developed at Eagle Ranch. The fresh nuts are packaged and shipped or sold at the retail store located on the farm. Daily farm tours, online shopping, gift shop, and more.

McGinn Family Pistachio Tree Ranch and Country Store
7320 U.S. Hwy. 54/70 North
Alamogordo, NM 88310
(800) 368-3081 or (505) 437-0602
www.pistachiotreeranch.com

You can take self-guided tours of the pistachio production, see more than 11,000 trees, buy unique and southwestern collectibles from their gift shop, enjoy pistachio ice cream treats and local wines in their tasting room, and much more.

Raspberry Products

Salman Raspberry Ranch
NM Highway 518
La Cueva, NM 87732
(866) 281-1515 or (505) 387-2900
www.salmanraspberryranch.com

Fresh raspberries in season (August and September) by the basket or pick your own (call for information on availability). Online and mail-order raspberry jam, topping, and vinegar (year-round) made from the berries, salad dressing mix made from vegetables grown in the gardens, seasonal fresh garden vegetables, fresh and dried flowers, honey from the hives in the raspberry field, and dozens of gourmet food products and handcrafted artistic productions.

Appendix D

Cookbooks

Available online through www.amazon.com or
www.barnesandnoble.com or through your local bookstore.

General Cookbooks

Café Pasqual's Cookbook: Spirited Recipes from Santa Fe
by Katharine Kagel, Barbara Simpson (Photographer), Bill
Leblond (Editor)
Chronicle Books
ISBN 0-81180-293-0

The Chile Pepper Encyclopedia
By Dave DeWitt
William Morrow and Company
ISBN 0-688-15611-8

Coyote Café: Foods from the Great Southwest
By Mark Miller
Ten Speed Press
ISBN 0-89815-245-3

Green Chile Bible
Compiled by Albuquerque Publishing Company
Clear Light Publishing
ISBN: 0-94066-635-9

Feast of Santa Fe: Cooking of the American Southwest
By Huntley Dent
Simon & Schuster
ISBN 0-67187-302-4

Jane Butel's Southwestern Kitchen
Or any of her many cookbooks on southwestern cooking
HPBooks, a division of Penguin Group (USA) Inc.
ISBN 1-55788-090-5

*Mark Miller's Indian Market Cookbook: Recipes from Santa Fe's
Famous Coyote Café*
By Mark Charles Miller, Mark Kiffin, John Harrisson, Suzy Dayton
ISBN 0-89815-620-3

The Red Chile Bible: Southwestern Classic & Gourmet Recipes
By Kathleen Hansel, Audrey Jenkins
Clear Light Publishing
ISBN 0-94066-693-6

The Santa Fe School of Cooking Cookbook
By Susan Curtis
Gibbs Smith Publisher
ISBN: 0-87905-873-0

The Whole Chile Pepper Book
By Dave DeWitt and Nancy Gerlach
Little, Brown and Company
ISBN 0-316-18223

Native American Cookbook

Indian Nations: Foods of the Southwest
By Lois Ellen Frank
Ten Speed Press
ISBN 1-58009-398-6

San Marcos Café
Santa Fe

Pie-O-Neer Restaurant
Pie Town

Craig Sharp,
Soirée cooking class
Albuquerque

Pie Town

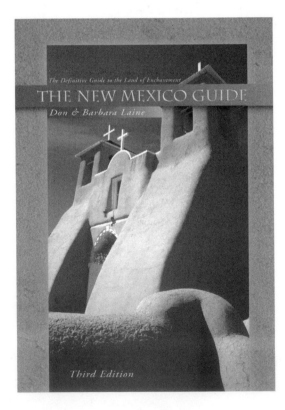